# A Gift for Ron

# A Gift for Ron

## Friendship and Sacrifice On and Off the Gridiron

Everson Walls

With Kevin B. Blackistone

Foreword by Frank Deford

LP

Lyons Press

Guilford, Connecticut

An imprint of Globe Pequot Press

Lyons Press is an imprint of Globe Pequot Press.

Text design: Sheryl Kober
Layout: Kevin Mak
Project editor: John Burbidge

Library of Congress Cataloging-in-Publication Data
Walls, Everson.
A gift for Ron : friendship and sacrifice on and off the gridiron / Everson Walls with Kevin B. Blackistone ; foreword by Frank Deford.
p. cm.
Includes index.
ISBN 978-1-59921-532-7
1. Walls, Everson. 2. Football players—United States—Biography. 3. Organ donors. 4. Springs, Ron. 5. Diabetic athletes 6. Kidney—Transplantation—Patients. 7. Friendship I. Blackistone, Kevin B. II. Title.
GV939.W323A3 2010
796.332092—dc22
[B]

2009031883

Printed in the United States of America

10 9 8 7 6 5 4 3 2 1

# Contents

# Foreword

Before you read any further in this book, the main thing to understand is that this is not a story about two football players. Of course, like just about everybody else, that's the mistake I originally made when I was assigned to do a piece on Everson Walls and Ron Springs for the HBO program *Real Sports with Bryant Gumbel.* But really, what's football got to do with it?

Still, that was what everyone naturally played up. Wow—the first time one football player had given an organ in transplant to another. Who had ever heard of such a thing? But then, when you stop to think about it, how often do we ever hear about one person who is not related to another *in any profession* doing what Everson did? It would be just as striking a story if it had been about two mechanics or two insurance agents or, yes, even two writers.

The fact is, Everson Walls is the only person I've ever known in my whole life who did what he did.

But then, I guess their story reinforced what fans want to believe, that players on any team in any sport are truly close to one another—*mates,* as they say in places like Australia. Teammates. But that's really just an idle myth. On any team, some guys like each other, some guys get along with each other, some guys abide each other, and, yes, some guys can't stand each other. Teammates are like any other group of people who are thrown together just because they have rather similar talents.

In fact, Everson and Ron simply just happened to meet on a football field a long time ago. By 2007, they hadn't been teammates for years. For that matter, neither one of them had even played football for years. So put football out of your mind. This is more a story about friendship that evolves into love.

And, of course, it's also about sacrifice. Everson is being humble when he titles this book *A Gift for Ron.* Everson gave so much more than one of his kidneys.

I'm lucky, in that I can understand what Everson did so much better than most people, because I had the opportunity to see the two men together. It was quickly apparent how close they were, how much they shared beyond that common body part.

As a journalist, I dislike interviewing two people together. It never works as well as one-on-one. You forfeit a certain amount of intimacy that leads to lesser responses when you try to talk to two people at the same time. Invariably, one of the persons talks more than the other, and both of them tend to hold back something, a bit fearful of speaking candidly in front of the other. But when I interviewed Everson and Ron together, none of those issues surfaced. They were clearly different personalities, but, altogether, they were seamless. I remember telling Mike Sullivan, the producer, don't worry about putting any shots of me into that section. I only get in the way. Just use the camera on the two men. Let people see them together, and, just seeing, then they'll understand so much better why Everson did what he did—and why Ron would surely have done the same thing had their situations been reversed.

Having said all that, I also know that because Everson and Ron had played football, their story does carry more meaning. After all, we do stereotype athletes, and it's natural to assume that football players are tough guys who don't do sweet things. And, of course, they can't avoid being that way vocationally—even if Everson swears he didn't like to tackle. (Of course, I don't believe that for a minute. Excuse me: An All-Pro *defensive* player who doesn't like to tackle? That's like me saying I don't much care for nouns and verbs.)

But it certainly is true that, once the game is over, football players can be rather everyday human beings. As Everson tells his story so well to Kevin Blackistone, football mattered a great deal in shaping his life. Certainly, this is true of Ron, as well. But there are so many other influences that made them both into the men they are and into the men who did what they did in that hospital in Dallas one day back in the winter of 2007.

*Frank Deford*
July 2009

# 1

# How Lucky We Are

Ron was dying. On that fall day in 2006, I could no longer pretend it wasn't true, no matter how hard I tried. My onetime teammate and longtime friend, the man who was the godfather to my children, as I was to his, was not going to bounce back like he had so many times on a football field after being knocked down.

We'd started working out in the gym near our suburban north Dallas homes whenever he felt up to it. I'd just helped him squeeze into an overhead triceps exercise machine, a maneuver a little more difficult than getting him in and out of his wheelchair. I braced Ron's two hundred-plus-pound body so that he could balance for a moment on the one foot—his right foot had been amputated—and shoved him behind and under the arm bars of the machine until he could plop down on the padded seat and lean against the backrest.

I then helped Ron extend his arms from his chest, where atrophy had caused them to retract, so that his elbows could slide onto the bars' pads. I feared I would break his arms because they were so stiff.

Finally, I carefully pried Ron's fingers and thumbs apart, scared that I might break them, too. These were hands Ron used as a running back in the National Football League for eight years to take handoffs, catch passes, and shed would-be tacklers. Now they were gnarled into little balls of flesh and bone, and I slipped each over the bar so that Ron could hold on with what little dexterity he could muster.

When I was done, I stretched out on my back on the carpeted floor—my hands clasped behind my head, my elbows extended like wings, my knees bent and my feet flat—and began to do sit-ups. I alternated twisting my torso left and right as I rose and lay back over and over, while Ron fought the triceps machine and the diabetes that was ravaging his body.

There wasn't much Ron could do about the diabetes now, except pray. It was all any of us could do as we watched him being whittled away by the crippling disease. Diabetes had taken his right foot, and it was threatening to take the left (two toes had already been amputated). It had shut down his kidneys at least once and sent him to the emergency room countless times. It left him in need of dialysis three times each week in order to make it to the next.

The only thing that could save Ron at this point was a kidney transplant, which he hoped would come soon from a nephew, Chris Springs. Chris was the latest relative who matched Ron's blood type and was in the process of getting tested to be sure he could donate.

Ron had not updated me recently on the progress with Chris, so on this day, at this moment, in between raising and lowering my upper body off the gym floor, I asked.

"Hey, how's it going with Chris?" I said to Ron, not even glancing his way.

"Oh, Chris had a bad kidney," Ron said.

I felt like I'd just been punched. All the air left my body. I stopped in mid sit-up.

"What?" I said with bewilderment.

Ron answered the same again.

"Shit!" I blurted out.

My eyes darted about the gym room. My mind raced. Ron is going to die, my mind screamed.

Ron was barely fifty years old, three years older than me. He'd been a physical marvel when I first met him twenty-five years earlier.

I was a rookie with the Dallas Cowboys then, and he was a veteran fullback. I'd never known any player so extraordinarily gifted. Ron was as big and as strong as his position demanded, and he possessed the speed and finesse of generally smaller and quicker halfbacks.

But now he was being waylaid out of nowhere by some disease. It didn't seem possible. It certainly wasn't fair.

I couldn't get Ron's wife, Adriane, who was the best friend of my wife, Shreill, out of my mind. I was thinking about Ron and

Adriane and their girls, Ayra and Ashley. They were so close with our kids, Charis and Cameron, that some people thought they were all siblings. I thought about Ron's son Shawn, born from a relationship Ron had in college, who was following in his dad's footsteps as a pro football star. I envisioned Adriane, Ayra, Ashley, and Shawn without the husband and dad they loved so much, and I just wanted to snap out of it.

This can't be happening, my mind said over and over.

All of a sudden, a flood of thoughts of what I could do to save Ron and help his family rushed over me. I'd been blessed with so much good fortune all my life that I figured I must have some to spare for a guy who'd grown from a teammate and mentor to best friend and someone I would entrust my kids to if any tragedy ever befell me.

I mean, I survived thirteen seasons in the NFL, and other than the occasional nicks, bumps, and bruises—including some internal bleeding once from a knee to the side that sidelined me for two games—I'd never been seriously hurt. Imagine that; I spent thirteen seasons colliding with some of the biggest, strongest athletes in the world, and I never once had to be helped off the field. I never broke anything more than a chinstrap or the tape on my ankles. I never got carted up a stadium tunnel. I never, ever, was rolled into an operating room as Ron had been several times now in retirement.

How lucky was I? I even got to play from the very start of my career, and for most of it, in my hometown, Dallas. Nine seasons. Think about it. How many guys got to do that? How many guys *could* do that? Ron never got to play with Washington, which was closest to his Williamsburg, Virginia, home. Tony Dorsett never got to play for the Steelers in his hometown of Pittsburgh. Too Tall Jones is from Jackson, Tennessee. There wasn't even an NFL team in Tennessee until the Oilers relocated to Nashville and became the Titans a little over a decade ago.

It just so happened that my hometown team was as famous and storied a team as the NFL has ever had, the Cowboys, America's Team. I grew up in a house a few blocks from where the Cowboys practiced.

My buddies and I used to ride our bikes from our neighborhood to watch them go through their paces. How many kids got to do that?

And how many NFL players got to do what I did at the start of my pro career? I drove from my mom's house to work as a cornerback for the Cowboys. That's lucky. That's something other guys could only dream about. A few times when I drove back to Mom's from work I brought Ron with me.

I never appreciated playing for my hometown team more than during my last few years in the league when I was in New York winning a Super Bowl ring and winding up on the cover of *Sports Illustrated* for the second time. The first time I was on *SI*'s cover was my rookie year, and it became one of the most famous sports photos ever. It was me flailing at that game-winning touchdown pass from Joe Montana to Dwight Clark in the NFC championship game in January 1982. People forget I had two interceptions, a fumble recovery, and seven tackles in that game, but I was immortalized for being between Montana and Clark for what became known as "The Catch."

Almost a decade later, in the 1991 Super Bowl, I was on *SI*'s cover again, this time exulting in victory at the end of the game, my hands reaching to the heavens. Ron was several years into retirement then, but he and his family were in the stands to cheer me on and in our hotel afterward to celebrate. My career had come full circle.

I never took any of my good fortune for granted, especially my health. After all, I played with guys and against guys whose off-seasons seemed to start with a trip to the team surgeon to get their knees cut on. I see some of them now, and they waddle or limp, or do both, because of the toll the game took on them.

But me? Other than the gray hair on my head, or on my face when I go a day or two without shaving, nothing has changed. I walk just fine. I even run a little bit, a few miles a few times a week around my neighborhood. The only time I ever visited a hospital, with the exception of greeting my newborn daughter and son, was to encourage someone who wasn't feeling well, like Ron.

I've worked at maintaining my blessing of good health over all these years, forty-nine and counting now. I try to eat right. I work out so regularly that Adriane calls me Jack LaLanne, then chuckles.

"Why don't you go work out with Jack LaLanne?" I can hear Adriane yelling playfully at Ron when he was still in good health, and I was newly retired.

Ron hadn't been as lucky as me, but you would never know. He's always been the funniest guy around. He has a joke about everything and a nickname for everyone. The first time he saw one of my best friends from childhood, Vernon MacDonald, Vernon was wearing an applejack cap, one of those hats with lots of billowing fabric attached to a baseball cap brim. Vernon has been "Applejack" ever since as far as Ron is concerned.

"Here comes Applejack!" Ron would bellow at the sight of Vernon.

Ron's the kind of guy who you hear before you see him.

I shouldn't call Ron just a onetime teammate and longtime friend, though. That would be selling him short. He's actually been much more than that to me, and me to him, I think. He's that big brother I never had; I'm that little brother he never had. He did a lot of talking, and I did a lot of listening, and a lot of laughing at what he had to say. When we first met during my rookie training camp, Ron did something that was very infra dig: He invited me, a greenhorn, to hang out with him, a wily veteran, at restaurants and bars he frequented. Other veterans never dipped so low.

I didn't know it then, and Ron probably didn't either, but that was the beginning of one of the great friendships of my life. I look back now on my relationship with Ron, and I realize that he was an embodiment of some of the most important life lessons that others, like my dad and my college coach, Eddie Robinson, tried to instill in me—about being a teammate, being a leader, being a friend. Most of all, Ron made me realize that to be lucky does not necessarily mean to receive gifts, but to be able to give them.

That sounds counterintuitive, but I am living proof, and Ron is, too, that it is true.

I learned the importance and the impact of giving on a daily basis after my retirement from the NFL in 1993, when I reunited with Ron, who was already several years into retirement and was returning to Dallas after living in Ohio and Washington, D.C. Ron had an idea for us to work at something we did on the side as Cowboys—help charities raise money by using our celebrity status as pro athletes, Cowboys no less.

We'd gather a few old teammates from the Cowboys, as well as some of Ron's teammates from Tampa, where his career wound down. We'd travel mostly through Texas and the Southwest, Dallas Cowboys country, but occasionally farther away as well, to help charities raise money by doing all manner of things. We'd hold autograph sessions. We'd participate in golf tournaments. We'd play in celebrity basketball games—our favorite thing to do.

The charities paid us an appearance fee and kept the proceeds from tickets bought for the autographs and golf tournaments and basketball games. It really had us running around. But it was for a good cause. We made a living helping others.

Sometimes during the day in whatever city we were in, we added hospital visits to our routine. That was something else we had done as Cowboys, especially around the holidays.

I'll never forget one afternoon when we went to a hospital where some kids were waiting for bone marrow transplants. We didn't know much about bone marrow transplants then, but the doctors explained the process and talked about how painful transplants were. Ron and I couldn't imagine a six-year-old going through something so trying. It hit us and all the other guys who made that visit pretty hard. There was nothing like seeing these transplant patients, so young and little, lying in hospital beds. We were big, strong football players, and they were so small and weak that they could barely move. Yet they were still happy to see us despite the great discomfort they were in.

We felt helpless. We saw the kids for ten minutes and then moved on. We knew there was nothing we could do for them other than bring a brief smile to their faces. We knew some of them might not have very long to live. It was a feeling we never forgot, and now that I look back, I realize that particular hospital visit was one of many stepping-stones making the path that led my life to where it is now.

That's the thing about life—you never really know where it is taking you. It is only when you look back that the signposts make sense.

I remember watching a local news report on TV during a really bad cold snap in Dallas not long after Ron and I visited the kids waiting for bone marrow transplants. There was a young reporter walking down a Fort Worth street early one morning, and he came across a bunch of little kids waiting for the school bus. There was a little white girl, and she was so bundled up she could hardly move. Then there was a Mexican kid, and all he had on was a thermal shirt. He was so cold he had the sleeves pulled down to cover his hands.

The reporter asked the Mexican kid where his coat was, and the kid said he didn't have one. I couldn't believe it. I mean it was *freezing* outside! No coat! I called Ron. Ron called a church in Fort Worth. The next thing we knew, we had put together a coat drive. Coats for Kids, we called it.

I always enjoyed helping people, but never more until then. When Ron and I saw the joy in the faces of the first little kids who got those coats, we felt so good. We felt like we left a bit of ourselves with them.

That's the lesson I learned for which I have Ron to thank, the gift of giving. I just never figured I'd have that feeling all over again with Ron as the person I was helping out.

☆

Over the years, as Ron and I spent more and more time together, I noticed that something was happening to him. I remember when we were at a meeting in Oklahoma and went to see a potential charity sponsor, some big-time businessman, a white guy. But he and Ron were more alike than not. They were loud and brash, joke tellers. They were firing away at each other, exchanging tall tales about business and one-liners about the Bible.

Ron grew up in a religious household. He knew his scripture. His mom knows the Bible back and forth. His sisters sang in the choir. His brother is a preacher. He was in his element joking with the businessman about the Bible.

I remember Ron reaching for a Bible on the businessman's coffee table and saying, "Yeah, I got one for you. Hold on, let me look it up."

As Ron flipped through the pages, he moved the book up close to his face and then farther away from his eyes. He was trying to adjust his sight, and the words weren't even that small.

"Damn, Ron," I said. "You need glasses already?"

Ron always had 20/20 vision, and at the time he was just into his forties. I didn't think much of it again until Ron and I were playing in one of our charity basketball games. I noticed he wasn't running as hard. He looked to be giving up on plays really easily, not running from one end of the court to the other like most everyone else. It was something he never did before. Little old guys who could hardly play basketball were stealing the ball from Ron.

Ron didn't say anything was wrong. He just kind of laughed it off.

I thought, Well, that must be the years catching up with him, from playing fullback.

But deep down, I worried that something else was going on. I remember one time when Ron was traveling to see his son, Shawn, play when Shawn was with the Seattle Seahawks, and Ron complained that his shoes were hurting his feet. I usually considered his complaints no more than minor distractions, and so did he. Guys, especially a couple of former pro football players, don't like to dwell on aches and pains. We didn't when we were playing. It's that masculine thing. We're supposed to be tough and not sensitive, fearless and not frightened. So Ron and I just moved on to some other discussion.

But one night Shreill and I were talking about her latest conversation with Adriane, and Shreill said she thought Ron was sick. "He's diabetic," she said. Shreill and Adriane talked all the time, and, unlike Ron and me, they talked about everything, worrisome and not. It was that feminine thing, I guess, being attuned to little things like feelings.

Adriane told Shreill that Ron learned he was diabetic as early as 1990, a type 2 diabetic he was called. By the time she confided in Shreill, more than a decade had gone by, and Ron had never said a thing about it to me, one of his closest friends, one of his boys.

Ron's family knew, of course. He just didn't say anything about it to the guys he hung out with. Like I said, guys don't talk about those things, especially football players. We didn't talk about those kinds of things in the locker room. We always kept any problems out of there. The team was our safe haven. The same was true of our friendships.

Now that I look back, it was really sort of a defense mechanism. The less we knew, the better off we figured we'd be.

It was a ridiculous mind-set. If there's one thing I've come to regret in recent years, it's that I didn't probe Ron more about what was going on with his health, and that he didn't volunteer any information about it.

After all, it was only after Shreill revealed that she'd learned Ron was diabetic that I found out how seriously diabetes was affecting Ron and how difficult his situation was getting. It was around January 2000, when Ron started wearing one of those bulky black plastic boots with the Velcro strapping. It went up to his knee. It was a walking cast like you'd wear for a broken foot or torn Achilles tendon. Ron told me he was wearing it because he had had his toe scraped.

Toe scraped? I didn't know what that meant. I figured it was a corn or bunion or something that had to be removed. But I'd never seen more than a patch or Band-Aid for that procedure.

One day, Ron was feeling a little more loquacious and told me he had had surgery and that some of his toe had been removed. I was stunned.

"Ron, what's going on, man?" I said. "You need to slow down."

"Nah," Ron assured me. "I'll be all right."

Ron kept on traveling. He kept going to see Shawn play all over the country. Ron kept trying to wear what we called his good shoes, too. He and I always had gator skin shoes, lizard skin loafers, ostrich boots, and all that. We'd go to a shoe store called Freedman's in Atlanta and stock up. Those shoes were so well made we could keep them the rest of our lives. We were professional athletes. We were always healthy. We knew we'd have long lives. We knew we would never be like the kids we saw in the hospital who needed transplants, the miracle gifts of life, to stay alive.

But trying to look good was doing Ron harm. I learned later that he was in pain.

Ron was in denial about what diabetes was doing to him. He refused to recognize that it was ruining the circulation in his body, particularly to his limbs. Ron thought he could just take some medicine, and everything would get better, the way he used to take a few aspirins after a particularly bruising game. But he couldn't do that with diabetes. It didn't work.

Then Ron had to go to the hospital for another scraping. Scraping. It sounded better than what it was—an amputation. The next thing I knew, a whole toe was gone from Ron's foot. That was when Shreill got really nervous.

"That's the same thing that happened to Mother," she said.

Mother was what Shreill called her grandmother. We looked at each other but didn't say a word. We didn't need to. We knew. After Shreill's grandmother lost a toe, she lost a leg. Eventually, she lost her other leg, and not long afterward she lost her life to diabetes.

But that was an old woman, I thought. That's what happens to elderly people. That's what happens to people who weren't professional athletes, former college and NFL stars like Ron.

I didn't know that's what happens to type 2 diabetics. I didn't know that more than half the amputations performed in the United States are due to diabetes. I didn't know that high levels of sugar in the blood ruin arteries and cripple extremities. When I was growing up, I never heard people talk about diabetes. I heard them say so-and-so wasn't feeling well because he had "the *shugah.*" That was all I knew about what was tearing down my friend.

Then Ron went in for another surgery, and they took another toe. He went in for another visit to the operating room, and they took his entire right foot. The man who had broken college rushing records and blocked for Tony Dorsett was suddenly in need of an artificial foot. His other foot looked to be headed toward the same fate.

I was devastated. I was witnessing the ravages of diabetes to the cornerstone of a family that Shreill and I adopted out of love and that adopted us for the same reason.

I watched as bit by bit the disease and doctors were whittling down the man I first came to know as a six-foot, 215-pound human boom box and battering ram. I watched a man who was expected as a fullback in pro football to clear the path for other players reduced to someone who now needed the help of others like me just to maneuver life's smallest obstacles, like getting in and out of a car or standing upright.

I'd gone from flying on the team plane with Ron, to carpooling our kids together, to traveling around the country with Ron on business, to shuttling Ron to and from a dialysis center because he could no longer drive himself, to pushing him around in a wheelchair.

I'd never been to a dialysis center, and after taking Ron, I never forgot it. It wasn't just what it looked like that shocked me, how stark and cold it was with people sitting back in doctor's office reclining chairs with tubes red with their blood hooked up to machines that whirred away softly. *Bzzzzzzzzzzzz.* It wasn't just the mood there, which was absolutely depressing.

No, what I'll never forget is what I learned dialysis is really for. It isn't for curing people of diabetes or other diseases that ravage the kidneys. It is for keeping people from dying. It is for artificially prolonging life for only a little while—a few months, a few years—rarely for a long, long haul.

The dialysis center was a place where people came to maintain hope while waiting for the lifesaving operation of a transplant. Ron was like everyone else who had to visit that dialysis center two, three, four, five times each week. It didn't matter that the other patients were old or young or had never been in tip-top physical condition in their lives. It didn't matter that they were black or white or men or women.

It didn't matter that Ron was a former college football star and a former NFL player. It didn't matter that he was still full of life. Ron was like everyone else in that dialysis center. He was holding on.

I didn't know diabetes was such a deadly disease and even more so for black people and black men. I felt as helpless looking at Ron sometimes as I did when I met those kids in the bone marrow ward we both visited years earlier. His body was getting carved up. His hands and arms were curling up and contracting into his torso. His sight was failing to the point where he couldn't have driven himself even if the rest of his body allowed it.

I didn't think there was anything I could do for Ron except be his friend, be that know-nothing rookie he figured I was when he first walked into my quarters at Cowboys training camp two decades ago. What could I do to stop Ron's downward spiral? What could anyone really do?

I went with Ron to the dialysis center several times, and Ron told me how he'd see the same people trip after trip, and then on another trip he would notice they were being whittled away just like him—a foot gone, a leg gone. Then sometimes, Ron said, he didn't see some of the same people anymore at all.

That was when I learned that someone like Ron would last about five years on dialysis. Ron was already three and a half years in. He'd been on the transplant list from his first trip to the center. He had a year and a half to go to get a transplant.

After that, most likely, Ron would be like one of the people he didn't see anymore. If he didn't get a transplant, he'd be dead. If he didn't get a transplant, the last time I helped Ron would be carrying him to his grave.

You wouldn't know how dire Ron's situation was from Ron. He was as selfish about his problem as he was selfless with his concern for others in the same boat.

Ron was a bright spirit in that dialysis center, just like he was when I met him in summer's dog days of my rookie training camp, and just like he was in the locker room after I was fortunate enough to make the Cowboys and become his teammate. He started tossing around jokes as soon as he rolled through the dialysis center's doors, trying to lighten the life-or-death load that weighed on everyone there, patients and caretakers.

"Here comes that crazy Ron Springs," someone would announce when we rolled him in. Everyone in earshot would chuckle if not laugh out loud.

Ron was praying under it all, though. So was I. We all were. We didn't say so to each other. We didn't want to, and we didn't need to. This was one of those times when deciding to pray was as frightening as it was necessary. You wanted to think that you didn't have to ask God to look out for a husband and father of three who sought in life only to make all those he encountered laugh and smile.

So Ron stayed Ron as much as he could. It was seldom that he let himself look less than upbeat. For one thing, he saw being on dialysis, which meant he was on the transplant list, as a blessing. He was certain a donation would come his way before his time ran out.

That was something else I learned from Ron: A challenge was no more than an opportunity. Those kids didn't have coats? No problem. We'll use our celebrity status to get them properly clothed.

So Ron asked me to start taking him to the gym when I went, which was almost every day. He said he wanted to stay in as good a shape as he could so that he'd be ready to take that transplant when it came and pick up his life again where the diabetes left off wrecking it.

"I want this vessel to be ready to receive that new kidney," he said.

I was glad because I felt like I was finally helping Ron feel better in earnest. It was like old times, too. Ron brightened up even more. We'd go to the gym, a new LA Fitness not far from where we lived. I'd do my workout. He did his for as long as he could. When he was ready to go, we left.

It wasn't easy. Sometimes Ron needed me to help him to the men's room. That was the hardest thing, harder than helping Ron stand and walk or pushing him here and there in a wheelchair. Helping another man in the bathroom was about dignity. But I did. It was necessary. And Ron and I moved on.

It didn't dawn on me then, but I was taking my onetime mentor under my wing. I was employing the lessons of teammate and friend that Ron cemented in me.

☆

One day, I thought our dreams had finally come true. Ron didn't make a big announcement. He just mentioned sort of matter-of-factly that his nephew Chris shared his blood type, which made Chris a potential donor, and Chris was willing to take all the medical tests a potential donor had to take to see if he could give Ron a kidney.

I was ecstatic. We all were. Ron's life was about to be saved.

Ron had been down this road before, though. A niece who shared Ron's blood type said she wanted to be his donor and even started the battery of tests to make sure she was healthy enough. It happened at a Springs family reunion. I'll never forget the niece making a dramatic, teary-eyed announcement that she was going to save her uncle's life.

But along the way it was discovered she had become pregnant. Ron's hopes were dashed. He was very upset with his niece for pledging her kidney to save his life but allowing herself to get disqualified by getting pregnant.

So Ron didn't talk more about Chris after first mentioning him. And then, on that one day while we were at the gym, Ron crushed me when he told me Chris was ruled out.

I remember that moment now like it just happened. I could see Shreill's grandmother. I was thinking about her funeral. I could see Adriane's face and the faces of Ron and Adriane's kids. I recalled Ron's niece breaking down in tears at the family picnic. I could see those Fort Worth kids who needed coats and how Ron figured out how to get them. I could see the kids in the bone marrow unit, and I wondered how many of them made it home. And I fought and fought to keep the vision of Ron's funeral from materializing in my mind.

"Damn it, Ron!" I shouted angrily. "What blood type are you?"

"O positive," he said.

To this day I don't know why I'd never asked Ron that question before. Maybe it was because I didn't think he wanted me to because he saw me as someone who could look after his family should he not survive. Or maybe I didn't ask because somewhere deep down inside I thought I might be like most everyone when faced with this challenge, this opportunity, and would look the other way. I don't know why I didn't seek that answer earlier, but now I had, and I realized what it meant.

"Me, too," I responded immediately. "Hell, I'll go by the hospital and see if I'm compatible. You won't ever get a kidney at this rate."

Ron thought I was kidding. He didn't want to think I was serious because he was sick of getting his hopes up only to be disillusioned again in the end. It was an emotional roller coaster he was tired of riding. Adriane, Shreill, and I and all the kids were tired of riding it, too.

So the next week I started the journey to save Ron's life. And along the way I found a new purpose for the rest of mine, or it found me. It's like John Lennon wrote: "Life is what happens to you while you're busy making other plans."

Although I didn't know it at the time, it was something my life had been preparing me for all along.

# 2

# Family First

My mom, Ouida Armstong Walls, now seventy-five, still lives in the one-story white wood-frame house I grew up in. It's on Rialto Drive in the Hamilton Park section of Dallas, and I lived there with my two older sisters and my dad, at least until Mom and Dad split up when I was about twelve. The pole with the basketball backboard, rim, and net, where my buddies and I often played hoops late into a summer's night, is still in the driveway.

I can still drive around the neighborhood, and often do, and point out who lived in which house and what they were all about, like the house on Galva Drive where Shreill and her sisters, better known as the Harris girls, were always on lockdown. Shreill eventually got out, became my high school sweetheart, let me follow her to Grambling State University, and in 1984 accepted my proposal of marriage.

I drive by the actual park in Hamilton Park where the basketball and tennis courts and open field still stand, and I can recall all the games we played as kids. I drive by a fenced-in tumble of rough ground and rocks we called Dead Man's Hill. We raced motorcycles there. I go by the red-brick Hamilton Park School where the first families in the neighborhood were able to send their kids from first grade through twelfth. I made it through the sixth grade there before court-ordered school desegregation forced me to be bused to a school out of the neighborhood. Now Hamilton Park School is an elementary school and goes only to the sixth grade.

I drive by the place where I spent every Sunday morning unless I had an excuse to end all excuses, a red-brick church with white doors that was long called First Baptist Church of Hamilton Park. It is now a Hispanic church with another name, and First Baptist, which I still attend, is relocated in the nearby suburb of Richardson.

I drive by a barbecue joint at the gateway to Hamilton Park on Forest Lane that was a hamburger stand—Biff's—when I was growing up. I don't know who started Biff's or who Biff was, but for years Biff's was owned and operated by my parents as a second source of income, and pride. It was *the* hangout for kids in Hamilton Park, just like that soda shop, Arnold's Drive-In, was for Richie, Potsie, and Fonzie on the *Happy Days* TV show we watched in the '70s. The Hamilton Park I grew up in was working class. It was nuclear families. Everyone knew everybody. It was a happy place. It just happened to be all black.

There aren't many more-famous neighborhoods in Dallas than Hamilton Park. It's about ten miles north of downtown Dallas and about twenty miles south of where I—and Ron and his family, too—live now in the Dallas suburb of Plano. But Hamilton Park isn't like either of those places. It may be the most unique neighborhood in Dallas.

Before my mom and dad moved there in the late 1950s, the plot of land where Hamilton Park took root was like most land outside downtown Dallas—it was farmland. I don't know what farmers here grew, but I can see that seeds of sacrifice were sown by the farmers' successors—the neighborhood's elders, like my parents, who came to call the neighborhood home. I was just one of the products. My wife, Shreill, was another. Our folks produced a pretty good crop.

Hamilton Park was born out of necessity, maybe even desperation. In fact, most of Hamilton Park's early residents were transplants, emergency transplants. Some came from around Love Field, the municipal airport, after a decision to demolish part of a black neighborhood adjacent to the airport that was needed for the airport's expansion. In November 1963, almost four years after I was born, President Kennedy arrived at Love Field and departed it in a coffin.

Other Hamilton Park settlers came from a community just south of downtown Dallas called, not so creatively, South Dallas. Large parts of South Dallas became home to many of Dallas's black residents after World War II, and as our numbers swelled, we began to trickle into formerly all-white parts of South Dallas. That didn't go over too well with some white Dallasites. Several black homes were bombed, just like they were in other cities in the South where neighborhoods were changing color, and Dallas began a quest to maintain the security of segregation, in an effort to prevent a race riot. That meant finding another and separate neighborhood for black Dallasites.

One area that won approval from white businessmen and black residents was the plot of land that they would name after a black doctor and community leader, Dr. Richard T. Hamilton.

Hamilton Park was planted on 233 acres and was secured by the Dallas Citizens Council's Interracial Association, which was a group of white and black power brokers who sought to keep Dallas from becoming another southern city strangled by racial tensions. Three Dallas banks financed the construction of water and sewer lines to the development, and the government guaranteed loans for potential home buyers. My father was among some black construction workers who helped cut some of the swaths that became Hamilton Park streets. Hamilton Park was built with the backbone and sweat of black people for black people.

Hamilton Park was dedicated in 1953, opened in 1954, and by 1961, two years after I was born, included 742 single-family homes, an apartment complex, a shopping center, the park, the school, a couple of churches, and no white people. Imagine that. It was a planned segregated community.

It was pretty much self-sufficient, too, like Harlem or the South Side of Chicago or any other black neighborhood you've heard of. It was just smaller, a lot smaller. We could walk the entire neighborhood, and did.

The only reason anyone left Hamilton Park was to go to work, and everyone worked. Mom worked at first for a white family who owned a car dealership.

I was very young then and couldn't have told you exactly what Mom did for that family, but I came to learn that Mom was a domestic. A lot of black women in Dallas did Mom's type of work, cleaning and cooking and looking after the kids for another family, usually a white family, before coming home to take care of her own. I didn't understand as a kid how difficult that may have been for Mom to do, to take care of someone else's household before taking care of her own. It couldn't have been easy. But Mom did it nonetheless. She did it for her children.

One time Mom took me along to the house where she worked, and I met the little boy who was part of her responsibility. He and I seemed to be about the same age, and he didn't appear to recognize the difference in our skin color. He just wanted to play.

The boy took me to a closet, exactly where in the house I don't recall. What I do remember is what was in the closet when he opened its door. There were toys and games piled in and stacked as high as the ceiling. I couldn't believe all of them were his. So we played and played and played some more until my mother's work was done, and she walked me out of the house for our trip back to Hamilton Park. That was when I turned to my mom and told her I wished I was white.

Mom didn't work for the family forever. At some point she found a new job not far away at Texas Instruments in the suburb of Richardson. I never knew exactly what she did there. I just knew it wasn't working for a family with a little boy who had every toy known to kids.

Mom got up very early to go to TI. I'd hear her moving about when it was still dark outside, and I'd sit outside the bathroom waiting for her to come out. I was and still am a mama's boy.

That doesn't mean I don't love my dad, who had one job for as long as I knew. He drove a dump truck from sunup to sundown, hauling dirt and debris from one place to another in what then was a booming construction business in and around Dallas.

Dad hadn't planned on being a dump-truck driver any more than Mom had planned on working for some white family. Dad planned on being an engineer if a fleeting dream of being a pro football player didn't work out. That was what he went to college for at Prairie View A&M University, a historically black college north of Houston and south of College Station, where gigantic Texas A&M University sits. Dad went to Prairie View as a football star from Elysian Fields in East Texas, which is where the Walls family tree is planted, and to study engineering. My mother's family tree is in East Texas, too, closer to Longview.

Dad was a fullback, just like Ron became with the Cowboys, and you can still tell today. He's still got those thick, rounded shoulders and big fat, strong hands. He doesn't move as fast as he used to, because of some heart ailments and other physical struggles brought on by age. But I found out years later that Dad set a freshman record for rushing at Prairie View.

Dad's football-playing career ended after his freshman year, when he found out my mother was pregnant with my oldest sister, Eartha. There was no question back in those days what Dad would do. Black men were more responsible then—to themselves, to the mothers of their children, to their families, and to their communities.

So Dad dropped out of college. He discarded dreams of being a pro football player. He left Prairie View to be with my mother back in Dallas and to get a job to support his budding family. His parents, especially his father—Herman Walls, the grandfather I called Pa-Pa—and my mother's parents expected nothing less. Eartha was born in 1954.

That was when Dad's dream of becoming an engineer came to an end. A dump-truck driver would do. My father could employ his physical gifts and make good money.

Then Mom and Dad had my second sister, Gigi. Gigi was born in 1955. I came along three days after Christmas in 1959. Mom thought I was the spitting image of a teddy bear and immediately pinned on me a nickname that stayed with me to Grambling—"Cubby." To this day, I don't know how everyone else I grew up with found out what my mom called me and decided to call me the same. But in Hamilton Park, in Dallas, and to a few at Grambling who heard Shreill call my name, I'm not Everson. I'm Cubby.

We were a typical Hamilton Park family, which meant, first and foremost, that every Sunday we could be found at one of the churches in the community. Ours was First Baptist Church of Hamilton Park.

Dad was a deacon in the church. My mom's brother, Uncle Robert, also lived in Hamilton Park and was a deacon in the church. My mom was the announcer in the church. I was always so proud of Mom in church because she spoke so eloquently.

Like a lot of families, we walked to church. It just took us a lot less time, because First Baptist was only one block from our house. If we didn't show up on Sunday, people started talking. You didn't want people talking.

If I got in trouble in church as a kid, by playing around in a pew or something like that while Dad and Mom were elsewhere handling their duties, Mom and Dad didn't have to worry about disciplining me. One of the church mothers, or other deacons, or maybe just another church member, would snatch me up and drag me into the foyer for a straightening out. They were expected to do it. That's how close-knit our neighborhood was.

Mom and Dad were well known and respected in Hamilton Park, in part because of their involvement at First Baptist and in part because of Dad's appearance. He always looked like and carried himself like a tough guy. His hands are so big and rough you would think he could change a tire, bolts and all, without needing tools. I think a lot of people were afraid of him. But Dad was soft-spoken unless he was around just his buddies. I never saw him threaten anyone. But I never saw anyone test him either. Dad was respected, and it was earned.

Despite long hours five days a week doing backbreaking work and spending much of Sunday doing church duties, Dad still found time—no, made time—to share with me his love for sports. He never said he was too tired. He never said, "Can't we wait until tomorrow?" Dad spent time to teach me everything he knew about football, of course, and baseball, too.

He got me into organized sports when I was in the fifth grade at the start of football season in the Spring Valley Athletic Association, which was a youth league in Richardson. Our team was the Razorbacks. Our coach was Dad. I've always said Dad was the best coach I ever had other than Coach Robinson at Grambling.

Playing in the SVAA was my first chance to line up against just kids my age and against white kids. In Hamilton Park, I was accustomed to playing only against other black kids and often against kids who were older than me and bigger. You got tougher in a hurry playing against older, stronger kids, and it showed when I went up against white kids my age and size in my first organized football season ever.

I played running back, and the first time I touched the football, I scored a touchdown. It wouldn't be the last time. I had eighteen touchdowns in six games in my first season in the SVAA. The kids who were my age in the SVAA just weren't as big and strong and fast as the kids in Hamilton Park I was accustomed to playing with and against. The SVAA kids couldn't catch me, and if they did, they couldn't bring me down.

I know Dad was proud of me. He just didn't show it a lot. Dad wasn't just my coach; he was our team bus driver, too. He'd stuff the kids he was coaching from Hamilton Park into his car and transport us to and from practices and games. No matter how well we practiced or played, he'd find something to rib us about. The idea was, I figured out later, that he always wanted us to be thinking about something we could do to improve ourselves.

That's the way Dad is. He's one of those guys who believe that you can fall as low as you might rise high, so he always keeps things in perspective. That's how I learned to look at life as I do, I guess, as always realizing there is a balance. It's something that I'd lean on later in watching Ron struggle with his disease and figuring out what I could do to help him.

Before my second season in the SVAA, the strangest thing happened. It was like a scene out of that John Sayles' movie *The Brother from Another Planet,* where two white men in black suits, who are aliens, invade a Harlem bar looking for a particular black guy, who is the brother from another planet. Two white men in suits came up to Hamilton Park and took me out of class. I was in the sixth grade then. They escorted me to the gym and weighed me. I'll never forget; I weighed 110 pounds.

By the time the second football season of the SVAA kicked off, the rules had changed. Kids my age couldn't play running back if they weighed more than a hundred pounds. There went my running-back career.

I didn't analyze what happened until I was much older, when I figured that the white parents weren't happy that black kids, two or three on each team, were taking playing time from their kids and some of the glory that went with it. So they changed the rules. With me no longer a running back and relegated to tight end, our team went from playing in the championship game my first season to winning one game in my second season. I think I scored just one touchdown because it was so hard at that age to find another kid who was good enough to throw the football any distance with any accuracy.

I played baseball in the SVAA, too, and, once again, Dad was my coach. I never liked baseball too much, but what Dad taught me about playing baseball made me, ironically, the football player I became.

I was a center fielder in baseball. Why, I don't know, because in the beginning I really wasn't very good at chasing down fly balls. I could handle a fly ball if I didn't have to move too much. I just couldn't draw that bead, as they say, on a fly ball if it was one that I had to chase after in order to catch.

Running after a fly ball seemed to make watching the ball like viewing a bad 8 mm home movie—it would bounce up and down erratically in my vision. My father told me my problem was that I was running flatfooted rather than on my toes. I was slamming my foot into the ground rather than tiptoeing, and that, he said, was causing the ball to dance in my line of sight.

So I started running on my toes. Slowly but surely, catching fly balls on the chase became easier and easier. I could draw that bead on the ball. That was one reason I came to make so many interceptions in high school, college, and the NFL. I learned how best to follow a ball in the air and watch it all the way into my hands. Baseball or football, it didn't matter. I owe that to my dad. I never forgot that lesson.

The only sport Dad didn't show me anything about was basketball. This is Texas. There's football and spring football, and whatever is in between doesn't matter much. Basketball was one of the whatevers in between. I learned to play basketball on my own down at the park. I fell in love with it like no other sport. That's what I wanted to be—a pro basketball player, not a pro football player.

I didn't play organized basketball until the seventh grade, when, for the first time, I was out of Hamilton Park on a regular basis. The busing craze that was sweeping across the nation from the East Coast and that ensnared me and my friends ushered in the only unhappy time of my young life, and my displeasure would last several years.

But it was also a period of my life when I encountered some events that would steel me for what I would confront with Ron. One was the separation of Mom and Dad. That was the first time I understood that I was witnessing what real sacrifice for others was all about.

All of a sudden, my mom was a single parent, and she had to figure out on her own how to take care of teenage girls preparing to go to college and an adolescent boy. Her life changed. My life changed. Our lives changed. It was painful. It was something that left such a deep wound in me that I've always said I will fight for my marriage, which I'm happy to say is now twenty-five years old. The last thing I want my kids to go through is the divorce of their parents. Family is very important to me. It's very important to Ron, which is one reason we became so close and I wanted to do whatever it would take to keep him around. His family loved and needed him.

Dad was still around after he moved out and eventually was divorced from Mom, but he had other concerns now. He had another family to take care of, which was what caused my mom and him to split up. So Mom picked up a second job at the Dallas Urban League in order to keep us in our Hamilton Park house. My sisters worked their way through college, starting at a nearby community college and finishing at North Texas in Denton.

Everybody sacrificed. I even picked up a job busting suds, as we used to say of busboy work, at a dinner theater not far away to lighten the load on Mom.

I didn't know it then, but Mom and Dad and my sisters were instilling in me the value of sacrifice that Ron would summon in me years later. So, too, was everyone else in and around Hamilton Park. Hamilton Park was the epitome of community. Everyone knew everyone. Everybody looked out for each other. If someone was in need, a neighbor was always willing to help. It was like that African proverb Hillary Clinton used. Hamilton Park was a village that raised its children well.

This was also the time when I met a kid who would become my best childhood friend. He didn't grow up in Hamilton Park but came from across the tracks, figuratively more than literally. Mike Terrell. We called him "T." I met Mike in seventh grade at a track meet. He lived across Stultz Road in the Stultz neighborhood. That was the sister neighborhood to Hamilton Park. It was on the other side of Forest Lane from my folks' hamburger stand. The kids on that side of Forest didn't go to Hamilton Park School; they went to Forest Meadow. We'd get together at youth league games and in the park.

Stultz was a step up from Hamilton Park; tall cotton, as the old folks liked to say. A lot of people from Hamilton Park moved to Stultz because the houses were better. Hamilton Park had wood homes; Stultz had brick homes. The families in Stultz were working class, too, but they made a little more money. Mike's dad worked for the airlines and traveled with the airlines. Mike's house even had a swimming pool. That's Stultz! So every weekend we were calling Mike to see if we could have a pool party. I was over there a lot with some other friends from Hamilton Park.

Mike came over to our neighborhood a lot to play basketball down at the park. That's where everybody hung out, the park, till two o'clock in the morning in the summertime when school was out. That was back in the days when kids stayed outside, and no one worried about them. There wasn't any talk about abductions and pedophiles, and the crackheads who roam the park nowadays were not a flicker in anyone's worst nightmare back then.

Parents who lived in the houses across the street from the park kept an eye on what was going on there. It was a safe haven without the little yellow signs they post now to designate a building a safe place for kids. We'd play basketball in the summer until we couldn't breathe anymore. We'd come in when we were ready, and none of the parents were worried because they knew where all the kids were—at the park—and what they were doing.

We had a tennis court down there, too. There was a little football field. There were picnic benches, swings. Everything was down there. There were plenty of things to do, including going to the theater. The park was across the creek from the Gemini Drive-In. We'd just walk over the creek and jump the fence into the Gemini parking lot to watch the movies. That was about the most real mischief we got into. I don't think we ever paid to see a movie there.

Mike had a girlfriend in Stultz, too, Felecia Allen. We called her Lisa. She was part of the crew that hung out poolside at Mike's house and came over to the park in Hamilton Park, where the girls milled about while the boys played basketball or football. Lisa went to Forest Meadow.

Until I started exploring whether I could save Ron's life, I hadn't thought about Lisa in a long, long time. I hadn't seen her in a long, long time. You know how it is. You go away to college, and you lose touch with a lot of the people you grew up with because they either go away, too, or enter other phases of their lives that don't intersect with yours.

That was the case with Lisa. I went off to college. She and Mike eventually went their separate ways, and the connection between Lisa and me was broken.

But I never forgot Lisa, not just because she was my best friend's girl, but because of the bond she had with her older sister, Gwen. They reminded me of my older sisters, Eartha and Gigi. Anyone our age who grew up in Hamilton Park or Stultz and knew Lisa and Gwen never forgot how tight they were either. And most everyone knew Lisa and Gwen because they were a couple of good-looking girls. Stultz had a lot of fine girls, which was another reason the guys from Hamilton Park liked to venture across Forest Lane.

I was graduated from high school and playing football at Grambling when some news broke back in Stultz about Gwen. Word had it that Gwen was very sick. Someone said she had the shugah. If I had known the shugah was the same as diabetes, it still wouldn't have made a difference, because I wasn't certain what diabetes was.

I've come to learn that my lack of knowledge about diabetes in my community is typical. I didn't know diabetes could cause heart disease and kidney failure and result in blindness or the need for amputations. I didn't know it could kill. I didn't know because no one in our community knew.

I didn't know that all the food we loved to eat growing up, what we proudly called soul food—salty fried fish and fried chicken and hot link pork sausages, leafy greens and green beans cooked all day in fat from ham hocks—was not as good for our bodies as our taste buds would have us believe. I didn't realize that the weight that it put on family members and friends as they grew older and became more sedentary made them more susceptible to a host of maladies like heart disease and high blood pressure, not to mention diabetes.

No one in Hamilton Park understood that the way we lived made us more likely to suffer from those sorts of debilitating disorders than other racial and ethnic groups. No one knew then that more than one in every ten black Americans would come to have diabetes, and at least one in four elderly black Americans would get it.

When you're a teenager and someone says one of your peers is sick with it, well, it just doesn't register what that means. You just assume they'll get better soon because that's what we do as young people—we overcome whatever ails us and live to get old.

Exactly how much Gwen was suffering from diabetes never made it all the way to me at Grambling. And I just figured, given that I didn't know anything about diabetes, that she'd get some medicine and she'd be fine. Like I said, we were young. No one I grew up with ever suffered any health problem worse than a really bad cold, as far as I knew. This was a similar thing, I thought.

But the few times I saw Gwen during my visits from college back to Hamilton Park, she didn't look as I remembered her. It was clear something had happened, or was happening, because Gwen was no longer the beautiful girl she'd always been. Her body was changing. She started gaining a little weight. One of her eyes seemed to have turned colors. She didn't look well. And when I saw her again, she didn't look any better. She looked worse. The change in her appearance was drastic to me because I'd only seen her every six months or so since I was away at school.

But I'd make small talk with Gwen and whoever I might see at her side whenever I'd bump into her. I never pried by asking her if something was wrong. I didn't like to dwell on potential bad news then any more than I did with Ron when his illness turned crippling. It wasn't so much a defense reaction to something I didn't want to know anything more about; it was, for me, a privacy issue. I figured that if she—or, later on, Ron—wanted me to know more, the information would come voluntarily. Gwen would speak up when she was ready. So would Ron. But they never did.

So I would just wish Gwen well and then, silently to myself, hope that the next time I saw her everything would be better. That she would shed the weight she'd put on. That her eyes would be clear again. I was certain everything would be normal again, because we were teenagers going on young adulthood. What could possibly be wrong with one of us?

The next thing I heard, Gwen needed a transplant and Lisa was going to be the donor who would give Gwen a kidney.

I didn't know quite what that meant then. It was around 1980. I was a college junior turning into a senior, and that was the first I'd heard of someone I knew being involved in a transplant. A transplant? I didn't even know that a live person could donate an organ. *What's going to happen to Lisa?* I wondered. None of us in Hamilton Park knew any better. We couldn't fathom diabetes being so serious and someone giving up a piece of himself or herself to help someone else live.

Lisa must have been about eighteen then and Gwen about twenty-two. I turned my attention back to playing football and staying on course to graduate from Grambling. It was a while before I got back to Hamilton Park again and saw any of the old gang.

I don't remember exactly when I saw Lisa or Gwen after Lisa donated her kidney to Gwen. I just remember hearing it worked. It sounded like a miracle. I didn't know how often miracles like that could arise.

# 3

# Friendships

I've heard it said that a lifelong friendship like the one Ron and I have is something that is earned. We are living proof that that is more than a saying and is an absolute truth. But I first came to learn the truth of friendship the hard way, when I started growing up in a single-parent household after Mom and Dad split up.

It was during that awkward period every kid goes through during adolescence. It was just aggravated for me.

When I was about to enter the seventh grade, busing arrived in Dallas, which meant that for the first time in my life I was going to have to spend a good part of my days outside Hamilton Park. That was difficult to conceive because I'd never considered it. No one had. Hamilton Park was our hood, always had been and, we figured, always would be, at least until we went away to college. But all of a sudden, I wasn't able to go to Hamilton Park School for my junior high and senior high years like all the older kids I knew. I wasn't allowed to walk a quarter mile to class through yards and down streets I could navigate in complete darkness without tripping over a single tree root.

Busing? I hadn't even been on a bus. But there I was, herded onto one of those yellow school buses I'd seen on the news and, with a bunch of other boys and girls from Hamilton Park, rambling out of our neighborhood to Richardson Junior High to be with kids we didn't know from families who didn't know ours.

Our new classmates were white kids, too. Busing was all about integration, of course. It was about breaking down the barriers of segregation. In Dallas, that meant disturbing the peace we all loved in Hamilton Park. I know that integration was why Dr. Martin Luther King Jr. marched and laid down his life. It was just that I don't remember ever hearing anyone in all-black Hamilton Park complain about being in all-black Hamilton Park.

Rarely did our bus pull up outside Richardson Junior High in the morning and not dump us off into a confrontation with the white kids. It was as if everything was scripted. We'd always make sure that the ninth-grade boys and the feisty boys from the lower grades, like me, Michael Warren, and Allan Foxall, got off the bus first. We were like the infantry. We took the first volley of incoming horse apples, those green grapefruit-sized, hard pebble–skinned, nasty balls of inedible fruit that grew on hedge trees all over Dallas. We came with our own arsenal of horse apples, too. It was war. There were skirmishes in the halls and cafeteria. It was hard sometimes to concentrate in class on what was being taught because I was thinking about who was sitting behind me and who I'd bump into when I headed to the next period.

Playing sports on the junior high team was frustrating because the white coaches had it in for the black kids and didn't treat us like the white kids. They knew the white kids. They knew their families. They came from their own Hamilton Park.

I remember one day I saw a kid named Lorenzo Jefferson pull off his pads and throw them to the ground because of the way the football coaches were treating him. He never played sports again. It was a real shame because he came from a family where everybody was a really good athlete. But that was the way it was. We knew we were better, but we couldn't get in a game even when our parents were in the stands watching.

It reminded me of something I used to hear my grandparents say: "You've got to be twice as good as the white guy." Most black kids in this country hear that at some point.

The last day of school that first year, the police even showed up. They came to make sure that what had been daily racial disorder didn't degenerate into something worse. It didn't.

After a couple of years, though, a bunch of us opted to transfer to Forest Meadow Junior High School for the ninth grade. We'd tired of the daily gauntlet we had to run at Richardson. It wasn't much different at Forest Meadow either.

It was the first time I began to dislike school. A lot of the guys from Hamilton Park didn't like the way the principals and teachers in our new junior high schools treated us. They didn't give us a fair shake any more than the coaches. We saw them as the enemy.

When we graduated to high school, we were split up even more. I wound up at Richardson Berkner High School, while some of my friends, depending on the boundaries, were sent to Lake Highlands High School. I was growing bitter about it all and becoming disenchanted. I stopped playing football because I didn't like the coaches. I wasn't alone.

I had to play something, though. I always played sports. So I wound up running hurdles and concentrating on basketball when I first got to high school. I chose basketball because I loved it, even though Texas was football country, and the high school basketball coaches were no fairer to the black kids than the football coaches were. At least it wasn't as physical. If there was one thing about football I never liked, it was tackling. That may sound odd for someone like me who wound up with tackling being an integral part of my game as a defensive player, but I never looked forward to running into the ball carrier and trying to knock him or pull him down. Basketball was just so smooth, poetic almost. There was nothing more pleasing than shooting a jump shot and watching it float through the rim and splash into the net. I wanted to be Walt Frazier or Earl Monroe or George "Iceman" Gervin. On top of all that, basketball was indoors, where I didn't have to get my Afro messed up in bad weather. Unlike football, I didn't have to smash it under a football helmet either. Little did I know my hair would wind up being an issue for someone else on the basketball court.

I was good at basketball. I made the junior varsity when I got to Berkner as a tenth grader and was excited about it. We had a basketball game on my birthday, which, as I said, is a few days after Christmas. As anyone born around Christmas knows, that means gifts get consolidated. One of my consolidated gifts that year was getting my hair braided before this game. I thought it looked so cool. All of my family came out to watch me play because it was the holidays, and everyone had a break from the normal routine of work and more work.

My basketball coach, Tom Everett, wasn't so taken with my braids. Afros and braids in the early '70s were a little threatening. They reminded people of the Black Panthers, a group I didn't know anything about at the time. I just thought it was a cool look, like the dudes on the TV dance show *Soul Train.*

Coach Everett thought otherwise. He punished me. He didn't let me play that day because of my braids, and I refused to take them out. I hadn't ever been so mad before in my life. I wanted to do what I felt like doing and I was becoming determined not to let anyone else influence me otherwise.

This wasn't cool, though. I had quit playing football. Soon basketball would come to an end. Playing baseball had become a historical footnote in my life. Dad had remarried and was rearing a new son, Greg. All of a sudden, I was going to have oodles of what my mom feared as she was rearing me on her own: idle time. She wasn't about to watch me come up with ways to while away the hours unsupervised. She just wouldn't have it.

Mom told me that since I wasn't as occupied after school, I needed to do something—like get an after-school job. So off I went in search of a gig as tenth grade wound down. I found one at a place called Granny's Dinner Playhouse, on the same block as the Cowboys' practice facility. You could have dinner and watch a play, usually a musical. Every now and then Granny's featured a well-known entertainer, but I missed all those big names, most painfully Tina Turner right after she broke up with Ike. I was a busboy, washing dishes, bustin' suds. Then I got another job doing the same thing at another dinner playhouse a little farther away called Country Dinner Playhouse. Playhouses were a popular thing back then.

The only thing I enjoyed that year was earning a little pocket change to buy cool clothes like window-pane jeans and platform shoes, and those silky disco shirts. Other than that, the rest of my sophomore year was bad. I got into more trouble at school. I got suspended for a few days for just being rebellious. Mom was scared of where I was headed. She had plans for me, or at least dreams. I was threatening to turn into a nightmare.

Mom was working a couple of jobs then to keep us living like we were accustomed to when she and Dad were together and Eartha and Gigi were in the house. Mom was doing everything she could think of to make ends meet. I remember she started keeping a lot of clothes in the house that she was selling on the weekends or late in the evening when she got home. She left the house when it was still dark for her job at Texas Instruments, which was not far away in Richardson, just on the other side of the big interstate highway loop called 635. Later in the afternoon, she went to South Dallas to work at the Urban League helping black people who were down on their luck. She pointed them in the direction of potential jobs and helped them prepare for job interviews. She helped them complete their education so they would have better opportunities. She taught them how to manage their money in tough times.

That was one thing that defined Mom. She was always trying to help somebody else. I still bump into people today who say, "Your mom helped me get my GED," and things like that. I picked up a lot of values from my mother, and I suspect one of the most important was the desire to lend a helping hand. Who knew that it would change the course of my life and that of someone else I didn't even know existed then?

My time together with Mom wasn't like it had been when all the family was together. Her work schedule, which was necessary, was so heavy, and much of the way I was spending my idle time, which was unnecessary, was away from home.

I was getting older and more adventurous and finding reasons to spend more time outside the house after school, after work, and later and later into the night. I wasn't doing anything but hanging out with the guys and chasing the girls, but Mom was concerned, and rightfully so. I remember one morning I came in the door as Mom was going out. I felt so bad. My behavior was just as disrespectful to my mother as mouthing off to her, which I never did, would have been. I told myself that would be the last time I did anything like that.

I was making new acquaintances then, too. I did so more out of necessity than anything else. My best friend T. was with his girlfriend, Lisa, more and more. I didn't have a girlfriend and didn't want to be their third wheel unless they invited me. So I started hanging out with some other guys in Hamilton Park, as well as some guys in some other neighborhoods.

I started going to South Dallas, which was all black by then. There was a place called Glendale Park in South Dallas where everybody came from all the black neighborhoods, even the suburb of Garland. People listened to music, played basketball, partied, and talked to the pretty girls from South Oak Cliff, which was a growing new black Dallas neighborhood even a little farther away than South Dallas. It was the first time I tasted the Bull: Schlitz Malt Liquor.

I was fifteen by then, and some guys who were even older, and had cars, befriended me and started taking me with them farther and farther from Hamilton Park. I was branching out, broadening my horizons in Dallas and worrying my mother more and more.

When I came home and got to my bedroom, I often discovered an article from one of the Dallas newspapers or a magazine, placed in the middle of my bed. It was usually some tale about a kid my age who stopped heeding the advice of his elders and wound up getting himself into trouble with the police, or worse. The planter of the messages was Mom, of course. She was trying to get me back on the straight and narrow.

I always told Mom not to worry because I wasn't that kind of boy. Then during the summer after my sophomore year of discontent, the police knocked at our door.

It was one of those not too frequent days when Mom and I happened to be home at the same time. Looking back, it was as if God had arranged that day so Mom could witness her biggest fears. I couldn't bluff anymore, though I tried.

Mom answered the door. The police asked for me. Mom called me to the front of the house with that concern in her voice that only a mother can muster.

"Cubby," she called me, with an eerie inquisitiveness.

Mom stepped back as I strutted to the door trying to summon some bravado to steel myself for what I had an inkling might be coming. It did.

The police asked me if I knew a couple of boys in the neighborhood they'd picked up for a holdup not far away. I told them I did know them. They asked me if it was true what the boys said, that they were over here at my mom's house with me during the time the victim said the boys were committing the robbery. The victim was a woman who worked at a dry cleaner on the edge of Hamilton Park almost next to the Cowboys' practice facility. I told the police it was true that the guys were with me at my mom's house. I could feel my mother's eyes looking me up and down from behind.

The cops then asked me if I would visit them later downtown at the station. I said I would. They turned and walked away. I closed the door and turned and faced my mother.

"Boy, what you talkin' about?" my mom said to me. "You know those boys weren't over here with you."

"Yes, they were, Mom," I said. "Don't worry about it."

I had disrespected my mother by coming in late when she was working long hours. Now I was lying to her face.

Hamilton Park seemed to me and most of the people who lived and grew up there to be nothing short of an idyllic place. But there were some bad seeds in the neighborhood, and I had started hanging out with a few of them from time to time because bad dudes always seemed to be some of the coolest. They drank. They smoked. Some of them were petty thieves who snatched a few things from stores. I was too scared to steal, but sometimes I served as their lookout.

One day, I volunteered to help some of these guys by agreeing to be their alibi for something they didn't quite fill me in on. That's how foolish I'd become. They went and did whatever they did, and I went the other way and didn't think twice about it again, at least not until those cops knocked at the door.

I didn't know all of what the cops knew, but I found out when I went downtown at their invitation. It was the first time I was in the police station beyond the front desk. The cops told me the guys I knew not only held up the dry cleaners but also sodomized the victim who was working there. Sodomized? I wasn't sure what it meant except that it probably wasn't good because it sounded like the word *Sodom* that I heard spat out like vinegar some Sundays by our pastor at church.

The cops didn't believe my story. They asked me to take a seat in a room with a large mirror that must have been a two-way. I wasn't there very long before the cops came in the room and arrested me. They said the victim identified me as one of the robbers and her attacker.

I tried to stay cool, but I was steaming inside, because the guys who I agreed to cover for hadn't done the same for me even though they knew I hadn't done anything except serve as their alibi. I was also angry because this was the "they all look alike" offense that often snared innocent black men.

I was frightened, too. I'd never been under arrest. The cops tossed me in a van and drove me to the juvenile detention center. They stuck me in cell P-15. It was right near the front door of the jail. I watched all the parents coming and going to see their kids or, if the kids were lucky, pick them up and take them home.

It was a Thursday when it all happened, and on Friday I was taken to a courtroom. I figured I'd be released there because I wasn't guilty of anything except being stupid enough to extend my friendship to a bunch of guys who didn't deserve it.

That was when it dawned on me how precious friendship really is. It isn't something you just toss around like bread crumbs to pigeons. It's something you extend like credit only to those who are worthy of it. You share your friendship with those who are deserving of it after all they've done for you, especially when you haven't asked them for anything, as I never have of Ron.

As I sat in that courtroom thinking about how I wound up there, I realized the mistake I'd made by confusing acquaintance with friendship. Those guys didn't care about me. They weren't deserving of what I did for them. I had suspected that whatever they were going to do was wrong, and I should have realized that they would be the first to run and hide, which they had done.

I'd done something I had learned from my mother, which was to help other people out. I'd sacrificed myself for others, but it was misplaced sacrifice, perverted sacrifice. That became painfully obvious when a prosecutor named Dee Miller stood before the judge, pointed to me, and said I was a "danger to the community" who should be locked up.

I'd never heard myself described like that, and no one who was close to me had heard such a description of me either. Cocky? Yes. Rebellious? Certainly. A threat on the basketball court or football field? Of course. A menace to society? Never. So the judge ordered me back to juvenile detention for the weekend.

My mother wanted to believe my fabricated story, too, and figured I'd be right back after I went downtown to see the cops. When I didn't come back, and she found out I was headed to court on Friday, she figured that would be the end of it, too, and I'd be released to return home, hard lesson learned. But now she had to come to the detention center to find out what was going on.

When I laid eyes on my mom coming through the door into the waiting room where we could talk, she was in tears. My dad was right behind her.

"Oh, Cubby," Mom said. "Where did I fail you? I thought I was a good mother."

Here was a woman I loved with all my heart, who'd seen to it that my two sisters made it to college and was doing everything now as a single mom to get me to college, too. But I'd done exactly what I said I wouldn't do again: disrespect her rearing of me.

"Mom," I said almost crying myself. "What are you talking about?"

Before I could say any more, like tell her what a great mother she was and how this was all a mix-up, she dropped the bomb.

"Why did you do all of this?" she said, holding a document from the court and pointing to it.

I grabbed the paper and started reading it. It said I robbed another place and assaulted someone else and stuck up yet another person somewhere else. On and on the charges seemed to go. It looked like I was being accused of every crime that happened in Dallas that summer.

I couldn't believe it either, and my sympathy for my mom snapped into anger.

"Mom," I screamed, with my dad looking at me, "I didn't do this shit!"

It was the first and last time I ever cursed at my mother, and it never should have happened then.

My mother was so upset I don't think my cursing even registered with her. Dad appeared only to focus on my denial of having done anything criminal.

I calmed down and looked at the document a little more closely. I noticed the dates and realized how trumped up the charges were.

"Look at this right here, Mom," I said pointing to a date. It was July 10. "Mom, remember this? We weren't even in the country."

That week Mom and her sister had taken me with them to the Bahamas. I remembered the date because that was Bahamian Independence Day, and we happened to be on the island there for the celebration.

"Listen, I was at Granny's Dinner Playhouse at work on this one," I said, pointing to another charge date on the document.

The tears that were streaming down my mother's face began to slow to a trickle. My dad looked at me and said, "I knew you didn't do this."

We hugged. Mom and Dad said they were going to get a lawyer, and then they left. I was left to think about what I'd done. It was the first time I read the Bible just on my own.

The lawyer my mom hired got a private investigator to track down my time cards from Granny's and the other dinner playhouse where I washed dishes. Mom and her sister had the tickets and hotel receipts from our trip to the Bahamas because they were keepsakes anyway, mementos of doing well as a black family. It was the first time we'd ever been out of the country.

Two weeks later, there was a second hearing before the judge and the same prosecutor, who couldn't sing the same song as before. I confessed the truth, which I should have done all along, and the other guys were rounded up and taken to juvenile to take my place. The charges against me, all of them, were dropped. I finally walked back onto the streets a free teenager, just in time for the start of school.

All the newspaper clippings and magazine articles Mom had left for me to see on my bed, all those cautionary tales, didn't have nearly the impact on me that those two weeks locked up did. I was scared straight, like those juvenile delinquents were by real-life jail inmates in that old film documentary of the same name. I stopped hanging with people who were up to no good and refused to extend my friendship to those who didn't deserve it.

Until then, I hadn't experienced any turning points in my life. I'd been knocked off course briefly by the breakup of my parents and then by the decision of Dallas to implement busing. But I'd never been spun around, and until then I never needed to be.

I didn't know that summer, of course, that those two weeks in the joint would lead me to where I am now and to the decisions I made with Ron, but they did. It was proof that sometimes you don't have any idea that you're standing at a starting line.

☆

For the first time, I couldn't wait to get back to school. I knew it wouldn't be any worse than what I'd just gone through and I was looking forward to trying out—no *making*—the varsity basketball team. There wasn't a sport I wanted to play more.

That was when something else I never envisioned happened. Just like Michael Jordan had happen to him in high school, I got cut from the varsity team. I was angry and dejected. I thought my not making the team had more to do with who I was, a black kid, and the way I carried myself, refusing to conform to the norms of Richardson Berkner. I had one of the biggest Afros in school whenever I untied the braids and let my hair out. Braiding put the pouf in the 'fro.

I thought my life couldn't have unraveled anymore, yet it had. I had been active in sports as long as I could remember and suddenly I was not. I finally fully realized my mother's fear for me and I was frightened about my future too.

So the first thing I did after the Christmas break my junior year was walk into the football coach's office and tell the coach that I wanted to play. Coach Allen Holladay wasn't sure I was serious. He'd heard about what I'd been through last summer. He questioned me. I wound up begging him to let me resume playing the game I played so well in youth leagues and junior high. He eventually acquiesced and let me join spring practice.

The other thing I did then was discover the best friend I've ever had in my life, Shreill Harris. I knew Shreill and her sisters mostly from school. But they weren't the types to hang out much in our neighborhood park or even just outside on the streets during the day or weekends. They were known as the Harris girls, and all the guys in Hamilton Park joked when we drove or walked past their house that if we saw them at all it would be playing peekaboo through the window drapes. Their father didn't allow his daughters to roam far from his sight.

We started talking a little at school before our junior years ended, and soon I made an introduction of Shreill to Mom, and Mom was bowled over by Shreill's intelligence and focus. Shreill wasn't trying to figure out if she was going to college. She already knew she was going to Grambling, where her uncle was an assistant football coach.

Mom was so happy that I was hanging around someone—as much as Mr. Harris would allow me—who was working toward something positive like college.

I expected to go to college, but I didn't really have a plan like Shreill. I just thought high school would end, and, just like my sisters, I'd wind up at the next educational level. I didn't even think about winning an athletic scholarship to college because I wasn't being recruited for basketball, and I had just started playing football again. A football coach wasn't going to reward a first-year high school player with a scholarship to play. My father starred at Prairie View as a freshman, and plenty of other guys in Hamilton Park went to college on football scholarships, but they were well-known talents in high school. I was all but forgotten until my senior season ended, and I'd done what I came to be known for, lead all the competition in interceptions.

That was when I really started liking football again. It took that long.

A few small schools inquired about me, like Abilene Christian, New Mexico State, East Texas State, and Sam Houston State. But I didn't want to go to any of those schools. Sam Houston State sat right next to the Texas death house in Huntsville, where they executed killers. I wasn't comfortable with that.

I really wanted to follow the new light in my life, Shreill. So I decided I was going to Grambling.

I knew Grambling like I knew Notre Dame. Everybody did. Because every Sunday morning before I went to church there was a Grambling highlight show on television just like the Notre Dame Sunday morning highlight show narrated by Lindsey Nelson, who famously fast-forwarded the replays with the phrase "moving on to further action."

I wasn't thinking about playing football at Grambling because I didn't think I was good enough, and the guys on TV looked pretty big. But unless I played football there, I wasn't going to be able to go, because Mom probably couldn't afford to send me. Dad was rearing a new family and was financially tethered to them.

But I put my mind to it, because I had no alternative if I wanted to be with Shreill, who was as important to getting me on the right track as Mom, my sisters, my dad, or that two-week scared-straight program I got myself into unwittingly.

My mom liked the idea because she knew Grambling, too, and knew of Coach Eddie Robinson. Everybody in our community knew of Coach Rob, as he was called. Grambling was as well-known a black institution as there was in the country, and Coach Rob was as famous a black person in America as any. Every time you saw Coach Rob on television, he looked very fatherly and very stern. In other words, he looked perfect for a cocky kid like me who had, if only for a short while, strayed off course.

I was doing my part to get to Grambling. I was behaving myself. I was working to get my grades up. I was holding onto Shreill with both hands as she helped pave a way for me onto Coach Rob's football team by telling her uncle all about her new six-two, 195-pound defensive back of a boyfriend who led his Dallas district in interceptions.

But I never heard from Coach Rob or anyone else at Grambling. So my mom decided that spring to pay the famous coach and famous school a visit with me in tow. She put on her newest outfit (Mom loved to dress and was always the most beautiful mom to me and the hippest to my friends), and she and I hopped in her Corvette and took off for Grambling. Mom always liked Corvettes, which was one reason everyone thought she was so hip.

I'll never forget how we passed through rural East Texas, where my parents hailed from and where I had visited many times, and my mother said, "See this? This is what Grambling is like." I was shocked. I thought a school with a national TV program was in a town more like Atlanta than their hometown of Elysian Fields, Texas. But I saw Mom was right when we pulled off Interstate 20 onto a narrow road lined with tall pine trees that after several miles dumped into Grambling, Louisiana, home to Grambling University and not much else. I discovered some small, low-level buildings scattered around. We had arrived on the campus.

We pulled up to a building near the gym, where Coach Robinson was supposed to be awaiting our visit. I must have looked like a city slicker in my platform shoes, window-pane jeans, and black leather visor cutting my Afro in half.

"Well, you kind of tall, son," was the first thing Coach Rob said to me when Mom and I were escorted into his office. "Maybe we could use you."

Then Coach Rob had another player walk me to the cafeteria where the players were dining, and I saw Doug Williams holding court. He was said to be up for the Heisman Trophy the next season, which would be his senior year and my freshman year, if I was so lucky.

I saw the rest of the campus over the next hour before being reunited with Mom, who had been meeting with Coach Rob. I said good-bye to Coach and hopped back in Mom's Corvette for the trip back to Dallas. When she pulled out of the parking lot, she gave me the news. Coach Rob was giving me a scholarship. It was his last.

Mom told me she explained to Coach Rob that I was a really good son and that she was rearing me as a single mother ever since she and Dad split up. She said she told him that she wanted me to have a male figure in my life who could be inspirational, and he was at the top of her list. Mom said she pleaded with Coach Rob for a scholarship because she didn't have the money to send me to college and that without a scholarship, she didn't know what would become of me.

This is how lucky I was: Coach Rob told my mother that he didn't have a scholarship to offer when we first contacted him, but one kid he extended an offer to decided not to go to Grambling. Coach Rob told Mom that he was impressed with me and with her and would give me that last scholarship.

Mom was on the road back to Dallas. I was on the road to pro football that ran me into that freight train of a personality named Ron Springs.

# 4

# Coach Rob's Team

I remember seeing a documentary on TV about Grambling Tigers football long before Mom and I visited Grambling that first time. The documentary was in color, but it was one of those grainy films, kind of like those 8 mm home movies parents back in the '60s made of family vacations and their kids opening Christmas presents. It was produced by Howard Cosell and Jerry Izenberg, the legendary New Jersey sports columnist. It was about how Coach Rob was using football to knock down racial injustice and erase stereotypes about black men. It was called *Grambling College: 100 Yards to Glory.*

The title didn't just come out of Cosell's head or that of some other producer of the film. When I got to Grambling, I learned that it came from a drill Coach Rob made everyone do before practice on our long, hard, dusty practice field.

He'd have two guys line up side by side and hit a two-man sled, a big metal contraption on slides with a pair of long padded rails standing up on the front and a platform for a man to stand on the back facing the padded rails. The sled would be placed on the goal line with all the rest of the field in front. The two guys would then have to smash into it shoulders first, hug it, lift it, and shove it halfway down the field, then turn and shove it all the way back to the goal line. Hence, one hundred yards to glory.

I don't know how much that sled weighed, but after pushing it for about twenty-five yards downfield in the hot Louisiana sun with a black helmet on just sucking in all the heat, it felt like I was pushing a grand piano up a San Francisco hill.

There was a lot of screaming and grunting. Everyone wanted to quit at some point. It didn't matter if you were a star or some monster-sized lineman who could lift other guys overhead. Everyone wanted to put those sleds down to catch their breath and let the sharpening pain in their legs and arms ease.

There were times I wanted to quit. There were times my boys wanted to quit. But you would make sure your guy didn't quit, and he would make sure you didn't quit, and somehow, some way, you'd get that damned sled to the fifty-yard line, get it turned around, and shove it back to the goal line, where you'd usually wind up hands on knees with your chest heaving as you gasped for air. Or you'd just collapse in exhaustion, wishing to expire rather than suffer through life any longer at that moment.

We thought the drill was to strengthen our legs and increase our endurance so that we'd be stronger than the other team in the fourth quarter. Maybe that was some of it.

What I realized years later, however, was that it was a drill designed to build camaraderie, to build support for each other, to build support for the Grambling program and bolster our pride in our school and our coach. It was about playing together for Coach Rob, who was using football to change the way the country looked at us as young black men and the way we as young black men saw ourselves in the country.

Coach Rob was big on legacy. At the start of every summer training camp, he would ask the newcomers whether they wanted to be just one of the hordes of Grambling Tigers who sprinted onto the field at the beginning of a game, or one of the Tigers who stood out from the horde when we ran onto the field. Coach Rob was big on how we'd be remembered after spending four years under his tutelage.

I had never thought about how I'd like to be remembered until I heard that Coach Rob speech every summer for four years in a row. How many teenagers or early twentysomethings think about their place in history? When you are that young, you are lucky if you are thinking about where you're going to be next weekend.

One hundred yards to glory was, at the end of the day, about learning to be a teammate in a struggle, small on Saturdays and large in life. It was a lesson I'd never really learned the importance of until then.

☆

I was never a real teammate in high school. Not that I didn't want to be. It was just that I didn't have time to be, or didn't take time to be. I was too angry and on edge about how the coaches were treating or mistreating those of us from Hamilton Park. All the athletes from Hamilton Park were like that.

We'd get suspended from teams because of our attitude. We'd get demoted from the starting squad because of our attitude. I got benched because I dared to wear my Afro braided. Taking the time to help each other out to become the best team we could be wasn't something we thought of. We were just trying to figure out how to get more playing time for ourselves.

I wanted to get minutes and maintain them at Grambling, too, but I learned while shoving that damned sled up and down the practice field that I needed someone else's help. I couldn't push that sled by myself. I was even having trouble moving it with a teammate. But there was no other way to succeed. It was either do it, or be done.

I wasn't sure I was going to manage one hundred yards to glory, or anything else the Grambling coaches threw at me. I was scared I wasn't going to cut it at Grambling. So many of the Tigers were everything I wasn't—big, strong, and fast. I was tall. That was about it. My knees sort of knocked together. I wasn't fast. I didn't have one of those (we would say this among ourselves) slave bodies, chiseled and ripped and all that.

I wondered if I wasn't in over my head. I worried that I was going to fail not just me, but, more importantly, my mom, who had done everything to get me into Grambling. After all, it wasn't as if Coach Rob sought me out like almost every other guy on the team. I wasn't even an afterthought. I sought out his program. I didn't have many options.

I really wasn't Coach Rob's type of kid. I was from outside Louisiana and from a big city. Coach Rob preferred Louisiana boys from off the country roads that snaked through the state. He liked boys he could mold into his vision of men, boys who hadn't seen bright lights, flown on planes, and traveled to places like the Bahamas.

My roommates, Mike Haynes and Jerry Gordon, weren't Coach Rob's type of guy either, which was why the three of us became so tight. Mike wasn't coveted by Grambling. He wasn't even recruited by the Tigers. He was from Louisiana, but from its biggest and slickest of cities—New Orleans.

Mike wasn't intimidated like I was. His mouth ran a mile a minute. He was nicknamed All World, a nickname conferred on him *by* him. "All World is here, Mike Haynes, All World," he'd say as he entered a room where the rest of us might be gathered. We would just laugh.

Mike had all the confidence of a superstar and none of the accoutrements, physical or otherwise. He wasn't a six-footer. The helmet they gave him made him look like a bobble-head doll because it was too big. The cleats they gave him were too large and appeared to flop, not unlike some circus clown's. If All World noticed any of it, he never let on.

I was uneasy and still trying to find my way and fit in when Mike came up to me during one of the earliest practices and said, "Walls"—which was what most everyone started calling me because they couldn't pronounce Everson—"we can cover these motherfuckers, man. C'mon!"

Mike didn't care that we were practicing against a Heisman-candidate quarterback, Doug Williams, who was throwing to some of the fastest receivers in the country. One was Robert Woods, a bow-legged little dude from Houston we called Speedy Gonzalez because he was so fast. Woods wound up selected in the fifth round of the NFL draft by the Kansas City Chiefs. Another was Carlos Pennywell, who was about my size, ran a 4.4 forty-yard dash, and got picked in the third round of the draft by the New England Patriots. That was the type of talent we went up against every day in practice at Grambling, and Mike, a walk-on with a bobble-head helmet and clown cleats, was certain he belonged. Mike wasn't even shy in front of the biggest sports media personalities in the country, like Cosell and Irv Cross, who was one of the first black national TV reporters I remember—all of whom found their way to Grambling to report on the national phenomenon who was Doug.

Mike just continued to talk about what he could do and daring Doug to test him.

My other roommate, Jerry, had an older brother named Dwight Scales. Scales starred at receiver for Grambling in the early '70s and now was playing receiver for the Los Angeles Rams, who chose him in the fifth round of the 1976 NFL draft. So Jerry had all of Dwight's professional knowledge to share.

Through Jerry, Dwight inspired me for the first time in my athletic career to continue practicing after the team was done. Dwight encouraged Jerry, Mike, and me to put in extra work with the upperclassmen after practice so that we could more quickly become an asset to the team. If and when the coaches called on us to enter a game, the upperclassmen wanted us to be ready because that would ensure that the entire Tigers football team would succeed. It was another lesson about the way to be a teammate.

So I'd hang around late and learn a few things about coverage and route running and clueing—watching the quarterback instead of just the man you are covering—from the older players. As I grew up in the Tigers' den, I would do the same for the new freshmen who came in.

What I was learning to do was sacrifice. I was taking the time, the extra time, to show someone else something that could make them as good as I was becoming. Maybe it would make them better than me, but that was fine. If we all got better, the team would get better, and we would win championships and attract the attention of the media and the NFL scouts.

Mike and Jerry refused to let my doubts defeat me. They generated a comfort in me about my talent, starting on that practice day when we first went up against Doug Williams. I wasn't so scared anymore. It showed in the very first game my freshman season.

It wasn't like high school, where I walked right into the starting lineup. Even if I had been that good from the very start, Coach Rob wasn't going to stick me in with the upperclassmen. But I did make the traveling squad for the opener against Alcorn State.

We met Alcorn at Memorial Stadium in Jackson, Mississippi, though, not on its campus in Lorman, Mississippi, wherever that was. That was one thing about Coach Rob's Tigers. We almost always played in a big stadium in a big city. We rarely played on some school's campus, except ours. We were a road show, and everybody came out to see us play. We had to be accommodated, and Memorial Stadium seated upward of 60,000. The stadium filled up that Saturday just like I remembered seeing stands on that Sunday morning Grambling football TV show.

The sky was clear, and the Mississippi sun was beating down. I couldn't sleep the night before because I was so excited. Mom was in the bleachers somewhere.

The game was no contest, as most of our games my freshman year would be with Doug. Doug just threw the ball up and down the field and lit up the scoreboard. He looked even more unstoppable than he appeared in practice. Coach Rob was letting Doug showcase his talent.

We must have been leading by five or six touchdowns in the fourth quarter when I heard someone on the sidelines yell my name. It was Fred Collins, my defensive coach. He had decided to put me in the game at strong safety.

I was scared as could be. I was trying to think how Mike Haynes would act—all cocky. But this wasn't practice. This was a real game. It counted. There would be consequences, at least for me. If I did the right things, maybe the coaches would play me again. If I did the slightest thing wrong, the coaches might send me back to Dallas. I was that nervous.

I knew there would be a chance of being in the spotlight because Alcorn was so far behind that it had no choice except to throw the football if it hoped to catch up. And that was just fine with me. I didn't want to run up and make a tackle, because everybody out there seemed bigger than any football players I'd ever seen before. I preferred to backpedal and chase passes, maybe even get close enough to bat one out of the air.

Sure enough, the Alcorn quarterback dropped back to pass on the first play I was in. I backpedaled a little, and the next thing I knew the football was wobbling through the air in my direction. I couldn't believe it. I settled under the ball as if it were a lazy pop fly on the baseball field and created a basket with my arms. It dropped right in. I cradled it and took off.

When those Alcorn guys caught up with me, my mom said she got a hot flash because one guy hit me low, and another hit me high, and I spun around in the air like a boomerang before landing on my head.

I was so happy to get off that field. And as it turned out, other than when I would run downfield on the kickoff squad, that first game turned out to be the only action I saw my freshman year.

As the season wore on, I was fighting with selfishness again. I wasn't afraid of the competition any longer; I wanted to play, and I was certain that I was good enough to play. But game after game, all I did was get winded running down the field with the kickoff team.

I remember we went to New York City to play Morgan State from Baltimore, at Yankee Stadium, of all places. That was the House that Babe Ruth Built, but, more significant to me, it was where Reggie Jackson was playing at the time. We checked in at some fabulous hotel, and I settled down for the evening, only to be disturbed by a knock at the door. I opened it, and there was Mom. I was so surprised and happy to see her. I couldn't wait for her to see me play on the field where just the year before Muhammad Ali and Ken Norton had fought.

But the first half of that game went by, and I didn't play. Then the third quarter went by, and I was still a spectator. The final gun sounded, and my uniform was as clean as could be. I hadn't been so steamed since my high school basketball coach benched me because of my braids.

I must have been the first one to board the team bus outside Yankee Stadium. I took the seat right behind the driver, hunkered down, and just stared out the window with a frown. I was like a little kid who didn't get his way. I was at that threshold between anger and tears.

The rest of the team started boarding the bus as boisterous as always. I acknowledged none of them. I didn't even look up—not until someone sat beside and me and said, "Hey, what's up?"

I turned for just a second to see who just invaded my space. It was Coach Rob. I was so concerned about me that I hadn't noticed I was sitting in Coach Rob's row. Mad and now embarrassed, I barely even spoke back to him.

Coach Rob was always a better man than everyone else, though. He didn't dispatch me to a player's seat. He didn't call me out. He just let me be. It seemed like the longest drive in the world back to our hotel downtown.

It took me a while to understand the way Coach Rob did things, and his reasons. I couldn't see then that his program was built on respecting elders, or upperclassmen, who passed what they learned down the line. I didn't realize he rewarded seniors for all their hard work over the years by giving them all the playing time. I thought he and Coach Collins were just out to get me. I wasn't the only freshman who thought that. I just handled it the most immaturely.

But what a method, to what appeared to be madness to me, Coach Rob had concocted. It made his team better because it made all the younger players like me want to practice harder. We wanted to prove to Coach Rob and his assistants that they were wrong not to play us.

So we went at every practice with so much gusto that you would've thought we were playing a game that counted. Mike kept running his mouth at Doug and Doug's receivers. His chattiness was infecting me. It became so competitive at one practice I remember that Coach Rob—who, it was true, was always an offensive-minded coach—watched Doug throw a touchdown pass against me and the rest of the defense and then screamed out the score with glee, "That's six!"

We were stunned. It was one thing for players to talk trash to each other, but not Coach Rob. So we practiced even harder. I still couldn't get in a game, though.

I did, however, look forward to the last game of the season even though I realized I wouldn't play. It was in Tokyo. Somehow, some way, Grambling cut a deal to play a game in Japan that year, and it was against Temple, not another little black school. It was arranged by the mastermind behind the curtain at Grambling, a nice guy from Shreveport, Louisiana, named Collie Nicholson. His title was sports information director, but what he really did was market Coach Rob and the football program to the rest of the country and the world. He was the one who put Grambling in Yankee Stadium the first time in 1968 to play Morgan State. He created the Bayou Classic in New Orleans right after Thanksgiving that pits Grambling against Southern University from Baton Rouge. He was the one who turned the Grambling Marching Band into the international sensation it became.

But when the travel roster came out for the Tokyo trip, my name was not on it. I wasn't mad; I was hurt. It was a feeling I would become accustomed to.

I worked hard at spring practice. Doug Williams was gone, and his little brother, Mike, had taken his place as quarterback. I was getting better along with the rest of the young defensive backs, and some practices went by where we didn't let Mike Williams complete a pass. Still, I didn't get to play with the defense again until the last game of my sophomore season.

It was against Florida A&M in the Orange Blossom Classic at the Orange Bowl in Miami. It was for the black college football title, and it didn't go well for us, which was why I finally saw some action. I was dispatched into the defensive backfield in the fourth quarter because the game was all but over. FAMU turned the table on us and was blowing us out. At least we could soothe our pride on Miami Beach after that setback.

That was one thing about little ol' Grambling. We not only played in the biggest venues in the biggest cities, but we stayed in the best hotels and flew everywhere we went, just like the big white schools. In Miami we stayed at the Eden Roc Hotel on the beach, one of the swankiest places you could be.

Coach Rob wanted to show us the best that life had to offer and show the world how we, as young black men from the South, could fit in. One of his traveling rules was that we dress in suit coats and ties.

That wasn't as simple as it sounds, because not everyone could afford a suit. And not everyone who did have a suit, what we all called "our Sunday best," could fit into it any longer, because we were getting bigger from working out and eating so many square meals every day.

If there was one thing Coach Rob and his assistants liked in their football players it was size. The bigger we were—especially the linemen—the better. So our training table, where the football team ate breakfast, lunch, and dinner, was always set with what seemed like a never-ending feast that could satisfy an army division. There was plenty of beef and chicken and pork. There was rarely any fish. The coaches encouraged us to eat and then eat some more.

There was never any concern about what we ate. No one ever thought twice about linemen we had who stood well over six feet and gorged themselves to tip the scales upward of three hundred pounds. We didn't know that obesity could lead to so many ailments, including diabetes, that affect black people more than anyone else. We just got up from our dining tables and headed back to the food line for seconds.

One year Grambling president Joseph Johnson implemented budget cuts that caused our training table fare to be pared back. We protested as a team.

So many guys on the team ballooned that a common fashion statement while on the road became draping the Coach Rob–required sport coat or suit jacket over your arm, because you were no longer svelte enough to fit inside it.

Traveling around with my teammates was more entertaining sometimes than the games we were traveling to, because a lot of these guys hadn't flown before, and they weren't too enamored with the idea. I'd never seen so many big men cry as I did when we hit turbulence one time on a flight to Tallahassee, Florida, to play FAMU. I remember when the plane landed, one of the biggest guys, Reginald "Big Squid" Irving, ran down the stairs onto the tarmac and dropped to his knees to kiss the ground. He was drenched in sweat.

I worked hard at spring and summer practice before my junior year. I was shutting people down. Most of the defensive backfield that was there when I was a freshman had graduated. This would be my turn, I figured, and so did everyone else.

But when the starting defensive backfield was announced before the first game, I wasn't in it. Mike Haynes made it. Robert Salter made it. James White made it. Sporty Williams, a senior, made it. It was an all-Louisiana backfield. I was named the first substitute off the bench.

My heart just sank. It was one thing not to play the first two years. It was another not to play my junior year when my roommate Mike and all the other guys I was coming up with were named starters. Mike and the other guys felt my pain, too. Then they demonstrated their friendship like never before.

They decided on their own that they weren't going to allow me to be left out, because they knew I deserved to play as much as they did. So in an ultimate athletic act of unselfishness, Mike and the guys went to Coach Collins on my behalf without telling me. They told Coach Collins that I should be playing, and they presented to the coach a proposal for how we could all get a chance to shine on the field. Coach Collins accepted the plan and unveiled it during a meeting of the defensive backs. He said that in the second half of every game I would rotate in and play each position—left corner, right corner, strong safety, and weak safety. I was stunned.

Football players don't often talk about being touched by someone's gesture or act or words. Sensitivity isn't our thing. But that was a touching moment. The guys I played with thought enough of me to sacrifice their playing time so that I could have some. Not only that, but they decided to give up some of their time during what generally is the most critical point in a football game—the second half—for my benefit. And with Doug Williams in the NFL now, there was going to be a lot more crunch time.

I was one grateful football player. I never felt better about my decision to go to Grambling than at that moment. I was so thankful for Mike and the guys. That was being a teammate. That was real teamwork.

They did what they did for me because we were all the best of friends. We were creating family where there were no blood ties. It was something I had no idea I would lean on so heavily many years later, the real meaning of team and teammates.

They didn't have to do what they did for me, and I don't think a lot of players would. I don't think I would have done the same thing had I been in their shoes. Sacrificing something, especially something you've earned, is a very difficult thing to do. To this day I don't think Sporty, the senior, had much to do with it, because he was the one who lost the most. He'd waited for that opportunity just like so many before him, and now he was only going to realize a part of it. But Sporty never said an ill word about it to me or anyone I knew then. He swallowed his pride for the betterment of everyone.

I made four interceptions playing in the second halves that season. Two of those picks I turned into touchdowns. That was when I first thought that maybe, just maybe, I could play football for a living like some of the Tigers who came before me.

I was turning into one of the BMOCs, too—big men on campus. Most of the football players were, but when you started starring, you definitely were a BMOC. I even got an apartment off campus that Mr. Harris back in Hamilton Park didn't know at the time was for me and his daughter Shreill.

During my senior year, I finally ascended to where I had hoped to be ever since my freshman year. With Sporty's graduation, I was handed a starting position, left cornerback. I wasn't just going to play the last two quarters; I was going to play entire games. I couldn't wait.

We opened the season against Morgan State back in New York at Yankee Stadium under the lights. Then we met Alcorn in Shreveport at Independence Stadium, where they play the season-ending Independence Bowl. I had an interception and some big pass breakups and tackles, but we lost the game, 29–27. It was the last game on the schedule that we lost.

One of those games was our homecoming against Tennessee State. Their quarterback had a reputation that preceded him—Joe "747" Adams. They called him 747 because he was as big as a wide-body airplane. They should have called him "Howitzer," because he could throw a football like a cannon could fire an artillery shell. Seven forty-seven wasn't just hype. He was the real deal. He came to Grambling with a preseason All-America label affixed to him and would go on to play in the Canadian Football League.

Everybody was talking about what 747 was going to do to Grambling. We were suggesting otherwise to anyone who wanted to listen. We couldn't wait for 747 to land on our field.

He was good, all right. That day he threw over fifty passes, completed more than thirty, and racked up over three hundred yards through the air and three touchdowns. In between, however, we picked him off seven times. Seven times!

We were such an impressive team at that point that CBS ranked us in its poll of the top twenty college teams in the country—out of all of them, Division I and Division I-AA, for the smaller schools, which we were in. We were that legitimate. We scored almost forty points per game that season and gave up fewer than two touchdowns per outing. Few Coach Rob teams ever topped those statistics, before or since.

We led the nation in interceptions, stealing thirty-two passes. Among the defensive backfield starters, I picked eleven, Mike Haynes and Robert Salter each grabbed eight, and James White snared a pair. I don't think Coach Rob ever appreciated how good we were. Even he had never coached a unit like ours. For the rest of the century, only one more Coach Rob team would win ten games in a year like we did when I was a senior.

We weren't done at regular season's end, either. The National Collegiate Athletic Association was just starting to experiment with a championship playoff for Division I-AA schools, and we got picked as champions of the Southwestern Athletic Conference and the black college ranks to participate. There were three other teams—Eastern Kentucky, Lehigh, and Boise State. We were dispatched to Boise, Idaho, which seemed sort of unfair for a small black school in the South, where we rarely if ever played in really cold weather.

We didn't complain, though. We were excited about yet another chance to prove we could play with anyone. Florida A&M proved black schools belonged in the same four-team championship tournament in 1978, which was the inaugural Division I-AA playoff. The Rattlers beat Massachusetts in Wichita Falls, Texas, for that title. So we knew that our being a little black school wasn't a detriment.

It was a little colder than we even imagined when we ran onto Boise's Bronco Field that December afternoon. It felt a lot colder than the 28 degrees it was supposed to be. I remember seeing trees on the ride from our hotel to the stadium that were shrouded in frost. The stadium when we arrived was enveloped in fog. You couldn't see clearly from our benches to theirs.

We held those dudes on their own turf. But we just never got warmed up. The game was tied at 7 going into the fourth quarter. It took a trick play to make the difference, a flea flicker.

The Broncos were about at their own forty-yard line when their quarterback, Joe Aliotti, handed off to a running back named Terry Zahner, who ran a few steps into the line, stopped, turned around, and tossed the football back to Aliotti. Aliotti heaved it downfield to a receiver named Kipp Bedard, who was wide open at about our twenty. He caught it and took off toward the end zone. I caught up with him inside the ten but couldn't bring him down before he crossed the goal line.

It was the first time I was caught by a camera's lens not being able to thwart another team from moving beyond mine to the championship game. We managed a safety after that and lost 14–9. Mike Williams, Mike Haynes, Jerry Gordon, and I always contended, of course, that if those guys had come to Grambling Stadium, we'd have sent them home on the short end and won the championship, which Boise did the following weekend against Eastern Kentucky.

I was disappointed my college career ended with a loss, but I felt so good about all that I had gained in my four years with the Grambling Tigers. That's the thing about my life that I feel so fortunate about. There has always been a balance. We lost that last game, but during my time at Grambling, I made invaluable friends for life in Mike and Jerry and some of the other guys I played with. I'd learned invaluable lessons, like what it means to be a teammate and how doing something for someone else, or several others, is more rewarding than doing something just for myself.

I knew then that I would be indebted to Mike and Jerry for the rest of my life for all the things they did for me—making me confident, if not cocky, about my ability to play football and just about anything else I set my mind to do. It was the ultimate lesson hammered into me by Coach Rob, too, which, I understood just a few years ago, made it possible for me to do what I would do for a pro teammate named Ron Springs.

# 5

# You Can Make It

You never know fate when you meet it. It isn't until after it is long gone that you realize it crossed your path. Ron and I tripped over fate, unknown to either of us at the time, on the last week of April 1981. Our fate was disguised as that year's NFL draft.

I was finishing up my senior year at Grambling that spring, spending most of my time trying to get through an accounting class. It was my biggest challenge in school since trying to defend passes thrown in practice by Doug Williams during my freshman year. My college football career was over, though, and it ended with a bang. We had lost the Division I-AA playoff in Boise, Idaho, to the hometown team, but we went there as winners of the black college football national championship for the first time since my freshman season. And I had led the nation in interceptions that year.

I also won All-America honors as a cornerback on two All-America teams—the black college team and the I-AA team. The I-AA team honored players in the college division for schools smaller than big colleges like Texas and Notre Dame and Ohio State. Coaches from those name schools never even considered recruiting me when I graduated from high school, even though I was the interception leader in my high school's district in twelfth grade.

As the NFL draft was about to kick off during my senior year in college, I thought about how I'd been ignored by the biggest college football programs just four springs earlier. I wondered if I'd be ignored by the NFL, too, because I didn't play at the biggest of schools.

I had reason to wonder. I'd watched the two best seniors from Grambling during my junior season be left with only free-agent contracts for entree to the NFL. No pro teams came to Grambling to work me out after the season as they had when Doug was about to graduate.

When I played in the black college football all-star game after the season, on a frigid weekend in Jackson, Mississippi, I met the Green Bay Packers' legendary defensive back from the '60s, Willie Wood. He'd just taken over as coach of the Toronto Argonauts in the Canadian Football League, becoming the first black head coach in the CFL. He offered me a contract then and there to play for him. I told him I'd think about it, which was not really true. I'd finished thinking about his offer as soon as he broached it. I had no desire to play in a minor league, and I had no desire to play in Canada, where it would be like it was in Boise, Idaho, for that Division I-AA playoff—cold.

Not long after, a friend of the family in California said he'd heard from Wood, who was a friend of his from Wood's USC playing days. He reported that Wood told him I was too slow for the NFL. So evidence was mounting in my mind that what should be a week of celebration for me could wind up being anything but.

April 28, the opening day of the 1981 NFL draft, was a Tuesday. I had my accounting class that afternoon. But first I joined a handful of teammates in the lobby of the athletic dorm, where there was a TV, to see if any of the local channels would announce if anyone from Grambling was drafted. I was doubtful but hopeful. I guess that made me wishful.

The Heisman Trophy winner, running back George Rogers from South Carolina, was picked first by New Orleans. The speedy linebacker Lawrence Taylor from North Carolina was chosen second by the Giants. The first defensive back, Kenny Easley from UCLA, was picked fourth by Seattle. Another Pac-10 defensive back, Ronnie Lott from USC, was selected eighth by the 49ers.

We continued to hear of names connected to big schools, the Division I-A schools. They continued to get called until the St. Louis Cardinals early in the second round picked a quarterback named Neil Lomax from Portland State. I'd heard of Portland State because basketball was my first love, and a few years earlier Portland State had a basketball player named Freeman Williams, who twice led the nation in scoring. Williams got drafted by the Boston Celtics. Maybe, I thought, someone would draft the nation's interceptions leader despite his being from a small school.

In the second half of the second round, a defensive end from Alabama State named Curtis Green was drafted by Detroit. He was the first player from a black college picked in the draft. But the second round went by without any more black-college players picked. Several more defensive backs I hadn't heard of were picked, though. Then the third and fourth rounds went by much the same way.

I wasn't surprised. I was disgusted. I picked up my books and left the lobby and the dorm. Everything was going as I anticipated. I was the best defensive back in the country, I was sure, and every other defensive back other than me was getting drafted. I was getting screwed, and I was ticked off about it. I had my accounting class to get to anyway. I wasn't about to allow my graduation to get derailed by wasting my time waiting for biased NFL talent scouts to do the smart thing rather than the safe thing.

Tuesday came and went, as did at least six of the draft's twelve rounds, without anyone contacting me to say I'd been selected. But before the second day of the draft began, on Wednesday, representatives from three teams arrived on campus to offer rookie free-agent contracts to me and Robert Salter. They came from the Saints, the Bills, and the Cowboys.

The pros knew what I suspected, and then some. I wasn't going to get drafted, and neither was anyone else at little ol' black Grambling. Our only entree to the NFL would be via rookie free-agent contracts, just like our best linebackers from a season ago. That meant that despite everything I had accomplished, I wouldn't be paid as much as defensive backs who didn't have my credentials but who were drafted. It meant I was being left to sign a contract for the bare-minimum pay in the NFL and with only a small signing bonus. The only question was which contract I'd accept.

I talked over the options with my best friends on the team, Mike Haynes and my roommate Jerry Gordon. There was no point in talking to Coach Rob, because I knew what he would say. I'd heard it before when his guys weren't drafted. "Hell, son," Coach Rob would say, drawing out his words as was his habit, "you can make it anywhere. This is Grambling!" Being drafted or being offered a free-agent contract didn't matter to Coach Rob. All he wanted was his players to continue their careers in the NFL, and he was certain that the talent he developed in us would carry us to long tenures in the league if not stardom.

I couldn't afford to make a decision based on pride. I had to make a calculated decision. This was about my future. This was for life.

Dallas's famous talent scout Gil Brandt called me about the team's offer. It included a $1,500 signing bonus. I told Brandt that I deserved more. It wouldn't be the first time I stated such a case to the Cowboys, and it wound up not being the last time the Cowboys told me, more or less, to take their offer or leave it.

The Cowboys knew they had me over a barrel. They knew, of course, that I was from Dallas. They were betting that I wasn't going to Buffalo even though Frank Lewis from Grambling was the star wide receiver there, and he was in the pantheon of Grambling greats with Coach Rob and Doug Williams and Willie Davis, who had a Pro Football Hall of Fame career before becoming an award-winning business leader. Buffalo was north. It was so close to Toronto it might as well have been in Canada. It seemed like every time I saw the Bills on TV, they were playing in snow. The Cowboys sensed snow was not an option for me.

The Saints had barely won a game the year before. They were being ridiculed as the "the Ain'ts," and their fans were wearing grocery bags over their heads in the stands. I wasn't going there no matter how familiar I was with New Orleans from playing Southern there every year in the Superdome.

I'd scouted the Cowboys, too, as a fan more than as a potential player. My study came in useful now. Mike, Jerry, and I watched the Cowboys escape the Falcons 30–27 in the 1980 season playoffs. The Falcons quarterback, Steve Bartkowski, roasted the Cowboys cornerbacks, Aaron Mitchell and Steve Wilson. A Falcons receiver named Alfred Jenkins caught 155 yards' worth of passes, including one for a touchdown. I knew I was better than the Cowboys corners, I told Mike and Jerry. I knew I could make the Cowboys. Mike and Jerry knew I could, too.

But Mike and Jerry didn't want me to go to the Cowboys because the Cowboys, they believed, had a history of thumbing their noses at players from Grambling despite the school being just four hours east of Dallas in Louisiana off Interstate 20. The only Grambling player we could think of who had played for the Cowboys was Ernest Sterling, Shreill's uncle. He was so big they called him Monster. Now he was Coach Rob's assistant coach, the one who had helped pave the way for me to get on the Grambling team.

I argued with Mike and Jerry that if the Cowboys wanted to win, they needed defensive backs like me. They needed defensive backs who could make plays, I said. They played a lot of man to man, and that was my forte. I talked Mike and Jerry into the decision I made, which, as fate would have it, united me with the teammate who became the friend for life who changed my life forever.

On Wednesday night, April 29, 1981, I agreed to a free-agent contract with Dallas.

☆

Ron was already in Dallas then. He'd been there two years since getting out of college, and his journey to my hometown seemed almost as destined as my return there. He wasn't as sought after by the NFL as he hoped at one point, either.

But that wasn't because Ron was from some small school no one paid attention to. He was from as big a school as there was in college football, a place everyone paid attention to, me included. Ron was a star halfback for Ohio State. He even played for a legendary, patriarchal coach like Coach Rob—Woody Hayes. His quarterback for a while was a guy I'd heard of from Dallas, Rod Gerald, who played at Dallas South Oak Cliff High School. That was all Ron and I had in common then, however, a legendary coach and a teammate of his from my hometown.

Unlike me, Ron had been a near-mythical figure before getting to the NFL. He was six-two and ran faster than the wind. In high school back in Williamsburg, Virginia, he set all sorts of rushing records. In junior college, Coffeyville Community College in Kansas, he set a rushing record that was still intact when he retired from the NFL. Ron always bragged that Woody Hayes wasn't keen on junior-college players until he saw what Ron did at Coffeyville.

In Ron's junior year at Ohio State, he led the Buckeyes in rushing and receiving. He caught sixteen passes. Hayes didn't have his team pass the ball much, so that was a lot. Ron was first-team All Big Ten, Ohio State's conference. He also anchored Ohio State's 4-by-100 track relay team. By his senior year, he had everything going for him. His personality and leadership made him such a team favorite that his teammates voted him to be a team captain. He was such a good player that Hayes couldn't help but approve his captaincy.

Ron's senior year was also when he suffered his first taste of bad luck. First, he lost Rod Gerald as his quarterback. Hayes demoted Gerald in favor of a freshman who was a star Ohio high school quarterback, Art Schlichter. Gerald was black, and Schlichter was white, and the black Buckeyes players were not happy about the switch. It was Ron's duty as a captain to talk to Hayes about the locker room's splintering and convince Hayes to reconsider the change at quarterback. Hayes refused, and Ron felt somewhat hardboiled by Hayes's dismissal of his plea. Ron didn't accuse Hayes of being racist. Hayes was one of a few coaches at big program in the 1970s who was letting a black guy quarterback his team. Ron just felt disrespected and he didn't talk to Hayes much the rest of that season.

To make Ron's senior year even less pleasant, in just the third game during the season in which he expected to work his way into the first round of the NFL draft, Ron suffered a physical setback for the first time in his life.

Ron and his guys were playing against Mike Singletary's Baylor Bears when Ron's freshman quarterback, Schlichter, ran a pitch play for Ron. Ron cradled the ball and started upfield, only to be met by Singletary, who smashed into Ron's left knee. Ron had to be helped off the field and didn't play for the next three games. His season was ruined.

Ron didn't do much the rest of that year, except be part of a play that is forever etched in college football lore, at least in the bizarre and unusual section.

It was Ron's final college game, on December 29, 1978. He and his Buckeyes were in the Gator Bowl playing against Clemson. The game wasn't for anything except pride and style points, but the Buckeyes, trailing Clemson 17–15 in the fourth quarter, were on the march for a come-from-behind win with two minutes left. They were inside Clemson's twenty-five-yard line. It was third down, and they needed five yards for a first down. Hayes called for a little pass play to Ron—"fire 23, halfback circle." Ron was supposed to curl out of the backfield into the middle of the field, where Schlichter, with any luck, would find him all alone.

The play looked to be unfolding as planned until Schlichter let the ball go. It was a horrible pass. It was so bad that a Clemson linebacker named Charlie Bauman had to put his hands up to stop the ball from hitting him. When he did, he caught the ball and scampered around a bit like a trapped squirrel until he was wrestled out of bounds on the Ohio State sidelines right in front of Hayes.

Hayes was always known for having a short fuse, and on this day it blew. Sixty-five years old and bespectacled, with his famous black ball cap on his head, Hayes snatched Bauman by the jersey. Then, to everyone's amazement, Hayes punched Bauman.

Hayes's fist landed just below Bauman's neck, and all hell broke loose. The sidelines emptied. Order had to be restored. Clemson eventually ran out the clock, and the next day Ohio State ran out of patience with Hayes. He was fired after being on the OSU sidelines for twenty-eight years.

Ron finished the game with ten carries for forty-two yards. He'd gone from being an All-America halfback candidate and potential first-round NFL draft pick coming out of his junior season to just another running back after his last college game. And even though he was at Ohio State and not at Grambling, and Woody Hayes carried more weight than Coach Rob and had more connections, and the Cowboys had drafted an Ohio State player before, his relationship with Hayes had soured since the quarterback controversy. He didn't figure he'd have Hayes to count on to get him into the NFL.

Although Ron didn't know it at the time, Hayes had set their differences aside and called Gil Brandt on Ron's behalf and lobbied for the Cowboys to take Ron. Why Hayes picked the Cowboys out of twenty-eight teams in the NFL I don't know. Whether he called other teams for Ron or why the Cowboys were the team to heed Hayes's words I don't know either. Fate doesn't explain itself. All I know is that two picks before the fifth round of the 1979 NFL draft ended, my hometown team, just blocks from Mom's house, selected Ron. He was the twenty-second running back drafted that spring.

The Cowboys didn't even need a running back. They already had Tony Dorsett, who won the Heisman at Pittsburgh in 1976 and was an NFL Rookie of the Year in 1977. Ron was the only running back the Cowboys drafted in 1979. By the time I arrived in Dallas as a rookie two off-seasons later, Ron was about to move into the Cowboys' starting backfield. He wouldn't beat out Dorsett. He would join Dorsett—as Dorsett's fullback.

Ron was always big for a halfback. His head was big, which I always joked with him about. His torso was thick. His arms were huge. But playing fullback in the NFL required even more bulk than the 198 pounds Ron carried in college. He spent his first two seasons in the NFL mostly getting bigger.

He wasn't alone in this effort as a young NFL player. But Ron refused to take the easy way to bulk up that was gaining popularity then—steroids. I remember my rookie year that there was a young linebacker who would come into the locker room to change into his practice pads and uniform from his street clothes with syringes dangling from his shirt pocket. The Raiders' 300-pound defensive line star Lyle Alzado admitted later that he'd been using steroids for ten years by the time Ron was a rookie. He died in 1992 at age forty-three from a brain tumor he said was a result of steroid abuse.

Ron just pumped iron to get bigger, and he could lift a lot of it. I recall watching him curl 225 pounds once and hear Tony Dorsett exclaim, "Ron, you're too strong!"

As Ron bulked up his body, he also adopted new skills to be mostly an everyday blocker rather than the game-breaking ball carrier he had always been. I didn't find out Ron had done this until years later, and it impressed me to no end, because what Ron did to make the Cowboys was an act of sacrifice. He'd set aside his particular talents as a running back for the betterment of others. It was a compromise, of course. He may not have been able to make it in the NFL had he not added the skills of a fullback. But his act ingratiated him to his new teammates.

☆

I didn't know Ron Springs from Hot Springs, when, for the first time in my life, I drove from my mom's house in Hamilton Park, where I'd moved back into my bedroom after graduating from Grambling, to the Cowboys facility I was accustomed to biking to as a kid. It was late spring 1981, and it was my first rookie workout as a member of the Cowboys.

I wouldn't have cared who Ron was then anyway. I was one angry guy at the time. I was mad at the world. I'd been slighted by the Cowboys and the rest of the NFL. I had a chip on my shoulder that was the weight of a boulder. I had led the nation in interceptions! But no one had thought enough of me to draft me.

I was all about me when I pulled into the team parking lot in my sister's hand-me-down copper brown Mustang Grande with more miles on it than the odometer could count. It'd made a lot of trips between Mom's house and North Texas State University, thirty-five miles up Interstate 35 in Denton, Texas, where my sisters went to college. It was an original Hooptie. There was a cinder block behind the driver's seat to keep the seat back propped up. I looked every bit like the free-agent rookie I knew I shouldn't be, and that made me even more upset.

There was a meeting for all the rookies with the coaches. It was the first time I met Tom Landry, and it would be like most meetings with him to come: brief. He welcomed us, wished us well in making the team and helping it win, and left the room. That was it. It was hardly as memorable as my first encounter with Coach Rob.

That was the difference between being an NFL rookie and a college freshman. As a freshman, my potential had to be tapped, because I was going to be relied on at some point during my four years. So Coach Rob made it his business to know who he was bringing in and to nurture each player.

As a rookie, a rookie free agent at that, chances were I wouldn't see Opening Sunday in the NFL unless I had a ticket. I probably wouldn't last long past the off-season workout, the schedule of which I was given during that inaugural encounter with Coach Landry. Coach Landry's lack of investment of his time in me at that moment made plenty of sense. I was just another guy, another body. Who knows how many of me Coach Landry had seen come and go, quickly, since he started coaching the Cowboys in the early 1960s? That I understood.

What I didn't understand was what I saw in that room that day after Coach Landry's quick hello and good-bye. I remember looking around at the guys the Cowboys drafted instead of me and wondering what they were thinking. I felt my anger building up. They drafted three other defensive backs: Vince Skillings from Ohio State, Ron Fellows from Missouri, and Ken Miller from Eastern Michigan. All I could think was that they didn't lead the nation in interceptions. I did! I went against Doug Williams every day in practice. They couldn't say that. That was part of my résumé, and I didn't get drafted. In twelve rounds!

I couldn't wait to show what I could do. This was about me. This was about self-fulfillment. I didn't care about the off-season weightlifting the Cowboys wanted the rookies to do. We didn't lift much at Grambling, and I hated it. I didn't care about all the running they wanted us to do because I didn't like that either, even if it was for my betterment and the team's, should I make the team. All I wanted to do was what I wanted to do, what I'd always done the most of to prepare for the season. I wanted to practice one-on-one against the Cowboys receivers and quarterbacks just like I'd done against Doug and his receiving corps at Grambling. I wanted to show how much better I was than the defensive backs the Cowboys thought were so good that they drafted them.

In a lot of ways, playing defensive back is for the selfish, or at least those not afraid to be selfish. Playing in the line or as a linebacker is a team thing. Playing running back is a team thing, too, because you have to run behind the blocking of others if you're not doing the blocking. Receivers have to run routes in coordination with other receivers. But defensive backs? We do what is best for us. Once the ball is in the air, each of us tries to get it. You leave whoever you are covering, ignore your responsibility, and try to make a play on the ball.

It took a month or so before training camp commenced, and I got my chance to show the Cowboys what I could do. Weightlifting and running were the only things going on for weeks at the training facility, and I got so bored I showed up less and less and looked anything but enthused. I spent more time playing basketball and tennis away from the facility because that was what I'd done most summers to stay in shape for the Tigers. My sister Gigi taught me how to play tennis at Hamilton Park, and I played a lot. I always thought the back and forth to the net and lateral movement were good for the footwork I had to employ as a defensive back.

There was nothing better than practicing the real footwork, though, and my moment with the Cowboys finally came one day when Pro Bowl receiver Tony Hill showed up. I was so excited. There were a few quarterbacks and receivers there, and they wanted to play a little pitch and catch against some defensive backs. I pushed myself to the front of the line. Let me see what this boy's got, so I can see what I got, I said to myself.

When my chance came, I walked right up in front of Tony as if I were going to employ the bump-and-run defensive strategy, shoving the receiver off line at the snap of the ball before backpedaling or running with him.

Tony looked at me and said, "Hey, Boss,"—he called everyone Boss—"I'm just trying to get loose." I said, "OK." So he ran a little curl route. I recognized it immediately and ran hard to the ball. He caught it, but I was right there, too close for his comfort once again, apparently. He turned and said, "Hey, rookie! I told you I'm just trying to get loose!" I told him if he was out there, I was going to cover him. A little more woofing ensued, and I assured him I'd see him again. That was my attitude. It was about me, and I was on edge.

I remember jogging on the track one day, trying to show I was part of the team, and I saw some veterans off to the side watching me. They made sure I overheard them talking about me. "Who's he think he is?" I heard them say. One of the guys was the Cowboys running back from Ohio State. It was the first time I'd seen him, Ron Springs, in my life.

☆

It wasn't until training camp commenced at Cal Lutheran University in Thousand Oaks, California, early that summer in 1981, that I finally met Ron, or, better yet, encountered him. It was the way anyone I ever knew who knew Ron described exchanging introductions with him. Ron's persona struck you, usually in a bellowing voice or laugh, before you actually met him. There wasn't any "Hello, how are you?"

It was about a week after I'd arrived at camp with the rest of the rookies. Like all the other players, I was staying in one of the dorm rooms on campus. I was one of five rookies staying in a quad, a dorm room for four. But that didn't last long. A guy named Love from San Diego State got cut a few days in, and we gained a little more space. It was me, another defensive back originally from Dallas named Michael Downs, a fullback named Worley Taylor from Oklahoma State, and a linebacker from a black school like me, Angelo King from South Carolina State.

Next door to us was another quad, and a week after we arrived four veterans moved into it. They weren't just any veterans, though. They were star veterans: Tony Dorsett, Robert Newhouse, Dennis Thurman, and the guy I overheard talking about me, Ron Springs.

You're always on edge in training camp the first time around. You want to impress and not make mistakes. An early morning knock on the door makes you jump because you fear it's the Turk. That's the nickname for the guy from the personnel office who tells you to pack up and hand over your playbook because you've been cut from the team. Why the Turk isn't just called the Grim Reaper I don't know, because he performs the same task. It was the Turk who knocked at our door the first week for that guy named Love.

But after you've not only survived a couple of training camps, but excelled in the league, training camp is pretty boring, and you're looking for ways to break the monotony. Ron broke his monotony with us, the rookies.

As soon as those veterans moved in, we could hear them. They were loud, and you could sense their confidence; as far as we could tell, they couldn't have cared less about us, the new guys in the dorm. But one day, this burly veteran appeared at our open door, blocking out the light coming down the hallway. He walked right in and just started talking.

He asked us where we were from. When he found out I was from Grambling and Angelo was from South Carolina State, he immediately began referring to us as Negro League players, like the old black baseball guys. All of us just started laughing—him, too. I don't remember the guy saying, "I'm Ron Springs." He didn't have to. He knew we knew who he was.

Ron was the Other Veteran. He was different. He reminded me of how the seniors at Grambling treated the freshman players. We made fun of the freshmen, too. But we didn't dismiss them, and Ron didn't dismiss us.

Ron invited us on his evening excursions to Thousand Oaks' restaurants and watering holes, and we were only too happy to tag along with a veteran. It wasn't a purely altruistic gesture on his part. What he really wanted was someone to drive him to and fro so he could concentrate more on the crabs he liked to eat and the beer he liked to drink. But as that first training camp ground on, we realized that Ron was also lending us a helping hand. He'd let us know what the coaches were saying about us. He'd tell us what we were doing wrong and what we needed to do more of. He gave us insight into what it would take to make the team, which was a remarkable thing, really. It didn't dawn on me at the time, but what Ron did was sacrificial.

After all, you have to be selfish to make a team. There are only so many spots on the roster. The last thing you want to do is give someone competing for one of those spots, especially yours, information that could subject you to a visit from the Turk. But Ron did just that even though he could be cut just as easily as a rookie because NFL contracts weren't guaranteed. He did it for me. He did it for Worley Taylor, who was trying to be a fullback just like Ron.

Ron never showed any worry about that. He was confident in his own abilities after all the success he'd had before making it as a pro, and he always reminded us of it. He was always talking about how he did it at Ohio State. That wasn't any Negro League school, he'd say. Ron was about to earn the starting fullback job during that training camp, too. We were just trying to seize any job on the team.

I was confident, cocky some said, about my abilities, too. I thought I would join Ron on the final roster from the first rookie scrimmage at Thousand Oaks. I picked out a rookie receiver named Doug Donley to go against because the Cowboys drafted him in the second round from Ron's school, Ohio State, and they really liked him. I knew that the coaches couldn't ignore me if I was playing against the guy they thought so highly of.

Doug and I went at it day after day, and I was getting the better of him. He was just six feet. I was six-two. I was learning the playbook and schemes just as fast as he was, and my position coach, Gene Stallings, started shoving me up the depth chart.

The next thing I knew, I was in the third quarter of the first preseason game with the punt return team. It was against the Green Bay Packers. Michael Downs was in, too. The ball was snapped. We rushed in. Downs blocked the ball. It hit the turf once and bounced up, right into my hands. Twenty yards or so later, I was in the end zone with a touchdown.

The second preseason game was in Los Angeles against the Rams, and I got my first interception. It came in crunch time, too, because a veteran defensive back named Randy Hughes from Oklahoma got hurt and couldn't return. In fact, he never really regained his health all that summer, and his loss opened the door for me to make the team.

In that preseason I went on to do what I'd done my entire college career—get interceptions. I got one in each preseason game. The Turk kept knocking on everybody else's door except ours.

The morning of the last day of training camp the team was summoned to a meeting. Michael Downs and I went downstairs, took our seats, and started looking around the room and counting heads. There was one too many defensive backs, we thought. Michael was already in the starting lineup. I wasn't.

Coach Landry came in the room and as coolly, or coldly, as he was known for being, he said simply, "OK, this is what we're going with." Michael and I looked around and realized Aaron Mitchell, the veteran corner, was gone.

"He's on the Whisper Jet," Ron told us afterward.

There was a passenger plane at the time called the Whisper Jet because it was supposed to be so quiet, and Ron said that was what happened to Aaron. They put him on it, and no one knew. Aaron was en route, we found out later, to Tampa. The Cowboys had traded him for a Tampa Bay draft pick.

Ron didn't say any more to me and Michael and the other rookies who ended up making that team. He didn't have to. The look on his face spoke volumes. It said welcome to the big time.

# 6

# Lesson from Landry

A sports reporter asked Coach Landry during my rookie season, when it was becoming evident that I had an uncanny knack for snatching opposing quarterbacks' passes out of the air, if he was surprised how well I was playing as a rookie free-agent cornerback in the NFL. Coach Landry, in what was his typical matter-of-fact way of speaking, told the reporter: "They catch some; he catches some."

If Coach Landry said anything else about me that year, I do not remember. I do not remember reading it. I do not remember hearing it on the radio or television. It may have been because I was too taken aback, too stunned, that *that* was the best thing he could say about me as a rookie. It turned out that that was about the best thing he could say about me as a veteran, too.

For most of my career playing for Coach Landry, compliments from him were nonexistent, and that always bothered me. It really hurt, actually.

I always wished he had looked at me differently. I always wished he had called me into the office to let me know he appreciated my effort, or to see if there was anything he could do to help me make the transition from Grambling to one of the most celebrated franchises in the NFL, one that he helped create as its first and only coach, which he had been at that point for almost a generation. He never did.

I tried not to take it personally. I watched how Coach Landry interacted with the rest of his players, and they didn't get much more from him than I did. There were a few exceptions. Coach Landry always talked to the media about what a great job Randy White did at defensive end, and how good Danny White was at quarterback. He talked about them like a proud father.

"That Randy White," Coach Landry would tell a reporter. "I wish I had fifty-five of him."

Ron was another exception, at least for a while. Ron was one of the few players who could knock Coach Landry off stride. He was one of the few who could create the crack of a smile in Coach Landry's stone-cold face. He could do it by saying something funny or, more likely, just by being himself.

Ron was as fond of hats as Coach Landry was. But Ron didn't wear just one type of hat, unlike Coach Landry, who famously almost always sported a fedora. Ron wore baseball caps. He wore Gatsby hats. When Ron started wearing colorful skullcaps from West Africa called kufis, and colorful smocks from West Africa called dashikis, Coach Landry not only noticed, he couldn't stop himself from querying Ron about his style.

The rest of us couldn't help but take note of Ron's dress either, just like we couldn't ignore his booming voice and constant wisecracks. We started calling Ron "Idi Amin" when we'd see him in his West African garb, because it made him look like the Ugandan president of that name, who had been at the height of infamy a few years earlier. Ron sounded like a dictator, too, whenever he barked out whatever was on his mind, which was often. Ron loved it. He just laughed.

After practice one day Coach Landry was stopped in his tracks by some lid Ron had donned. "What's with the hats, Ron?" Coach Landry asked.

Ron looked at him a little bemused before shooting back, "Coach, you got more hats than I do. What you asking me for?"

Coach Landry and everyone in earshot got a chuckle.

I never got that kind of reaction from Coach Landry. I never got much of any reaction from him at all. If I did, it was generally a negative critique, or something close.

I was always perplexed by how Coach Landry dealt with me. I wondered what I was doing wrong and what more he could have wanted from a guy who made his team and his starting defense despite not being drafted. After all, I picked up in my first real game where I left off in preseason, making interceptions, and against the Redskins, Dallas's reviled rivals, and on the Washington's home turf.

I wasn't a starter on that first regular season game of my pro career, which was probably a good thing. I was too excited, and Washington's stadium, RFK, was as raucous as it looked on television when I was growing up. I couldn't believe the things Redskins fans yelled at us, like "Fuck the Cowboys!" Nothing was nice. It was a maniacal atmosphere. I remember there was a guy in a wheelchair festooned with an American flag giving us the finger. And when the Redskins fans cheered, they jumped up and down and made part of the stadium's bleachers bounce off the ground.

I was scheduled to be the first defensive back off the bench when the "nickel package" was inserted. That would come whenever Washington was in an obvious passing situation, and our defense called for a fifth defensive back—me, the nickel back—which surprisingly turned out to be often.

Washington had a new coach that year, Joe Gibbs, who was a disciple of Don Coryell, the San Diego coach nicknamed "Air" because he liked to pass the football so much. The new-look Redskins decided to throw all day in this season opener, whether or not the down and distance dictated it. They threw rather than handing off to burly running back John Riggins, who was most likely to use his size and power to run over would-be tacklers, or to scat backs like Joe Washington and Terry Metcalf, who were most likely to use speed and quick moves to run around defenders. As we figured it out, our defensive linemen just reared back and ran roughshod over Washington's line, most of which was new. They gave Washington quarterback Joe Theismann fits. It made for easy interceptions for those of us in the defensive backfield. By the end of the day, we'd picked off four of Theismann's passes.

I got to play more and more as the game went on because Steve Wilson, one of our starting cornerbacks, went down with cramps, and Michael Downs pulled a hamstring running with an interception. On one play in the second half when I was in, one of our linemen either hit Theismann as he was throwing or tipped the ball as it left Theismann's hands. The ball fluttered through the air and started tumbling out of the sky toward me. It looked a lot like the first pass I intercepted at Grambling.

I settled under it as if it were a beach ball being tossed my way. I caught it and rolled into a fetal position on the turf until someone piled on me to make sure I didn't get up and run, which was the furthest thing from my mind. We won. It was the first of eleven interceptions I made during my rookie season.

Our second game was at home against the St. Louis Cardinals. I was less nervous about playing in front of Cowboys fans for the first time in a game that counted than about how I was going to get my whole family and Shreill's into Texas Stadium to see it. I felt like that kid I was during the basketball game on my birthday when I had my hair braided. I was thinking more about getting everything else in place than about the game.

Ron knew how to make the most of being a professional athlete, especially being a member of the Dallas Cowboys. He showed me which restaurants and bars liked to be able to brag that Cowboys dined and drank there, which meant they gave us free dinners and drinks in exchange for showing up. One of our favorites was the Million Dollar Saloon, a lavish strip club with a great chef, on Greenville Avenue not far from the training facility.

More crucially for this first home game, though, Ron showed me the ropes for getting lots of tickets, and I needed plenty in my hometown, about twenty-five or thirty. The Cowboys gave each player two complimentary tickets to each home game. If you wanted anymore, they were $26 apiece unless you bartered for some from your teammates. I bought some from everyone I could because I needed twenty-three for each game to accommodate my family and friends. That was the one downside to playing for the Cowboys and being from Dallas. It was expensive. Then Ron told me I needed some more tickets for another reason.

"You can't be no Cowboy driving that car," he told me, cracking on the hand-me-down Mustang Grande I was driving with the propped up driver's seat.

He told me to buy some tickets for the whole season and trade them at a car dealership that liked being associated with the Cowboys—and they all did—for a new car. I did. My rookie year I got a five-speed Toyota Celica Supra in which Shreill and I learned to drive a stick shift. Ron definitely made my $32,000 rookie salary go a lot farther. I managed to get all my family and friends to that home opener, which we won, and I acquired an entire lot of tickets for the rest of the season. Back in Hamilton Park, people were looking at me as the big man in the neighborhood because of my newly acquired largesse.

The third game was back on the road, and it was my first *Monday Night Football* contest. We were meeting the Patriots in Foxboro, Massachusetts, and it was scary.

It wasn't the game that unnerved me. It was the trip to the stadium from our hotel to this outpost of Boston called Foxboro.

I had never been to New England, and I'd never thought about there being country roads up north. But the farther we went down a little road off the main highway, the darker it seemed to get, just like in East Texas. The closer we got to the glow of the Patriots stadium, the more harrowing the trip became.

We had a police escort, but it didn't matter. The police couldn't get us, in our caravan of big buses, through the crowd of Patriots fans that lined the road. We kept stopping and going, stopping and going, what seemed like every few feet. And every time we came to a stop, the fans started screaming and pounding on the side of the bus, rocking it. It took us so long to negotiate the crowd that we didn't have time to go through our normal warm-up. We basically just went on the field and stayed till kickoff. Confronting the Patriots themselves was a relief after running the gauntlet of their fans.

On my first play, which came on a third down as the nickel back, I was lined up against Harold Jackson, a Pro Bowler who had been a legend at Jackson State. Harold was fast but not as tall as me. He ran a corner pattern into the end zone, and his quarterback, Matt Cavanaugh, tried to drop the ball in to him and over my head. I saw it all the way and picked it out of the air before it got to Jackson.

It was one of two interceptions I had in the game. I got the second one in the fourth quarter, after our defensive coordinator, Gene Stallings, sent me in with the starters after Steve Wilson went down again with an injury. My second interception sealed a 35–21 victory. The other star in the game was Ron, who caught eleven passes from Danny White for seventy-two yards.

Seeing me for the first time in the pros, Howard Cosell raved about me, friends told me later, and said the Cowboys had finally found the play-making defensive back they'd been lacking. Cosell called me "Emerson." A Dallas sportswriter referred to me the next morning as the "big-play rookie." Still, I didn't get a compliment from Coach Landry. Not one of those "atta boys" or "nice jobs." Nothing.

At our first team meeting upon returning to Dallas, Coach Stallings pulled me aside and said I'd be starting at left cornerback in the next game. I said OK. End of conversation.

Inside, I was jumping for joy. I couldn't wait to tell Shreill and Mom. I told everybody. My sister Eartha couldn't believe her little brother was the starting cornerback for the Dallas Cowboys. It felt so good to have come that far. I was one of the twenty-two starters along with Ron. I told him he had to rely on a Negro League player now, and he couldn't help but laugh.

On our first day of practice the next week, I walked into the defensive huddle, and Dennis Thurman looked at me, nodded, and said: "Hey, man, way to go." Dallas reporters called Coach Rob and asked him about me, and he told them he knew I was going to make it all along. I could just hear Coach Rob's high-pitched voice drawing out those words: "Hell, we knew he was a pro the first time we laid eyes on him."

The only thing that would have made me happier was if the man who made the decision to start me had acknowledged as much. But Coach Landry never said a word.

I started thinking Coach Landry just didn't like me. I figured he didn't care much for me after I griped to Gil Brandt about what I felt was a paltry rookie free-agent contract. I thought Coach Landry wanted me to prove my worth before I demanded higher compensation that I was certain was more commensurate with my talent.

But what I came to realize was that Coach Landry just didn't like the way I played defensive back. He didn't like that I didn't do it the way the textbook indicated, but I was still successful.

That wasn't an uncommon attitude among a lot of coaches toward players from black colleges. Big white schools were considered superior. Black schools were thought to be inferior. The players from black schools needed to be shown how to do things the proper way. We were renegades. We were sandlot players.

Coach Landry knew the cornerback position as well as anyone. It was his position. He starred there for the Giants back in the '50s. He was a thief just like me. He picked off thirty-two passes in a playing career that lasted just eighty games. Then he coached defense on the Giants while Vince Lombardi coached the offense. They went to the NFL Championship three times in four years. Defense was how Coach Landry made his reputation before the Cowboys made him their head coach, in 1960, when they came into the league.

So it was hard to tell Coach Landry there was another way, especially by the time I got to Dallas. He was in his twenty-first season as a head coach then and had long been an NFL legend. There was Coach Landry's way, and there was the wrong way. Nothing else existed.

I remember a rookie defensive back came up to me during one training camp after I'd been around a few years and had been to the Pro Bowl a few times, and he related to me something that happened in a defensive backs' meeting that for some reason I'd missed. He said the room was dark, and they were watching film, when all of a sudden the door opened, and the hallway light flooded in. Everyone turned around to see who had the temerity to interrupt a meeting. It was Coach Landry.

"Guys, I know you're watching film from last year," the rookie told me Coach Landry said. "Whatever you do, do not try to do what Everson Walls does. If you do, it's a quick ticket out of here."

Coach Landry never got over the fact that I was an undrafted free agent. Once a free-agent rookie, you're always a free agent in the NFL.

You were not what the coaches were banking on. They always have doubts about you. They see you as a fluke. They wait for you to slip up and fail.

What coaches were really doing was warding off doubts about themselves. If I was as good as I was turning out to be, then Coach Landry and Gil Brandt and their scouts weren't as good as their reputations suggested. They would have drafted me—and high up—if they had known better.

But I wasn't the fastest guy or the strongest guy. I wasn't long-limbed like Michael Downs. I wasn't from a big-time college program like Ron with Woody Hayes endorsing me.

I found a way to compensate for my lack of speed, and it bedeviled Coach Landry. What I did that he didn't like was what I learned to do in Coach Rob's secondary. It was what was called "clueing." All the guys at Grambling did it. They weren't the only ones either. Some pros did it, too. I covered a receiver by watching the quarterback and sensing where the receiver was going to run, instead of watching only the receiver and running with him, which was the textbook way of playing defensive back.

Since I wasn't fast enough to just run with a lot of guys, I played a little farther back off the line of scrimmage. I stood almost as far off the line of scrimmage as the linebackers and, like the linebackers, kept my eyes on the quarterback almost the entire time.

When the ball finally was snapped, I started to backpedal, keeping the receiver in front of me and continuing to look at the quarterback, waiting to see where he was going to look.

I was a fast backpedaler, fastest on the team, if not in the league. Sometimes I thought I could run faster backward than I could forward. I always thought it came so easy to me because of all the backpedaling I did during the off-season playing basketball and from what I learned from Dad playing outfield in baseball. I tried never to turn my back on the ball. I'd turn my shoulders and swivel with my torso, but I tried never to turn my back. That allowed me to keep an eye on the quarterback, so when the ball was finally thrown—to my receiver, or elsewhere—I'd see it immediately and take off in its direction. That was the way I got to so many passes before the receiver did, or another defensive back. That was the way I got to a lot of tipped passes and deflections. I was already headed that way.

In my mind, I was getting the job done. In Coach Landry's eyes, I was being greedy, I was being interception happy, and I was more interested in my statistics than in the game.

Coach Landry thought I was selfish. Me—the kid who spent two weeks in juvenile detention to save the hides of a couple dudes who didn't deserve my friendship—selfish. Me—the college player who accepted a platoon role in order to let an upperclassman have his turn—selfish. That hurt.

Here was a coach who as a defensive back himself had picked off all those passes. He knew you had to be a little selfish back there, especially at cornerback, because it's just you and the other guy. If you're going to do your job, you've got to want the ball more than the guy you're covering and as much as any of your teammates in the backfield. If that was being selfish, then I was guilty.

But if I got beat, Coach Landry thought it was because I did something the wrong way. He thought it was because I was peeping into the offensive backfield at the quarterback rather than watching my receiver.

I did get beat sometimes. Pittsburgh's Mel Blount and San Francisco's Ronnie Lott, who were superstar defensive backs in the league at the same time, got beat sometimes. Everybody got beat now and then. Hell, receivers got paid to outmaneuver us, just like we were paid to stop them from doing so. The difference with me was that I didn't have the pedigree other guys like Blount and Lott had. Blount was a veteran Pro Bowl player who had won several Super Bowls, and Lott graduated from the University of Southern California, a big-time school like Ron's. If I got beat, it was because I wasn't good enough or didn't know what I was doing.

That couldn't have been further from the truth. Sometimes the wide receiver figured me out, and I had to come back and figure him out at the next meeting. That's the thing about football, especially at the professional level. That's the thing about sports in general that's so challenging. It isn't just that you are always pursuing perfection but not always achieving it, which is true of any endeavor. It is that in sports you are doing so in an arena in which everyone can watch you and judge, immediately. So you have to learn to keep your head up and keep striving no matter the critiques. In Coach Landry's system, achieving perfection was even more difficult than in most other systems, particularly for those of us who played cornerback.

Coach Landry was the mastermind of what he called the flex defense. It was not a defensive back's friend. It was made for linebackers.

A linebacker in the flex who was quick and a sure tackler was bound to be a star, because the flex was designed by Coach Landry to stop the run. The linemen didn't play in a straight line at the line of scrimmage. At least two of them were a couple of yards off the line of scrimmage, while the other pair was, quite normally, nose to nose with the offensive linemen. Each lineman and linebacker was then instructed not to run directly to the ball carrier or quarterback, but to flow in that direction, a kind of controlled run, I guess you could call it. The linemen were to maintain spacing, while the linebackers filled the gaps between them and, if it all worked, catch the ball carrier after he picked a gap to try and run through.

Meanwhile, the cornerbacks were left all alone. It was us and whoever we were covering. It was one-on-one, just like I'd practiced so many times at Grambling. The difference with Coach Landry's system was that as a cornerback in the flex defense, I was sacrificed for the desire to stop the run. Linebackers didn't drop back too much into pass coverage to help. We were on our own.

I didn't mind, though. I relished one-on-one. What I didn't appreciate was being criticized when I came up short in a team system in which I, unlike most everyone else in it, didn't get any support.

It was an all-around learning experience going from college to the NFL. But the big lesson was going from Coach Rob to Coach Landry.

I understood the difference, though. Coach Rob had a vested interest in you for four years and had a greater mission in mind than just football. He was preparing young black men for life. Coach Landry only cared if you could play football when called upon, period.

But Coach Landry wasn't a bad guy. He was just aloof, just as he appeared to be, especially with me.

☆

Near the end of the regular season in my rookie year, Landry called what I learned was an annual special meeting for the team. It was to announce who on the team had made the Pro Bowl, which was the league's all-star game. The Cowboys veteran defensive back and one of Landry's favorites, Charlie Waters, liked to talk about how this particular meeting unfolded.

Coach Landry read the names alphabetically. Pat Donovan, the left tackle. Dorsett. Too Tall Jones. Herbert Scott, a guard. Rafael Septien, the kicker.

"Everson Walls," Coach Landry said, then "Danny White."

That was it. There was some applause, some "way-to-gos," and that was it—until we hit the practice field.

With me now playing for the Cowboys, my boys from Hamilton Park had new reason to roll over to the practice facility and stand at the fence and watch us go through our paces. I spied my boy Vernon MacDonald and couldn't contain my glee at what I'd just learned. Charlie Waters always laughed telling what happened next. I yelled across the field to Vernon with a childish enthusiasm the Cowboys weren't accustomed to: "Homeboy, guess what? I made the Pro Bowl!"

Charlie was on his last leg then, literally. He was a longtime veteran strong safety who was coming back from a knee injury that was so severe he missed the entire 1980 season after undergoing reconstructive surgery. He was playing on my side as my safety net and was really struggling because of his knee.

But no one ever said anything because Charlie was a great guy and had been a great player on five Cowboys Super Bowl teams, two of which won it all. He was as much a part of the blue star as any player.

So when things happened like what did in a game against the Cardinals, Charlie was absolved. It was a point in the game during the second half, when the Cardinals were driving, and we were in a defensive scheme specifically to stop the Cardinals receiver Roy Green. The cornerbacks were supposed to cover the outside, and the safeties were to stay inside. Green broke down toward the goalpost, and Cardinals quarterback Jim Hart fired the ball his way. Green made a one-handed catch for a touchdown under the goalpost on my half of the field but in Charlie's quarter of it. When I got back to the sidelines, the coaches asked me what the hell I was doing.

I was trying to play team defense. That's what I was doing. I was doing what they asked me to do. I wasn't freelancing, which was what their line of questioning suggested. But that's the way it was for the rest of that season. I was the whipping boy whenever something like that went wrong. I hoped it was just because I was a rookie, but time didn't bear that out.

Charlie never joined in the criticism, though. He really was a great guy. He only had words of encouragement for me and said I was doing a great job whenever anyone asked.

Charlie became to me in the Cowboys secondary what Mike Haynes had been to me in Grambling's: He was my cheerleader. He was the one who helped me keep my head up. That's what you want as a player. You like a little pat on the back every now and then. It makes you more confident. Charlie gave me the reinforcement that I never got from Coach Landry, and it meant a lot, because he was held in such high regard. During a training camp a year or two later after Shreill and I were married in 1984, Shreill said she was coming to camp to see me. Coach Landry was a big Christian and, consequently, big on family. But he had a rule about players being with their wives during training camp. You had to get his permission.

So for the first time since I'd become one of Coach Landry's players, I approached him after practice for a face-to-face meeting. I told him Shreill was headed to town, and I wanted to stay with her. Coach Landry denied my request. I was shocked. I was mad. And I ignored him.

The coaches did bed check that night, and I was gone. The next morning in a team meeting Coach Landry didn't mention me by name but said the team couldn't afford to have players who put their wishes ahead of everyone else. That prompted me to have my second face-to-face meeting with Coach Landry.

I reminded him that I requested time with my wife just as others had done. I told him that the others had the time away granted to them and that I thought he treated me unfairly by not allowing me the same privilege. He said something about misunderstanding what I'd asked him the day before. That was that. I thought Coach Landry knew he hadn't been fair with me but just couldn't bring himself to say so.

☆

I never had an odder relationship with any coach than I had with Coach Landry. It wasn't dislike. It wasn't love-hate. It was just confounding. But it taught me that you can't judge people by what they say or don't say; you can really only judge them by what they do.

Coach Landry appreciated my talent enough to start me as a rookie free agent. He appreciated me, and all his players, enough to ask others about what went on in our lives away from the field. I learned that as our training camp in Thousand Oaks, California, was winding down in August 1984.

Shreill was pregnant with our first child. She was due in late October or early November, but the pregnancy had not been going smoothly. There had been a couple of close calls, so Shreill and I were as nervous as we were excited.

The good news was that she had a lot of support around her back in Dallas while I was on the West Coast. There was her family and my mother and her new best friend, Adriane, Ron's wife. I couldn't wait to get home to be with all of them.

After the last practice, as was our custom, players went out in Thousand Oaks to toast the town good-bye. Ron and I had tied on a pretty good headache knocking back margaritas (tequila was our spirit of choice) and beers. After all, there was nothing to do the next day but get on the flight back to Dallas and fall asleep.

But when I got back to my room, I had a message to call my mother, immediately. I did, and when my mother answered the phone and heard my voice, all she said, very excitedly, was: "Cubby, Shreill 'bout to have this baby!"

Shreill was just six and a half months pregnant. I sobered up quickly, but there was nothing I could do except pray. I just wished the morning flight back to Dallas could leave right then.

I don't think I slept that night or on the plane in the morning. When we landed, it was late. I got a ride home so I could pick up our car to get to the hospital. All of my family was at the hospital as well as Shreill's. Shreill hadn't delivered, and the doctors said she was fine, but they wanted to keep her under observation at the hospital just to be sure.

I went back home at some point to change clothes and get a little bit of sleep. I was feeling a lot more comfortable about the situation. I don't remember what time I finally got home, but I do remember being awakened from a deep sleep by the phone ringing at seven o'clock the next morning. It was a nurse urging me to get back to the hospital as fast as I could. I ran red lights as if I were driving a cop car with sirens blaring.

Our daughter, Charis Walls, was born. She was two and a half months premature. She weighed two pounds, fourteen ounces. She was put in an incubator and hooked up to a respirator, and the doctors told us she would be there at least a month. They guaranteed nothing. Among the visitors there that day were Ron and Adriane. We prayed.

I was at the hospital all day every day that week, but I had a game on Saturday, and I had to get back to work. I was drained emotionally and mentally. I felt like I was sleepwalking when I came into our locker room at Texas Stadium for the game.

Everybody knew what I was going through because Ron let them know why I was absent. A lot of guys asked me if I was all right and wished Shreill and me and our baby their best.

I suited up and went out on the field for pregame stretching and warm-ups and then returned to the locker room for the final game instructions that Coach Landry gave to everyone while standing in the middle of the locker room. Then he gathered us closer as he always did for a prayer before doing battle.

Coach Landry told God that Everson Walls and his wife, Shreill, were new parents of a baby girl who was still in the hospital after an unusually early birth. He asked for God to look out for Charis and Shreill and me and had the team pray for us. They did. That was that.

Coach Landry had left me stunned again, this time with my eyes welling up with tears.

We left the locker room, walked down the ramp, and played a football game of which I have no recollection.

Thank God the doctors were right. After some time in the incubator, Charis was unhooked from the respirator. She was breathing on her own and getting healthier. About a month after she was born, the doctors gave us the go-ahead to take her home.

I remember that day like it was yesterday. It was the third Sunday of September 1984, and we had our home opener at Texas Stadium against the Eagles. We won 23–17 and picked off Eagles quarterback Ron Jaworski three times.

We walked up the ramp and into our locker room, and the door slammed shut behind us. Coach Landry walked to the middle of the floor to give us his postvictory congratulatory talk and hand out the game balls to the most outstanding players on the day.

I don't recall what I did that afternoon. All I remember is that Coach Landry told everyone my daughter that day was released from the hospital and had finally gone home to her mother. He then gave me the game ball, and I had that feeling again that I had after he said a prayer for Charis.

# 7

# Shreill and Adriane

I don't trust a lot of people. I haven't since my blind faith as a tenth grader landed me in juvenile jail for a couple of weeks. That experience made me leery not only of strangers, but also of those I knew casually. Outside of a few guys I knew well from having grown up with them, like T. and Vernon, I began to live my life among others very differently after I got out of the hoosegow.

One reason, other than getting locked up, why I began to close myself off to others was my growing relationship with Shreill, my new high school girlfriend in the eleventh grade who became my college sweetheart and, on Valentine's Day 1984, my wife. If juvenile jail scared me straight, Shreill was my insurance that I continued down the right path.

It wasn't anything she ever said. It was what she did. I just kind of followed her. She worked to be a good student; so I learned to do the same. She never thought twice about *not* going to college; I began not to either. She picked Grambling; I picked Grambling.

The only path I didn't follow that Shreill cut was toward other people. She has always been more outgoing than me. I joke that it might be because Shreill's father never let Shreill and her siblings, especially her three sisters, roam Hamilton Park too much. They always seemed to be cooped up in their house, just a few blocks down the street and around the corner from my mom's. Mr. Harris, bless his soul, probably would have chased me from Texas and across the Mexican border had he known that Shreill and I in our senior year at Grambling rented a trailer off campus to live in together.

We were rarely there alone, though, because Shreill always had people coming over from campus, especially when she made her red beans and rice with chicken. I would have a couple of my friends from the football team drop by, like Mike Haynes and Jerry Gordon, but

Shreill had everyone come over. That's just her bubbly, big-hearted personality.

But I'd heard rumors about NFL wives—backstabbing and envy and sniping—before I made the Cowboys. The stories were just like those that wound up on that short-lived television show about home life in the NFL called *Playmakers,* where wives worried about other women trying to pry loose their husbands, and players worried about other players trying to take their wives or girlfriends. Shreill and I had a special relationship that helped turn my life around and give me a comfort that I'd never felt before, and I wasn't about to let anything sink that.

Shreill was aware of the new world we were about to enter, too, and adopted a little of my cautiousness about the new people with whom I was working and their friends and family. I remember the first time I brought Ron to my mom's house to meet my mother. It was early in my rookie season. I'd mentioned Ron to everyone plenty of times, but they and he had never had the pleasure of meeting.

Ron and I walked in the door, and the first person we saw was Shreill. She was in the kitchen with Mom. Shreill wasn't working then. It was just a few months after we got out of Grambling, and she was enjoying time for once to do nothing. She was over at my mom's house just about every day then. She was doing everything at Mom's house except living there, although it looked like she was doing that because of all the clothes she was keeping there.

I introduced Ron, and we stayed and talked and laughed for a while in the kitchen. Then we excused ourselves, got in the car, and Ron started laughing.

"Boy, don't let any other girl walk up in your mom's house with you," Ron said through his chuckling. "Shreill's gonna be sittin' right up in that kitchen with your mom just waiting for you."

One day, Ron returned the favor and invited me by his house after practice with a few other guys from the team. Tony Hill lived across the street from him then, and he came over. We were just hanging out in the house talking and laughing and drinking a few beers when the door opened, and in came a beautiful woman with a mocha-latte complexion like Shreill's. Everybody in the room knew her except me. It was Adriane, and she looked none too happy.

She was just coming in from work at Lone Star Life Insurance in North Dallas, where she was a legal adviser. I think she expected a little peace and quiet in which to wind down. Instead, she found her home filled with a bunch of guys with their feet up on the furniture engaging her husband in his boisterousness. She sort of glared at us. Ron introduced me and said something more that Adriane simply dismissed. It was the first time I saw someone put Ron in his place.

But that was what Ron always said about Adriane, that she didn't take any of his guff. And she didn't. He could throw his barbs at her, and she would throw them right back, with a few of hers for good measure.

Ron liked to hang out a lot, and he told a story once about slipping back into the house in the wee hours of the morning, being sure to take off his shoes so he wouldn't make too much noise and wake Adriane. Well, she was waiting for him this particular time. He said he closed the door, and the next thing he knew Adriane was on his back trying to put him in a headlock and demanding to know where he'd been and why he was returning so late.

Ron laughed whenever he told that tale. He could because he and Adriane have a special relationship, just like Shreill and I do. The tenor of theirs was just a little different, but it was still one of love and respect.

The more I saw of Adriane when I was with Ron, the more I liked her for all of those reasons and then some. I just liked the way she carried herself, how smart she was, and how she handled Ron. Ron always wanted the last word, but it wasn't always the right one. Adriane never minded telling Ron he was wrong, and she always had something very sensible to say, sometimes something you hadn't thought about.

What Adriane did for me was explode whatever myths I harbored about NFL wives, or at least she proved that some NFL wives and girlfriends were exceptions. She certainly was. So I gathered the nerve once to bring Shreill with me to a get-together at Ron and Adriane's house.

I felt cautious. Even though I was always talking to Shreill about Ron and Adriane, I had left Shreill to be friends only with the girls she grew up with. By the time I dared to take her into Adriane's presence, apart from when we'd bump into Adriane after games, Shreill was pregnant with Charis, our first born. That was after the 1983 season, my third NFL campaign.

To my surprise, when Shreill and Adriane finally got to spend a little time together, it was as if they were long-lost sisters. It surprised Shreill, too, I think.

I remember once when, against my better judgment, I dropped off Shreill at a baby shower for one of my teammate's wives, smack dab in the middle of all the women I wanted her to stay away from. And, as I feared might happen, I couldn't get back in time to pick her up, which meant she'd be immersed in that pool of gossip even longer. Adriane volunteered to give her a lift home, and they must have stayed at our kitchen table sipping wine and yapping for the rest of the night.

Then they showed up together at one of the off-season charity basketball games Ron and I and some of our teammates played in often. I was as stunned as I had been when my mom turned up in New York on my first big road trip with Grambling. Adriane asked Shreill if she wanted to go, and Shreill said she'd be more than happy to tag along.

Who knew that these two women would hit it off so well so quickly? And the more Shreill's pregnancy began to show, the closer she and Adriane became. After Ron and I departed that summer for training camp in California, Shreill and Adriane were hanging out together and talking on the phone almost every day.

The day after Charis was born in August 1984, Adriane stayed at the hospital with Shreill, while I went to work at Texas Stadium for a preseason game. After Shreill was released, the next Monday, Adriane volunteered to drive Shreill to the hospital whenever I couldn't so that Shreill could see Charis while she was being held until doctors deemed her fit. That went on for an entire month, and Adriane was a working woman.

Adriane may have been at Shreill's side more than I was during that time, and I was grateful for it. Shreill couldn't drive herself because she was still healing from the cesarean section the doctors performed on her to deliver Charis.

Sometime later I remember overhearing Shreill ask Adriane when Adriane was going to have children. Shreill said Adriane didn't think she was ready to have a child then because she felt a bit like a foreigner in Dallas. Adriane was from Cincinnati, and she didn't have any family in the area. Shreill said Adriane, who worked a nine-to-five job, was worried about who she could trust with her baby during the day. That was something family did, Adriane told Shreill.

After watching Charis survive a premature birth, Shreill told Adriane that child care should be the least of her worries and volunteered her mother and my mother as potential babysitters for any children Adriane had. That was how Shreill felt about Adriane—she was family.

By the time Charis was a year old, Shreill was planning a baby shower for Adriane, who then delivered a baby girl she and Ron named Ayra. The only suggestion Adriane didn't take from Shreill was to leave the baby with my mom or Shreill's.

Instead, Shreill and Adriane took care of their babies together. Adriane took leave from work, and she and Shreill had each other as baby mamas to hang out with. They did so every day, like it was part of a schedule. After Ron and I went to work with the Cowboys, Shreill and Adriane bundled up their babies, grabbed their strollers, loaded the babies and strollers into a car, and took off for one of the malls. They wouldn't split up until late afternoon, when they would head back to their respective homes and prepare dinner for their husbands. It was their routine while they were young first-time mothers. Shreill and Adriane were together even more than Ron and I.

They were so close that Shreill all but suffered withdrawal when Adriane packed up Ayra to move with Ron to Cleveland after Ron's NFL career summarily ended in Tampa Bay in February 1987. Ron had been in Tampa since just before the 1985 season started, when the Cowboys soured on him and cut him loose. Adriane moved to

Tampa with Ron at first but didn't like it and returned to Dallas. After Adriane got to Cleveland, she and Shreill were on the phone every night, it seemed, with Shreill filling in Adriane about what she was missing back in Dallas, and Adriane filling in Shreill about how Ayra was doing, and occasionally Ron, too.

The next time Shreill became pregnant, Adriane got pregnant, too. After Shreill delivered our son, Cameron, we left him and Charis with our parents and took off to Cleveland to see Adriane and Ron and their family that had now also expanded with a second daughter, Ashley. Ron and I wondered if our wives were now planning both of our families. The truth was that they were making our two families one.

# 8

# Erasing Defeat

It wasn't until I was a few years into my NFL career that what Coach Rob was trying to get across to us, about our place in history, finally sank in. Shreill and I were at an NFL awards banquet in Chicago, and I bumped into the San Francisco wide receiver Dwight Clark there.

Clark and I shared a few things in common. We were both from the South; he was from North Carolina and played football at Clemson in South Carolina. We weren't highly thought of coming into the NFL, but at least he was drafted, in the tenth round by the 49ers.

My rookie season ended in the NFC championship game in San Francisco when Clark caught a pass from Joe Montana with his fingertips in the back of the end zone, while I reached in vain to knock the ball away. There was less than a minute left in the game, and the 49ers held on to win by the margin of the extra point after Clark's touchdown, 28–27.

The photograph of Clark's grab became immortalized overnight as The Catch, with him as high in the air as he could stretch his six-four frame, and me still earthbound right behind him. The Kodak company made it part of a commercial, and it ran on television over and over and over again. It was really a great spot. Barbra Streisand sang "The Way We Were" in the background—you know, "Memories, light the corners of my mind, misty water-colored memories, of the way we were. . . . " I just never liked the ending of the commercial any more than I did the ending of that game.

Clark liked it all, though. He spotted me before I spotted him and called my name from across the room. "Everson," I heard someone say.

Clark always seemed like a nice guy. We'd met before and had some fun exchanges. Once we took a picture together reenacting The

Catch at another function. I'd seen Montana since that game, too, but he was always in his own world, it seemed.

Clark and I walked toward each other and shook hands. Then he asked me if I had received my money.

"What money?" I answered.

"From Kodak," he said.

Clark said that he and Montana got checks from Kodak for the photograph that was running in its commercials on television and in glossy ads in magazines.

I was stunned.

I was as much a part of that photo as Clark and Montana, and Kodak paid them but hadn't volunteered to do the same for me. I was mad. Clark was surprised, too.

"You need to go get your money," he said.

"I'm already there," I told Clark, thanking him for filling me in.

When Shreill and I got home, I called my agent, Steve Weinberg. Weinberg called Kodak. Following a long wait for a response, it became clear that Kodak wasn't going to be fair with me. The *Dallas Morning News* reported under a headline that read "Walls Fails to Catch on with Kodak":

> *49ers receiver Dwight Clark received about $15,000 from Kodak for the use of his picture in "The Catch" in print and television ads.*
>
> *Cowboys cornerback Everson Walls, who defended on the play that sent the Niners to the Super Bowl in 1981 and is prominent in the picture, found out from Clark that he got paid and asked Kodak for money as well. They offered $1,000 and a camera. Walls rejected it.*

I was tired of being overlooked, dismissed, and mistreated. I'd had my fill of that as a rookie free agent. This time, I told Weinberg to get a lawyer. We filed a lawsuit against Kodak in November 1987.

*Dallas' Walls Files Suit Against Eastman Kodak*

*DALLAS—Dallas Cowboys cornerback Everson Walls has filed suit against Eastman Kodak Co., accusing the film and photo processing company of using his picture in advertisements without getting his permission.*

*Walls' suit, filed Wednesday in state district court, complains about Kodak's use of a picture of a catch by Dwight Clark of San Francisco in the 49ers' 28–27 victory over the Cowboys in the 1982 NFC championship game. The picture shows Walls attempting to defend against Clark and identifies Walls by name.*

*Walls' suit said "such publication constitutes an unwarranted invasion of plaintiff's privacy, his right to be left alone, to live a life of seclusion free from such intrusion, and unwarranted publicity."*

I wasn't just amazed that Kodak so arrogantly dismissed me and then tried to stuff a thousand bucks in my pocket and one of its cameras in my hand to make me go away. I was also shocked that The Catch had taken on a life of its own and defined, in the eyes of much of the public, the careers not only of Clark and Montana, but of me.

I didn't want to be remembered for that play any more than I did for any other single play. I especially didn't want a losing moment to become my legacy, and I sought then and there, feeling Coach Rob's spurring, to create another memory of my time in and around football. I didn't know what it was going to be, but I knew I had to make it.

This was just another instance in my life in which I was misunderstood. I wasn't a loser. I never had been. I wasn't a loser in that particular championship game either. It just so happened that one play was so consequential that it overshadowed everything else I'd done up to that point in the game, as well as everything my teammates had done.

☆

As with a lot of my experiences in life, the game in San Francisco against the 49ers was about disproving a first impression, in this case not a first impression of me but of our team. The Catch had taken place during our second meeting of the season against the 49ers in their place. The first trip there, in October 1981, didn't go well at all for me or anyone else wearing the blue star.

It was the sixth game of the season, and we were coming off our first loss, which came in St. Louis against the Cardinals. We figured that was an aberration and looked to rebound against a 49ers team that was off to a 3–2 start and hadn't been very good the year before.

But when we ran onto the field at Candlestick Park, it was like running on quicksand; it was like some of the really bad fields I'd played on with the Tigers at small black colleges, or even at Grambling on the few occasions when we played on campus. Every step we took, our feet sank. We couldn't push off. We couldn't gain traction. I thought I could make it work to my advantage because it would slow down the 49ers receivers, but I was wrong.

First of all, like everyone else on our team, I was wearing short cleats. In soft turf, I may as well have been wearing Chuck Taylors. The cleats didn't dig deep enough. We were slipping and sliding like we were playing on an ice rink. The 49ers knew better and were outfitted in long cleats. They led 24–7 at the half. We changed our cleats before the third quarter to longer ones, but it was too late. San Francisco's momentum never waned, and they won, 45–14.

It was the first poor showing of my NFL career. I got beat by a little bit of everybody, from Freddie Solomon to Clark. I gave up a couple of touchdowns as Montana passed for over three hundred yards and never seemed to miss.

I didn't doubt myself or my teammates, though. I just wanted to get the opportunity for me and everyone else to redeem ourselves. It came in the most important football game I'd ever played in twenty-two years on earth: the NFC championship game on the second Sunday of 1982 at, once again, San Francisco. This time, we were prepared for the beachlike turf. Everybody had on long cleats.

It promised to be a great game, because it featured two great coaches, Bill Walsh and Coach Landry, strategizing against each other.

It also featured two play-making defenses. The 49ers had a great secondary led by Ronnie Lott, and we had a really good pass rush led by Harvey Martin, Randy White, and Too Tall Jones. The 49ers had a newfangled offense called the West Coast, and we had the Cowboys aura and Coach Landry's flex defense. The 49ers had finished the regular campaign 13–3, and we'd compiled a 12–4 record.

I was so anxious. I wanted to show that the blowout loss we suffered back in October was a fluke. I wanted to show Walsh, a guy who was supposed to be a coaching genius, that I wasn't a weak link in the Cowboys secondary because I was a rookie from a black school. I had always felt that other coaches, and some of those I played for, thought less of us "Negro League" players. I was fueled by that sense of underestimation I felt when I first came into the league and would feel for the rest of my career.

It was a perfect football-weather afternoon when we kicked off. The sun was out, and there was a crisp breeze coming off San Francisco Bay, not those swirling winds that could compromise the contest.

It didn't look good for us on the 49ers opening drive. They shoved us down the field before Montana found Solomon for a short touchdown pass. That was the way things had started back in October before they blew us out.

This time we bounced back, even though we lost Dorsett for much of the first half after he was kicked in the eye. Rafael Septien booted a long field goal. Tony Hill caught a twenty-six-yard touchdown pass from Danny White.

Then Montana took over again and threw a twenty-yard touchdown to Clark. It was like that for most of the rest of the game. It was back and forth, back and forth. Neither team really grabbed the momentum, but I helped set up our go-ahead touchdown with just over four minutes left in the game when I recovered a fumble. Danny White followed it up by passing twenty-one yards to Doug Cosbie for a 27–21 Cowboys lead. So it was up to those of us on defense to salt away tickets to the Super Bowl, and we had the 49ers right where we wanted them, pinned deep in their territory.

The 49ers were at their eleven-yard line. We went into our special defense called three-man, eight-man, which we always used to close out games. It sent the linebackers to the sideline in favor of three defensive backs. There was only one problem with it, and San Francisco knew what it was. It was extremely vulnerable to the run.

We didn't anticipate them doing much running from their eleven with so little time left. But we were wrong, and we didn't adjust in time.

We held them on the first two downs, and then they handed the ball off to Lenvil Elliott on third and long, and he scampered for another set of downs. It was demoralizing, but they still needed to go eighty-nine yards to get into the end zone. They went eighty-three.

There were fifty-eight seconds left on the clock. The 49ers faced a third down at our six-yard line and needed three yards for a first down. The roar cascading down Candlestick's stands was getting louder and louder as we got backed into that end of the stadium. It sounded like we were standing at the base of a massive waterfall.

The 49ers called time out, and Coach Landry put our linebackers back into the game. We all discussed our assignments. Michael Downs and I were to double team Clark on the left side of the end zone.

Montana settled in under center. The ball was snapped. Then everything went into slow motion.

I saw Montana drop back and drop back some more, and then I didn't see him. But I was still watching Clark, and I was right with him. I was just waiting for something to happen, and it seemed like time was going on, and nothing was going to happen.

All of a sudden, I spied the ball. It was in midflight. It was high and away. It looked like it was going into the stands. Then it started to drop, like a pitcher's changeup. In a split second it was headed in another direction. At the beginning of the play Clark broke to the inside. Now he was reversing to the outside and apparently saw Montana all along.

Clark leaped as the ball was coming down toward the corner of the end zone. I saw it happening and could only hope it went over his head. It did, but not beyond his outstretched fingers. I swung in that direction but wasn't nearly close enough. Touchdown, 49ers. Clark was a half yard from being out of bounds.

I got back to the sidelines, and everyone was just deflated. I was upset, too, of course. But having grown up watching Cowboys quarterback Roger Staubach turn what looked like certain defeat into victory, I didn't slump on the bench. I stood close to the sidelines to watch what I knew was going to be a short drive to set up a long Super Bowl invitation–clinching field goal.

Sure enough, thirteen seconds after The Catch, just as I envisioned, White dropped back and saw Drew Pearson streaking across the middle. White threw a perfect strike. Drew caught the ball in stride. He looked like he was going to make it to the end zone until 49ers cornerback Eric Wright caught his shoulder pad and would not let go. Drew was high kicking trying to get away, and Wright was bulldogging him like they do steers in the rodeo. Drew eventually was dragged down after thirty-one yards across midfield, at the 49ers forty-five.

A hush came over Candlestick. We were jumping for joy on the sidelines. We knew we needed maybe fifteen more yards, and Septien, who was headed to the Pro Bowl with me in a few weeks, could send us to the Super Bowl with a game-winning field goal and turn The Catch into just another touchdown.

White dropped back to pass again. Tony Hill ran a sideline route and was open. But just as White began to throw at Hill, he was hit from behind by defensive tackle Lawrence Pillars. White went down in a heap, while the ball came loose and fell to the ground. Another defensive tackle, Jim Stuckey, fell on it before any Cowboys in the area could. There were thirty seconds left. Our dream was dashed.

I dragged myself into the locker room, and as I passed one of our star defensive ends, Harvey Martin, who was visibly dejected, I said, "Don't worry, Harvey, we're gonna get 'em next year."

The next day, Martin was quoted in the paper criticizing me for talking about coming back the following year rather than winning that season. I was offended, but there was nothing I could say. I had two interceptions, a fumble recovery, seven tackles, and had broken up three or four passes. The only thing anyone remembered, though, was that I didn't break up Montana's last pass. *Sports Illustrated* captured The Catch for its Super Bowl cover, just Clark and me. The 49ers went on to win the Super Bowl.

I never thought that some people would try to define me by that one famous play, which was in the penultimate play of my Pro Bowl rookie season. That, however, was exactly what happened.

I was really surprised that Montana-to-Clark became lore. I guess I was too close to the trees to see the forest. I recalled watching football games growing up that were just as good or better, with plays just as big. We got six turnovers against the 49ers. They got a couple against us. It wasn't a clean game.

I was never one to let failures outweigh accomplishments. But I'd never had that approach to life tested so mightily as it was in the aftermath of that championship game. This was where that outlook was steeled. The next season, just as I had predicted to Harvey, we did get back to the championship game, but we lost again—to Washington. Washington went on to win the Super Bowl.

I first went to the Super Bowl, as a fan, that year, in January 1988, to watch my old college teammate, Doug Williams, become the first black quarterback to win the ultimate game playing for Washington. I had a ticket package for two, all expenses paid, as part of the settlement Kodak reached with me to withdraw my lawsuit.

Shreill couldn't make it because she was pregnant with our son, Cameron. I took my best friend from Hamilton Park, T., and when we realized we were witnessing Doug Williams make history, I said, "Thank you, Kodak, for being so hardheaded."

☆

That ended up being the only way I got to a Super Bowl with the Cowboys. We were falling apart. We hadn't been to the playoffs since the 1985 season. Quarterback controversies with Danny White, Gary Hogeboom, and Steve Pelluer seemed to plague us each season. Dorsett was getting older. Herschel Walker was brought in from the folding U.S. Football League for a ton of money, which rubbed some of us the wrong way. Ron was long gone to Tampa. In 1988 we won a total of three games. Not long after, the team was bought by an Arkansas oil man named Jerry Jones. Jones asked Landry to step down. Landry said he'd think about it.

Jones wasn't interested in waiting, so he fired the only coach the Cowboys ever had and brought in his old teammate from the University of Arkansas, Jimmy Johnson, who'd played with Jones on the Razorbacks 1964 national championship. Johnson was the championship coach for the Miami Hurricanes then.

Then we hit rock bottom. We won just one game in 1989, with a rookie head coach and a rookie quarterback named Troy Aikman.

Jimmy Johnson liked me. He respected me, I think, because I was a veteran, and he could trust that I knew what I was doing. He made me one of the team captains, which was the first time someone had entrusted me with so much responsibility.

But losing grates on everybody, especially when you're accustomed to winning, as Johnson and I were. It boiled over in a mid-November loss to the Cardinals in Phoenix, where the Cardinals had moved from St. Louis a season earlier. I didn't play particularly well that game and got beat for a touchdown. The loss came on the heels of what would be our only win that year, at Washington.

When the game was over, I stopped to talk to Cardinals receiver Roy Green, a longtime nemesis and friend of mine, before leaving the field. I don't recall what we chatted about. We probably just exchanged pleasantries and bemoaned being on losing teams and cracked a joke or two about it. It was nothing out of the ordinary for those of us who'd been in the league for a little while.

Jimmy was a newcomer, though, and he didn't see it that way. He lit into me when I got into the locker room for, he said, "fraternizing" with the opposition. I was shocked by his reaction. The lacing I took leaked into the media. Jimmy was trying to instill his way of playing football, and he couldn't afford a veteran—a captain, of all people—doing it another way.

My playing time started to dip after that. I rode the bench a long time on a cold day at the Meadowlands in New Jersey against the Giants. I thought I was going to freeze to death.

I knew then I wouldn't be around Dallas much longer. I was thirty years old and expensive. My three-year contract with the Cowboys made me the second-highest paid cornerback in the league, and it was about to expire. The new ownership and coach wanted youth and refused to offer me a new deal. I was a free agent again, and in February 1990 I started looking for a new football home.

It looked for a while like Denver, where Dorsett finished his career in 1988, would be my next stop. Then Seattle tried to sign me, but I wanted to look a little longer. I did my homework just like I had done when I got out of Grambling, and I thought the Giants would be a good fit for me. They were coming off a 12–4 season that blew up in the first round of the playoffs. Their defense was solid, but if it had a weakness, it was the secondary, which Rams quarterback Jim Everett shredded in the playoffs for 315 yards and two touchdowns. So I called the Giants coach, Bill Parcells, while I was working out at the Dallas YMCA, and he agreed to give me a look.

When I arrived at the Giants facility in New Jersey, I was greeted by Parcells's defensive coordinator, Bill Belichick, whom I'd never met, but he embraced me like a long-lost child. I was surprised and pleased by Belichick's welcome. I'd never felt that kind of love from my coaches in Dallas.

They decided not to work me out. They just interviewed me. I told Parcells that I was the piece he needed to win a Super Bowl. The Giants offered me a deal, and I took it.

I look back now and can hardly believe what good fortune that decision was for me. I'm able to say I played for four of the greatest coaches of all time—Coach Rob, Landry, Parcells, and Belichick.

☆

By the start of the 1990 season, I had wrested the starting right cornerback job from Perry Williams, who was a couple of years younger. I felt rejuvenated.

For the fourth game of the season, we traveled to Dallas, and I walked down the visitors' tunnel onto what had been my home field. I remember Parcells told the *New York Times*: "I thought he was worth taking a look at. He's practiced and played well here."

Parcells suggested the Cowboys should have tried to keep me but that he was glad they had not. He needed a veteran cornerback, and the Cowboys needed youth. My final contract with the Cowboys expired at just the right time for the Cowboys and for Parcells.

We won easily, and I played well. I went on that season, my tenth, to play better than I had in years. I was having fun being part of a defense stacked with Lawrence Taylor, who had starred with Ron in high school, and Pepper Johnson, Carl Banks, Steve DeOssie, and Leonard Marshall. We were the stingiest defense in the league.

Belichick's creativity kept everyone, especially me, excited. He started moving me to safety on third-down passing situations because he knew I was a ball hawk. I wound up leading the team in interceptions with six. I even did a couple of things I'd never done before in the NFL. I got a sack when Belichick sent me on a blitz, something the Cowboys never allowed me to do, and I took an interception for a touchdown.

☆

By the time we got to November, we still hadn't lost. We started the season 10 and 0 and became favorites to get to the Super Bowl. That was about the time I got a phone call from Ron.

Ron was out of the league by then. He'd been released by Tampa Bay, wasn't picked up by another team, and had scooped up Adriane and Ayra in Dallas and moved to Cleveland to work in the construction business. Shawn was living with Ron's mother, Ethelyn, in their hometown of Williamsburg, Virginia. The Cowboys had let me go when I was thirty, too. But Ron was done as an NFL player at that age.

We had stayed in touch but only sporadically. Mostly what I heard about Ron then came from Shreill because she was still very close to Adriane, and they talked all the time. It had been a while since Ron and I had had a conversation of any depth.

I remember hearing Ron's voice, and he sounded like a broken man.

"Why's everybody always picking on me?" Ron said.

He was talking about rumors that swirled around the league about his last days in Dallas, rumors that he felt were keeping him from getting another job. People were saying Ron, the life of the locker room, was a bad influence on his teammates. I couldn't believe what I was hearing. It didn't jibe with my interpretation of how Ron acted, which was that he stood up for his teammates, and the coaches and Gil Brandt and the Cowboys' longtime president and general manager Tex Schramm didn't like that. It was a classic case of labor against management.

I recalled in 1983 when the Cowboys cut Benny Barnes, who had been playing defensive back for Dallas his entire NFL career, eleven years at the time. A lot of guys were upset because Benny was a good guy who we all thought could still play. Nobody spoke up, though, except Ron.

When Ron had heard the news about Benny, he stormed into our training camp locker room, pulled a chair into the middle of the room, and stepped up onto it like some street corner preacher in Harlem standing on a milk crate.

"How long are we going to take it?" Ron preached. "How long?"

After a few seconds we realized he was serious and not just clowning around to break up the monotony as he so often did. So we responded, "Not long."

That was Ron. He was always willing, never afraid, to take up someone else's cause. He never thought about the consequences he might face by putting his neck on the line to help another guy. He wasn't fearful of what others thought, especially those in charge.

I didn't know what to say to Ron that day he called me in New York to moan about having been dealt what was undoubtedly in my mind an unfair hand. I just let Ron get it off his chest. I told him to hang in there. He was happy for my success but embittered that he wasn't granted the same opportunity to continue his career with a winning team. There really wasn't any reason for Ron's career to end so early and in an outpost like Tampa. He was just in his prime then. He didn't have any nagging injuries. He appeared to be in tiptop shape. He was starting in the Buccaneers backfield. Ron was knocked out of the game by fear. Front office managers and coaches were scared he would inspire other players to stand up for what they thought was right.

☆

The Giants continued to roll through the rest of that season, but we sleepwalked through a few games, tripping up and finishing with a 13–3 mark instead of a perfect record. We beat the Bears in the divisional playoffs, then found ourselves in San Francisco for the conference championship.

That game meant the world to everyone on the team. But it meant the universe to me. There I was, back on the same field where the worst memory of my career was born ten years earlier. It was a memory that had stuck in my mind like so much muck in my cleats on a muddy field. I thought this might be an opportunity to exorcise that memory and be rid of it once and for all.

The Giants did that for me with a too close for comfort but very satisfying 15–13 victory. I could see the summit, finally. I could see The Catch disappearing in my memory's rearview.

I didn't hear from Ron again that season, but that changed when I got to Tampa for Super Bowl XXV in January 1991 against the Buffalo Bills. Ron and Adriane surprised me and everyone else by turning up.

My entire family made the trip from Dallas. Shreill and the kids and my parents, including my stepmom, came down. My sisters, my stepbrother, my nephews, and even some cousins made the trip. But I was most pleased to see Ron, because his being there was absolutely unexpected. I'd reserved rooms for my family, but I didn't have one for Ron and Adriane because we didn't have a clue they were coming.

It reminded me how close Ron and I were, that he would come out of his way to cheer me on. It couldn't have been an easy trip for him. He was coming back to the town where his NFL career ended. He was coming to watch a game he dreamed of playing in. He would see his friend and former teammate try to win the trophy he always wanted.

Ron was talking trash and said he was going to put down a bet on us to win even though the Bills were favored. It was a typically comical Springs gesture, and it relieved some of the pressure that I couldn't help but feel building up.

When I finally strode onto the Tampa Stadium field the last Sunday afternoon of that January, I was as calm and focused as I'd ever been. I'd even been entrusted with a new assignment. To avoid being stymied by Buffalo's no-huddle offense, Belichick had decided to have someone on the field call the defensive signals. He ordered me to do it.

So it was Bills quarterback Jim Kelly versus me calling plays. I kept it simple and leaned on the talents of the guys around me. I also played mostly safety in a game for the first time in my career, because Belichick inserted an extra cornerback to thwart the Bills passing attack.

It all worked right away. We forced the Bills to punt on their opening possession. Then Parcells helped us out on defense by unleashing a ball-control rushing game plan that kept Buffalo's quickstep, high-scoring offense on the sidelines.

It was a back-and-forth tense game. It was one of those games where any mistake was going to be costly.

I couldn't help but think about that San Francisco title game as this Super Bowl went on. I was thinking about my pledge to myself to make a new memory to overshadow that. I was thinking about what Muhammad Ali said, that he wasn't going to be what others wanted him to be. He was going to make the impression he wanted to make.

We were clinging to a 20–19 lead late in the fourth quarter when the Bills were marching on what looked like a Super Bowl–winning drive. Only two minutes remained in the game, and the Bills faced a third down with one yard to go for a first down at their own nineteen, when their running back Thurman Thomas broke through the line and looked like he had a clear path to the end zone, as clear a path as Drew Pearson had in San Francisco on a catch from Danny White that could have turned The Catch into just another touchdown in the record books.

I took off after Thomas. I knew that if I didn't catch him, no one else would. I could be the hero this time instead of the goat. I had to make the surest tackle of my life, and somehow I did, twenty-two yards later.

The Bills managed a few more plays before they were forced to stop the clock with eight seconds left at our twenty-nine-yard line. Their kicker, Scott Norwood, lined up for what would have been a forty-seven-yard Super Bowl–winning field goal. He stepped to the ball and, with a thud, gave it a ride. It sailed to the right of the goalpost. The referees waved that the kick missed. The game was over.

I was so excited I must have run for thirty yards, in what direction I don't know, and jumped higher than I'd ever jumped before. Upon landing, I bent backward, reached to the sky, and, I learned the next day, was captured doing just that by a *Sports Illustrated* photographer who wound up having the picture chosen for the magazine's Super Bowl cover.

My career had come full circle. I'd made the memory I wanted on my terms.

I remember trying to answer a reporter's questions afterward only to open my mouth and start crying with joy. I'd shed that monkey from my back, that image of defeat from my career. I finally was getting the respect I always thought I deserved and was defining my being, not just in sports but in life.

# 9

# The Doctor's Plan

When I was growing up, I thought respect was something you earned that couldn't be taken away, kind of a diploma or a war medal. I thought that I'd proved my worth in the NFL just like Coach Rob said I would. He even bragged to reporters about me when they called after my rookie season to ask about the Grambling kid stealing all those passes.

But I had begun to think differently about respect as my NFL career blossomed quickly, long before I made it to the Super Bowl. I was in the Pro Bowl as a rookie after leading the league in interceptions. I did the same in my second season, 1982, which was shortened to nine games by a players' strike.

But after two NFL seasons, two Pro Bowls, and twice leading the league in interceptions, I was still getting paid the same salary that the Cowboys gave me out of college as a player neither they nor any other team had deemed good enough to spend a draft pick on.

At my second Pro Bowl, I told San Francisco safety Ronnie Lott and Oakland Raiders cornerback Lester Hayes what I was making. I told them what the Cowboys were offering in a new contract, and Lott and Hayes broke out in laughter. Hayes, who was from Houston and had become a star cornerback with the Raiders when I was still in college, counseled me—ordered me, really. He told me, simply, "Go get paid."

He didn't tell me how, though, and I certainly didn't have a clue. But I was determined to find one.

It was one thing for the league to overlook me in the draft coming out of Grambling. It was another for the team I won a starting spot with as a rookie to continue to treat me like that same undrafted free agent.

I didn't share my frustration with too many people outside of my family, but one with whom I did, and in detail, was Ron.

I was just getting to know Ron really well then, when he protested the Cowboys' release of Benny Barnes. Here I was on a defense with perennial Pro Bowl players like Randy White and Too Tall Jones and practicing against Dorsett, the best running back in the league, but the personality on the team that grabbed my attention the most was this boisterous, motor-mouth, stand-up comedian of a fullback named Ron Springs.

Ron was a born leader, as Woody Hayes discovered when the Buckeyes voted Ron to be one of their captains. He should have been a captain with the Cowboys, but management never would have endorsed it. Slowly but surely, the Cowboys brass came to see Ron as a threat to their authority.

Ron was an outspoken black man at a time when outspoken black men weren't much tolerated in a place like Dallas. I knew that because I grew up there. Ron was getting himself into deep water, but he didn't care. Ron and I started hanging out together a little more after he stood up for Benny Barnes. We would work out with each other during the off-season. We'd grab a few drinks and maybe a meal after practice with some of the other guys, just like we did during my rookie training camp. Shreill and Adriane were getting to know each other through some of the team functions for families. Ron came by my mom's house, where Shreill and I were still staying because we hadn't pulled together enough money to do what we wanted: buy a house and start a family. Ron and Adriane didn't live far away. They were on the other side of Abrams Road, which was one of the main arteries not far from the Cowboys practice facility and my home neighborhood of Hamilton Park.

One day Ron and I were sitting in the kitchen of my mom's house gearing up mentally for another monotonous training camp. We were knocking down some beer and tequila. It wasn't an unusual gathering—we often got together over drinks and my complaining and his counsel. I liked to make margaritas and thought I could make them better than anyone. Ron liked to drink them as much as I did, and he also liked vodka drinks. We both enjoyed cold beer, so we'd have that, too. I was always on the lookout for a bag of potato chips, because I was always just finishing up one. I wasn't concerned about liquor and lots of salty snacks, and Ron wasn't either. We were professional athletes, and there was no harm food could do to our bodies, we figured.

I told Ron how fed up I was with not being able to get from the Cowboys what I felt was my fair share. I hadn't gotten it when I signed with the team as a free agent. I didn't get it after I made the team. I wasn't even getting it now after I'd been selected to back-to-back Pro Bowls.

Ron was all ears.

Training camp was right around the corner, and I told Ron that the only reason I was going to go was because I couldn't afford what would be a $1,000-a-day fine for not showing up. That was a lot of dough in those days. The million-dollar contract, which I didn't have, was still very new. I couldn't afford to pay $1,000 every day to express my displeasure. I made $32,000 my rookie year and $37,000 my second season. The Cowboys had offered me another meager raise before my third season, and I wanted something more commensurate with how I was performing.

Ron agreed with all my complaints, but he wasn't being the talkative guy I'd come to know. It was almost as if I could hear the wheels spinning in his head.

Then, all of a sudden, Ron blurted out, "Why don't you just announce your retirement?"

"Retirement?" I said in disbelief.

I was twenty-four years old. I wasn't even at the first base camp on the climb up my career's mountain. I couldn't even conceive of what it looked like on the other side of the hill sliding down to another chapter in life. Retire? Shreill and I hadn't yet married. We didn't feel financially comfortable enough to start a family. We were still living in the neighborhood we grew up in at my mom's house. Retire? Football was all I wanted to do, and it was all I thought I knew how to do.

That was when Ron pointed out that I couldn't be fined if I was out of the league.

"Really?" I answered with wonder.

Then the wheels in *my* head started spinning. I could satisfy my gut feeling to show the Cowboys the level of my dissatisfaction by staying away from camp. And all it would cost me was, well, nothing, because contracts didn't kick in until the first kickoff of the season. Most important of all, I stood to get what I knew was rightfully mine: a lot more money.

After I thought about it a minute or two, and knocked back another swig of beer and tequila to be sure, it became obvious that Ron had come up with a brilliant negotiating strategy. After all, the Cowboys needed me. That we all knew. I was a two-time Pro Bowl cornerback who led the league in interceptions my first two seasons. I possessed the skills the Cowboys so badly needed before they tapped me and all those other rookie and free-agent cornerbacks in 1981. They'd be forced to sit down at the table with me.

On top of all that, my retiring would cause a little controversy, and I always enjoyed a little controversy.

It was obvious to Ron, too, that he'd come up with a brilliant strategy, because if it worked, he could say it was his idea in the first place. He enjoyed boasting as much as I enjoyed controversy. And if it didn't work, Ron had nothing to lose, certainly not our friendship. I appreciated the brainstorm.

I told Shreill what Ron and I had decided I would do. She thought it was absolutely crazy but figured we knew what we were doing. We really didn't, though.

As far as we knew, what I was going to do was a first. Plenty of guys had held out before, but no one who wanted a better deal had ever used retirement as a ploy. It wasn't something that would dawn on any player as young as me.

I called my agent, Steve Weinberg, and had him set up a meeting with Gil Brandt so I could tell the Cowboys in person how mistreated I felt. A few days later I was sitting in Gil's office as Gil listened to my story of woe and then dismissed me as he'd done when I tried to negotiate for a higher paying rookie free-agent contract. He didn't think I was really going to go through with my threat to retire at twenty-four years old. He didn't realize I was committed to the strategy Ron and I had set my mind to.

I still had my beat-up, hand-me-down Mustang. I had to drive it during the off-season because it was only during the season, when I had the Cowboys tickets, that I could barter for a nice new car from some car dealership, which was a trick that Ron had turned me on to. So I drove home to Mom's from that meeting with Gil in my damned Hooptie, sat down at a typewriter, and composed a letter to Pete Rozelle, the NFL commissioner, announcing my retirement. I waited to mail it until just before training camp commenced.

Then Shreill and I disappeared. The only people other than our parents who knew we'd left Dallas were Ron and Adriane. He was getting a kick out of all the plotting going on, secrets only he and a few others in my inner circle were privy to.

Shreill and I took off for New York. It had been my favorite place to visit ever since my disappointing inaugural trip there as a Grambling freshman when my mother surprised me by showing up, and then I didn't get to play. One of the things I liked about New York was that you could be so alone, maintain such great privacy, while being in the midst of so many people. There was so much to see and so much to do and great places to dine.

Shreill and I just wanted to be left alone. I certainly did, at least. I didn't want anyone to see any apprehensiveness in me, which I'm sure was evident. This was Ron's experiment, after all, and in a way I was his willing guinea pig.

Shreill and I got a room first at the Sheraton Hotel in the financial district and settled in. We didn't know how long we'd be there. Training camp lasted for a little more than a month. Worry was racing through my mind. What would happen if the Cowboys found some rookie free agent from another little ol' black school who could play, and they really could get by without me? Suppose some veteran defensive back with another team became disgruntled during his team's training camp and demanded a trade, and the Cowboys acquired him. I wasn't as certain now about this gamble as I was when Ron dreamed it up.

After a few days in the financial district, Shreill and I moved on to the Sheraton on Fifty-third Street in Midtown Manhattan not too far from Times Square. There was no news, not a peep, from the Cowboys management. Ron was keeping me posted on how it was shaking down at home.

Back in Thousand Oaks, California, the Cowboys started training camp, and their Pro Bowl left cornerback was nowhere to be found. The front office, coaches, players, and fans wondered where I was and when I would arrive. Word got out, thanks to Ron, that I had opted to retire rather than play for less than I believed I was worth.

Everyone was stunned. This was a first. With each day, everyone at training camp expected me to stop my unprecedented protest and show up at the dorm with my tail tucked between my legs. Some of the guys, like Tony Dorsett and Robert Newhouse, would ask Ron if he'd spoken to me and how I was doing. They knew Ron and I had become pretty good friends by then.

But Ron was biting his tongue, which was a huge task for him. He told our teammates that he hadn't talked to me, but that he assumed I was doing just fine.

Ron was fibbing, of course. He knew where I was and was providing updates from the home front. He took great glee in all the interest everyone was taking in him to get to me.

The guys would tell Ron how they overheard the coaches whispering about my whereabouts. One day, Ron told me, he witnessed it himself. Tex Schramm walked onto the field while everyone was stretching in preparation for practice. Ron said Schramm surveyed the practice field, obviously looking for me, and when he didn't see me, he quickly motioned for Coach Landry and Gil Brandt, who were on the field, to come to him. Ron said the trio drifted away from the field and huddled off to the side for quite a while before Schramm turned and headed back to his office.

Who knows if they were talking about me? But phone calls started coming in from the Cowboys front office, and from some of my teammates, to my mom's house looking for me. Guys grilled Ron more and more, too. I'm surprised they didn't haul him into an interrogation room like they do in the movies and threaten him with bodily harm if he didn't fess up. Reporters were looking for me as well, camping outside my mom's house at one point. She was none too pleased.

When we had been at the Times Square Sheraton for a couple of days, my cell phone rang. I had the latest technology—it was one of those things about the size of a brick, and you carried it in a soft case with a shoulder strap. With a cell phone hanging off my shoulder, something not many people carried in those days, I looked even cooler than when I showed up in Coach Rob's office for the first time in platform shoes, window-pane jeans, and a disco shirt.

"Walls," the familiar voice on the other end boomed. "It's the Doctor!"

Ron didn't just have nicknames for everyone else. He also had them for himself. "The Doctor" was one of them. "Governor" was another. Why? Who knows? That's something that makes Ron Ron.

I could hear a lot of chatter in the background. I recognized the voices as Dorsett, Newhouse, and Dennis Thurman. They were yelling at Ron.

"We knew you knew where he was!" I could hear them screaming. "Damn it! Let us talk to him! Where is he?"

Ron was just laughing. He hung up before we could even have a conversation.

Ron had held his tongue as long as he could. He told the guys he could get in touch with me anytime he wanted and wanted to prove his boast by calling me with them in the room to witness it. He never told them I was in New York. He just said I wasn't in Dallas. He told them Shreill was with me. He told them he knew everything about what I was doing because it was all his idea.

Ron was doing what Ron did best: bragging. All the information he had on this affair further cemented his status as king of the clubhouse.

Shreill and I were in New York for just a week or so when word got to us that the Cowboys wanted to talk. A sense of satisfaction swept over me. One week, and they couldn't get by without me. I showed them, I thought.

Shreill and I ended our vacation immediately and flew back to Dallas, and I booked a flight to California. I called Greg Aiello, Dallas's public relations man, and told him my flight to California was scheduled to get in late at night and that I'd prefer not to speak with the media until the next day.

But when I showed up at Thousand Oaks late in the night, reporters were waiting. The Cowboys screwed me again. I had to do an impromptu press conference.

The next day, I was on the practice field with Ron and the guys, but I still didn't have a new deal. What I agreed to with Gil Brandt took another year to get finalized. It wound up being a $125,000 signing bonus and a $120,000 salary. The first thing Shreill and I did with our newfound wealth was get married, on Valentine's Day in 1984. Then we bid farewell to my mom's house and bought our own, which was as far north in Dallas as you could be without being in the suburbs. Finally, we purchased our first new car, a burgundy BMW 635.

The only reason I didn't feel indebted to Ron after getting my new contract was that Ron never made a friend feel like he owed Ron anything. He never made you feel like he expected something in return. I wouldn't have blamed him had he felt otherwise, especially because what Ron did for me and others wound up biting him. Ron was content to boast to everyone about how he put together the strategy to get my new deal. I must have heard him tell that story one hundred times, and it got funnier with each rendition.

☆

I often wondered how Ron had developed his personality; he was so unselfish that it made most of those who encountered him act in the same way, toward him and others.

About a year later, shortly after the '84 season ended, I got a chance to return the favor Ron had done me when he showed me the ropes of contract negotiation.

Among the many advantages of being a professional athlete, particularly a member of the Dallas Cowboys in Dallas, is that people always want to give you something for free. In addition to the new cars the dealership let me use in exchange for season tickets, and the food and drinks we regularly got from restaurants around town, Ron showed me how to get suits from the best haberdasheries, for as close to free as could be. It was great publicity for an establishment to be able to say one of the Cowboys was a frequent customer.

I've mentioned the Million Dollar Saloon. It was a strip club, but not just any strip club. It had furniture covered in crushed velvet and architecture accented with gold paint. It served top-shelf liquor and had a humidor. The chef made the best tenderloin steak medallions in the city. The owner was a Cowboys fan, and the joint was not far from our practice facility. As a result, the owner always maintained an open-door, no-cover policy for us and gave us the best seats in the house, or any we wanted, whenever we ventured in. We gladly accepted, and often. It was too good a deal to pass up, but one Friday in late January 1985, Ron probably should have turned down the freebie.

Ron and a Cowboys defensive back, Steve Wilson, decided to stop by the saloon after practice this particular day for a free meal. When they went through the front door and began to walk past the cashier into the club, a guy Ron had never seen stopped them and asked them what the heck they thought they were doing. Ron said they were coming in for dinner, and the guy told Ron he was the new manager, and Ron and Steve would have to pay. Ron told him he had never had to pay before, and the guy said he didn't know anything about that. The guy told Ron and Steve to leave if they weren't going to pay.

The next thing Ron and Steve knew, a Dallas police officer, a woman, showed up at the saloon. Someone at the saloon had called the cops. The female officer attempted to arrest Ron, and Ron wouldn't let her. More cops showed up, and Ron couldn't keep them

My mom and dad at their prom. EVERSON WALLS COLLECTION

rrying the load for Ohio State. THE OHIO STATE
ENT OF ATHLETICS

ight) posing with my Grambling defensive backfield teammates, James White (23), Mike "All-World" Haynes (28), and Robert
ey Bear" Salters (6). EVERSON WALLS COLLECTION

Me and Coach Rob. EVERSON WALLS COLLECTION

Ron jogging to the end zone. DALLAS COWBOYS

Me with my Cowboys' defensive back teammat
THE *DALLAS MORNING NEWS*

Ron and me enjoying a break during a Cowboys' charity basketball game in Gallup, New Mexico.
DALLAS COWBOYS

Celebrating the 1991 Super Bowl victory with my Giants' defensive coach Bill Belichick and teammates.
EVERSON WALLS COLLECTION.

My second *Sports Illustrated* cover shot, taken during the Super Bowl celebration. AL TIELEMANS/*SPORTS ILLUSTRATED*

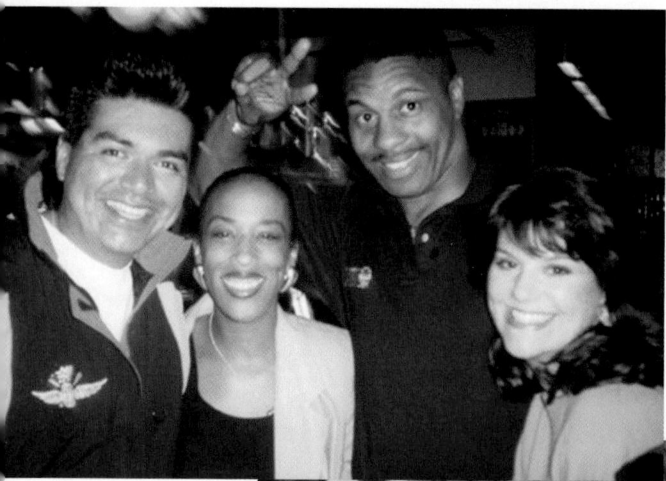

Shreill and me flanked by comedian Georg
Lopez and his wife, Ann, who donated a kid
to George. EVERSON WALLS COLLECTION

Ron and me being interviewed at a Players Ink II event.
THE RON SPRINGS AND EVERSON WALLS GIFT FOR LIFE FOUNDATION

Adriane and Ron. EVERSON WALLS COLLECTION

n's family and mine at the December 2006 press conference announcing my decision to donate a kidney to Ron.
COVINO, COVINO PHOTOGRAPHY

Ron and me being interviewed before the transplant. THE RON SPRINGS AND EVERSON WALLS GIFT FOR LIFE FOUNDATION

Me pushing Ron to midfield to be honored by the Cowboys at the 2007 season opener. JOE COVINO, COVINO PHOTOGRAPHY

l and Adriane. EVERSON WALLS

on in rehab. THE RON SPRINGS AND EVERSON WALLS GIFT
R LIFE FOUNDATION

Ron wearing one of his goofy hats.
EVERSON WALLS

Me and Ron. CHARLOTTE CALDWELL

from cuffing him. They shoved Ron into a patrol car and hauled him to the nearest station. Ron was charged with assaulting a police officer—which was aggravated assault, a felony—two misdemeanors, and criminal trespass.

It was big news. It happened at a topless club, which the holier-than-thou guys on the team pretended to frown upon. It involved a woman police officer claiming to have been manhandled by a six-foot, two hundred-something-pound Cowboys fullback.

There was a time when Ron bragged about his relationship with Coach Landry. Coach Landry seemed to like Ron not only because of how well he played but because he always lightened the mood in the locker room. Ron was one of the few players who could get Coach Landry to grin and chuckle. Alicia Landry, his wife, even got a kick out of Ron when she'd see him after a game or at a team social function.

But Ron was coming to be seen by management as a rabble-rouser rather than a locker room jester after he had concocted my retirement scheme to get me the money I thought I was due.

Nobody back in the locker room could believe what happened when we heard about it. Everybody knew the protocol at the saloon, including the wives and girlfriends, who knew we visited the saloon like a lot of well-known businessmen in Dallas. Ron and Steve said the incident was exaggerated by the officer, and we believed them. Everyone knew Ron didn't possess the kind of personality to incite a police officer to arrest him. If anything, he had the type of personality that would have left the officer clutching her sides in laughter. Something was amiss, we were sure.

Ron wasn't as shaken by the episode as were those of us closest to him. Few things got him down. While his case dragged out over the winter and spring and into the summer, he remained his old gregarious self, even though Coach Landry and the rest of the Cowboys brass started acting coolly toward him. Then, despite the thin ice that appeared to be freezing under Ron's feet, he chose to champion the cause of another teammate—Tony Dorsett—against management.

Maybe unselfishness was something Ron gleaned from being a fullback, a position that really demands more sacrifice than anything else, especially on a team with a halfback as talented as Dorsett. Dorsett got the ball the most. He got most of the acclaim. Ron helped clear the way for Dorsett's glory and never got rewarded in any special way for it.

But when Ron decided to help Dorsett negotiate a path to get more money like he'd helped me, the Cowboys took notice, and Ron got penalized for it.

Ron was waiting for his case to wend its way through the system when he jumped to Dorsett's aid. Ron by then had us all believing his case wouldn't amount to much, and spirits were rather high all around. I had my money and Shreill, and I had our first child, our daughter Charis, who was a healthy one-year-old by now. We felt blessed. And Adriane was pregnant with her first child, too. Shreill had thrown a surprise baby shower for Adriane, bringing Steve Wilson and his wife in from Denver, where Steve was playing then.

The team was coming off a disappointing campaign of nine wins and seven losses and was hopeful for a good season for '85. But something was brewing with Dorsett and management. Dorsett had been to the Pro Bowl three of the previous four seasons but didn't feel like he was being remunerated properly. He was feeling like I'd felt and had even more reason to complain, given his longer list of accomplishments.

There was a special urgency for Dorsett, however, because he was having some financial problems, and his problems had found their way into the news. He accused the Cowboys of leaking his money problems to the press in an effort to show he wanted more money just because he'd squandered what he had earned. Dorsett had something called a tax-shelter straddle that was popular in the late '70s but got outlawed by the Internal Revenue Service in 1981. He was hit with an additional tax liability of more than $300,000 after the rule was rescinded. On top of that, Dorsett's new agent had decided to sue him for $70,000. The *Dallas Times Herald* sports columnist Skip Bayless called Dorsett "His Indebtedness."

Dorsett was also ticked off because the Cowboys gave defensive star Randy White a bigger contract without much dickering.

He was angry. So he demanded that his contract be renegotiated, and he decided not to show up at camp until it got fixed.

Dorsett didn't retire as I had. He was already making a lot more than I was and could afford to be fined despite his financial woes. But it was a dicey situation for all involved, especially Dorsett. His '84 campaign hadn't been up to his normal standards. He fumbled a lot. He didn't seem as unstoppable. He was a thirty-year-old NFL running back then, at that threshold when even the greats start to offer diminishing returns.

But Ron wasn't hearing any of that. Dorsett was his guy. Ron was even tighter with Dorsett than he was with me at the time, because they'd been teammates longer, they were roommates, they were a tandem in the same backfield, and they had both gone to big-time schools, not the Negro League. So Ron appointed himself as Dorsett's spokesman in Dorsett's absence.

Almost every day during Dorsett's holdout, Ron put on press conferences for the media. He gave reporters updates on his roommate's position as if he were a press secretary holding court for the president in the White House briefing room. It was hilarious to witness because Ron acted so serious, and the media ate it up.

Ron was being serious, but he was also doing it for entertainment purposes. The Cowboys brass, however, didn't find it humorous. They had a financial system that they thought was important in making the team successful—it included finding diamonds-in-the-rough like me and Michael Downs and getting us cheap, and it meant maintaining a tight hold on the purse strings when it came to more expensive players like Dorsett. Ron had constructed my successful stonewall for a better contract, and now Dorsett was demanding a more lucrative deal. Management didn't want contract renegotiation to become a trend.

Ron told me some years later that Dorsett had cautioned him about his advocacy. "Tony told me, 'You've got to chill. Tex [Schramm] is getting mad.'"

But Ron didn't wilt. He just reared up even more, sticking out that barrel of a chest of his and exaggerating his strut even more.

In mid-August, Tony Dorsett got the raise for which he'd held out. He had stayed away from camp for a month, steeled in part by Ron's counsel that he was doing the right thing. And Ron had started in Dorsett's position while Dorsett was holding out.

Ron told the press when Dorsett returned, "I was driving a Rolls-Royce. Now I'm back to driving the same old Chevy with black wall tires."

Ron had never been so wrong. A little over two weeks later, just a few days before we were scheduled to kick off the 1985 season on Monday night before a national television audience against our biggest rivals from Washington, the Cowboys discarded Ron. They cut him. He wasn't traded. He was given a pink slip. And because it happened before the official start of the season, his contract, which like all NFL contracts was not guaranteed, was voided immediately.

The morning after, a *Dallas Morning News* sports columnist named David Casstevens penned a farewell ode to Ron that described him as "the Bre'r Rabbit of the Cowboys. Sassy. Smilin'. Laughin'. Bein' himself. Speakin' his mind." Casstevens quoted Dorsett later in the column as saying that Ron's philosophy was not to "take life so seriously, when you're gonna die anyway."

Ron was all but despondent. So was I. For the first time in my pro career, my mentor was not only going to be missing from my side, he wasn't even going to be working in our profession. I started to worry that Ron misjudged his court case, too, which was still lingering and carried a potential jail term of one year.

We kicked off the season hosting the Redskins with a rousing 44–14 victory. Dorsett ran for seventy yards and one touchdown, and Timmy Newsome, filling in for Ron, rushed for thirty-three yards and a touchdown and caught fifty-one yards' worth of passes. I intercepted a pass. It all felt like a pyrrhic victory after the loss of Ron. He was still unemployed and facing trial. The next Thursday, Ron finally got his day in court. Dorsett and I told him not to worry and that we'd be there with him. We knew that wouldn't be easy, though. We would have to miss practice. Given the way the team's relationship with Ron had soured over the past couple of seasons, Dorsett and I were pretty sure how Coach Landry was going to react to Ron's predicament and our desire to show our support for him. Practice would come first. He wouldn't want us to go.

Sure enough, Coach Landry told us we would have to practice on the day of Ron's hearing.

I'd never had a great relationship with Coach Landry, and this instance didn't help it any. His preaching about the importance of family never seemed to jibe with the way he acted with me when it came to a family matter. It reminded me of the time at training camp when he wouldn't let me spend the night with Shreill when she visited. I had never really forgiven him for using football as a wedge in my marriage.

Few people felt the way that I did about Coach Landry, because of his collected demeanor and the apparent high morals he lived by. But to me, he was a confounding man. He was rarely more confounding than he was with Ron and the rest of us during this strip-club incident.

We'd hoped that the court appearance would be scheduled for early in the morning or late in the afternoon when we wouldn't have to be at practice. But it was smack in the middle of the day. The way Dorsett and I saw it, there was only one choice. One of our family members, a former teammate, was in need of our help. We ditched the afternoon practice session and went downtown to the courthouse for Ron's hearing. Ron would have done the same thing for us.

Shreill and Adriane were there, too. Dorsett and I didn't just sit in the courtroom; we offered testimony on Ron's behalf as character witnesses.

Everybody knew who we were, including the judge. It was almost impossible to be a Cowboy and not be known in every corner of Dallas. We were seen as more than celebrity athletes. We were seen as heroes, which was a bit too much for most of us to accept.

The jury took our testimony into consideration, as well as the argument that it had been a simple misunderstanding involving the new saloon manager, the police officer, and Ron. But this was still Dallas. The police were mostly white, Ron was black, and this was a case about entitlement, which was something a lot of Dallasites frowned upon if a black athlete like Ron appeared to possess it.

A jury deliberated for about four hours. The longer we waited, the more frightened we got. Our fears weren't assuaged when the jury returned, and the first decision its foreman issued was guilty as charged.

Our hearts stopped until we heard it explained that Ron was being convicted on a lesser charge of resisting arrest and was found not guilty of the more serious charge of assaulting the arresting officer. The next day the same jury sentenced Ron to forty-five days' probation and a $2,000 fine and ordered him to pay $1,300 in medical expenses incurred by the female officer. Ron told the press, "I feel real good about it. I feel good about not going behind those cold steel bars."

The next day, Ron got better news—sort of. On the eve of our second game of the season at Detroit, Ron got a one-year contract offer from the Tampa Bay Buccaneers for what he had been scheduled to make from the Cowboys. The downside was that Tampa was the NFL's Siberia. It was the worst club in the league.

The Buccaneers, who were an expansion team in 1976, were the end of the plank in the NFL at that time. It was where once-good players went to rot. John McKay, Tampa Bay's original coach and a legend for running USC for many years, was gone. So, too, was Doug Williams, my old quarterback at Grambling, who had quarterbacked the Buccaneers to three playoff berths in four seasons.

Ron didn't deserve to be there. He was a winner in high school, junior college, college, and the first six years of his pro career. He had been with Ohio State and the Cowboys—programs that were better run than most. The Buccaneers in 1985, Ron's first season with them, were coached by Leeman Bennett. He'd managed three winning seasons as head man in Atlanta before taking over Tampa Bay just as Ron got there in 1985. The Bucs lost their first nine games in '85. They wound up with a 2 and 14 final record that year.

Meanwhile, we started out 6–2 in Dallas and went on to make the playoffs, where we got shut out in Los Angeles by the Rams.

I missed Ron's presence. Our locker room missed him, too, and management knew it. Coach Landry rarely addressed personnel issues in front of the team—he rarely addressed anything other than football in front of the team. But when they jettisoned Ron from Dallas, a guy who had stood up—literally—for teammates like Benny Barnes, Coach Landry knew he couldn't let it pass like Ron had just been some free-agent special-team player.

Coach Landry didn't call a team meeting to acknowledge Ron's forced departure. He just used a general assembly of the team one day to talk about it. He spoke about Ron as if he were a beloved uncle in the family business who'd just died. Coach Landry said something about football being a business and the need for everyone involved to pick up the pieces and move on despite the loss. It was a pretty short speech, but for Coach Landry it was a lot to have said.

☆

It probably wasn't a coincidence that '85 was the last season we were really any good in Dallas. It ended with a thud with our loss in the playoffs, and although we didn't know it at the time, it foreshadowed what was to come. The team went steadily downhill with losing seasons for the next three years—my last three seasons in Dallas.

A big reason was the loss of Ron's personality, which had buoyed everyone through tough times on the field and off. With him gone, when we started to deflate, there was no one in the locker room to pump us up. Looking back, I realize that's what was happening.

The great drafts Gil Brandt had long engineered, picks that made him a legend in pro football history, stopped happening; he seemed to have lost his touch at finding those diamonds in the rough. The cornerstones of the team were starting to weaken with age. Too Tall Jones was in his late thirties. Drew Pearson had retired in 1983. Harvey Martin went into retirement after that season, too. We had quarterback controversy after quarterback controversy, it seemed. Clint Murchison, the longtime owner of the team and an oil magnate, sold it to another oil magnate, Bum Bright, who got caught up in the oil business collapse in the late '80s and didn't get along with Coach Landry, who was aging, too. Bright even suggested out loud what others were starting to think: The game was passing Landry by.

In the middle of our late-'80s decline came another and more devastating walkout strike that divided the team so wide, only a Ron Springs could have bridged the gap, and he was nowhere nearby.

"The whole thing with Dorsett contributed to my demise," Ron told me years later. He didn't have any idea that the Cowboys would punish him so harshly, forcing him to look for a job just as the season was commencing and almost every teams' roster was set.

It hurt Ron, and it hurt me. I felt as if I'd lost one of the best friends a person could have, someone who had always been there for me.

# 10

# Walking the Line

My understanding of the daring kind of leadership that Ron demonstrated in the mid-'80s was planted back in 1982. We opened that season at home full of confidence and excitement, only to fall flat on our faces against the Steelers, whose championship core—quarterback Terry Bradshaw, running back Franco Harris, and linebacker Jack Ham—were just about out of tread. We rebounded the next weekend in St. Louis against the Cardinals and Roy Green, the receiver I had probably the most difficult time covering in my career. I chased Green around that day, as did most of my defensive backfield mates, watching him catch ten balls for 170 yards. At least we didn't let him in the end zone.

But just as quickly as the '82 season, my second in the NFL, kicked off, it came to a sudden halt.

The third game never happened. The day after the Cardinals game, the players' union called a strike. It was called at midnight right after a Monday night game between the Packers and the Giants.

There were rumors going around that the NFL Players Association would tell its membership to walk. Few of us believed it would, though, because players never had struck before. That was a baseball players' thing, we thought.

Few of us wanted a strike, because it meant we weren't going to get paid for a spell, and we didn't know how long that spell would last. I had just begun earning what for me was a lot of money, and even though I knew I should be making more, this was before I was prepared to take a stand to demand a fairer share.

Not only that, I was itching to get back to where we'd left off a season before: the NFC championship game. If no one had known who I was before my rookie season started, they sure did when it ended. I'd picked off 49ers quarterback Joe Montana twice, made seven tackles, and recovered a fumble before we lost out going to the Super Bowl by a point after The Catch.

If our quarterback, Danny White, hadn't fumbled when we got the ball back, we could've kicked a field goal to win the game, The Catch would've been forgotten, and, of all the ironies, I would have been the MVP of the game. Catch or no Catch, everyone knew how good I was as a rookie. I had gone to the Pro Bowl. I couldn't wait to pick up where I'd left off.

But that wasn't going to be the case. That summer, the union convened a meeting for its individual team representatives and any interested players in Albuquerque, New Mexico, to prep them on the possibilities of a strike. The union wanted more of the gross revenues the league was pulling in because the league had just cut some new TV deals that would make it even richer. The Cowboys union rep was one of Ron's training camp roommates, Robert Newhouse—"House," as we called him.

I was getting to know House the way I was getting to know all the guys in the veterans' squad. Like everyone else, House had heard me complaining all the time about how the Cowboys treated me, or mistreated me, in my original free-agent rookie negotiations. He saw my spunk when I challenged Tony Hill and Drew Pearson in practice. I guess he saw the rebel in me, because over the course of my rookie season, he talked to me a lot about the union and whether I was interested in working with it. When the union convention was set to meet in Albuquerque, he invited me to go.

I just wanted to stay home and work out and hang out with Shreill, but my mom told me I should go—mothers know best, right? It turned out to be one of the most important learning experiences of my life.

That trip to Albuquerque taught me how the league worked. It laid out why management wasn't to be trusted and why players so often got the shaft. It showed me how much the owners made and how little they shared with those of us who were laying our well-being on the line.

Just a few years earlier, in 1978, there had been a horrific collision between Raiders defensive back Jack Tatum and Patriots receiver Darryl Stingley. It left Stingley in a wheelchair, paralyzed from the neck down, a quadriplegic. (He would die, in 2007, of complications from his injury.) There wasn't a player in the league for whom the story of that accident wasn't a constant nightmare. We knew we played a very dangerous game, and considering how short our careers were likely to be, even for the luckiest of us, we knew we deserved a lot more than what the league was offering.

I came back from Albuquerque a convinced union member, and I encouraged other players to agree to the strike.

The first Sunday and Monday night of the season, stadiums all across the country were empty. The parking lots may as well have had tumbleweeds blowing across. It was eerie. We sat for fifty-seven days that fall of '82, before all but caving in to the league's owners. They didn't give us more money. They didn't guarantee us a percentage of the revenues that we generated for them, which was one of our demands. And they didn't even end up feeling much pain from the strike—the average paid attendance in 1982 was 58,472, the fifth-highest in league history. So the owners still got paid while we didn't. It was a bitter pill.

The only thing we gained was the legal ability to share individual contract information with each other, which gave us more bargaining power in contract negotiations because we knew what other guys made for playing the same position for the same number of years and with how much success.

☆

I was happy to get back to playing, but I always felt a little resentment in the back of my mind; I vowed to cleanse the feeling if I ever got the opportunity. Little did I realize it then, but I was being prepared for the chance to do just that, and become something I'd never really been—a leader.

I'd wound up in juvenile detention for a couple of weeks as a teenager because I followed some guys, without thinking through the situation for myself. I was never named captain of my high school team or Grambling's. I was always more likely to tag along rather than point the way. I was never the guy who took the initiative.

But that started to change. It wasn't just House's counseling, the meeting in Albuquerque, and the strike that shaped me then. It also came from watching Ron, the way he took up the causes of others and gave the quiet among us a voice. He wasn't afraid to walk the walk for the right reason. He would have made a great players' union rep. But for some reason, he never sought an official position. He wasn't against the union, but he never joined in union activities either. When I asked him about it, he just said that wasn't his way of doing things. Ron was never one to campaign for his leadership role; he preferred it to be given to him because of the way he stood up on his own for everyone.

But in 1987, when the next showdown between players and management developed, Ron was gone. He was three years removed from the Cowboys, and, after two miserable seasons with miserable Tampa Bay, he was completely out of the league. He had been cut by the Buccaneers in early 1987. It was the second time in four months the team had released him. The first time was in the middle of the 1986 season, when the Bucs purged their roster of several veterans like Ron just to save money. The team's management didn't care that Ron was the starting fullback. But they were forced to bring him back a few weeks later after several of their running backs got injured.

Ron started ten games for Tampa Bay and played in twelve, rushing for 285 yards on 74 attempts and catching 24 passes for 187 yards. He had been with the Cowboys for six years. In the eight seasons he survived in the NFL, he rushed for 2,519 yards, caught 249 passes for 2,259 yards, and scored 38 touchdowns.

Ron was still good to go, but no one would have him then. I certainly could have used him at my side in Dallas because our locker room needed some leadership, including a new union rep, and not too many guys were gung-ho about taking the reins. After all, things hadn't gone too well for the union in '82, and there was a feeling that reps, if they dared to do anything, would get blacklisted.

I was one of the few guys for whom that sounded attractive. I'd entered the league with a black mark and hadn't shed it. I was still ticked off about what went down in '82 and how I had to scrap and fight to get what I knew was due me from the Cowboys front office.

So I volunteered to walk out on a limb as the union rep. The last time I'd gone out on a limb, in high school, it was for the wrong reasons. I was trying to help a couple of guys I thought were my friends who were up to no good. I was a lot wiser in 1987 when I was summoned to help others again.

I threw my name into the Cowboys helmet during the quick locker room vote and was handed the job of team rep—or, it might be better to say, the job was tossed to me like a live hand grenade.

I got a letter from Ron upon my victorious election. It was not congratulatory. Ron was worried for me. He reminded me that the Cowboys hadn't been playing up to par and said that management would use extracurricular activity like union organizing as a way to scapegoat me and ship me out of town, just like they'd shipped him out for encouraging people to renegotiate their contracts. He told me to watch my back and be careful about what I said to the media. He told me to play harder than I ever had so the Cowboys couldn't blame me for any of the team's struggles.

I tucked the letter away at home. I greatly appreciated Ron's guidance, and I took it to heart.

But I believed in the union, too. I believed in what it was trying to do, because I was a victim of the control the league owners and the executive office had on the players. The union wanted to get us more money, and it wanted to reunite its membership, which had been fractured, if not broken, after '82. I thought of myself as a players' player. I hadn't much cared for management ever since I had to "retire" to get a contract I knew was due me.

The union also wanted to get us the ability to ply our trade with whatever team we desired, the way everyone else in America had a right to work for whomever they wished. As it was, we could move from one team to another, but only after the expiration of the contract under which we were working and only if our old employer didn't match whatever new contract we were offered by another team. Gene Upshaw was four years into being the NFL Players Association boss and was trying to resurrect its image when I picked up the torch for his office in Dallas. The union was a mess when he took over. It was broke from the '82 strike and had lost most of its support in the nation's locker rooms.

But Upshaw had some positive things going for him. He had been a fellow player—one of us—and a great one, no less. A Pro Bowl offensive lineman with the Raiders, Upshaw was voted into the Pro Football Hall of Fame in January 1987.

Not everyone was ready to follow Upshaw's lead against the owners when the collective-bargaining agreement with the league expired in the fall of '87, and Upshaw and the owners hit an impasse in negotiations. He wanted to run the same play that so many were certain was the reason we'd failed five years earlier. He wanted to strike.

This time, I was ready from the get-go to stomp out of the locker room. I wanted to show management we meant business this time. I had no problem carrying the boss's message to the membership in Valley Ranch, the new state-of-the-art training facility the Cowboys opened not long after they jettisoned Ron to Tampa Bay.

It wasn't going to be easy. I knew that. One of our first votes to strike confirmed my fears.

After much debate one morning, it seemed most of the guys were on board to strike, when Randy White and Don Smerek, one of White's defensive line mates, showed up to our meeting late. Everyone was pretty fired up, and White was animated when he walked in. I told him the team had almost decided to side with the union boss's wishes and vote to strike. Randy seized the floor with his indomitable personality and said he thought it was a bad idea and why.

Then Dorsett stood up and told Randy that he was wrong and why. Their debate got more and more heated, and everybody's favorite offensive lineman, Nate Newton, had to step in to separate them. Some fists were swung before everyone calmed down a little.

That was the way it was in a lot of locker rooms around the league—hotly divided.

That was just the way management wanted it, of course. Management was united, and they knew that a divided union would easily be defeated. All we knew right then was that Randy wasn't going to be on board, and neither was his buddy Smerek. They weren't the only ones. But we eventually carried enough votes to authorize another strike.

That was when I really picked up the mantle from Ron. Just as he'd come into my room when I was a rookie and started teaching me the ways of the NFL, I pulled aside some of the younger guys and told them what to expect and what they needed to do. I told them what it was like the first time around five years ago and what we did and didn't do that cost us. I implored them to stick together.

They listened. It helped that my reputation for standing up to management was near legend in the Valley Ranch locker room. A lot of them knew about Ron's "retirement" strategy that got me paid. So they trusted me early on. If nothing else, everyone in that locker room, young and veteran, who was ready to walk, knew that the last person to let them down would be me.

That was what players wanted from their union rep. They wanted a guy who wasn't going to sell them out, and there wasn't a chance I was going to do that. I would be there for them just like Ron was there for me when I held out in 1983, and I was there for Ron when he was in that courtroom in 1985. This was what being a teammate ultimately was all about: not being a sellout.

We weren't certain exactly when the call to walk would come. We opened the season at St. Louis with a colossal fourth-quarter collapse in which the Cardinals scored three touchdowns to win 24–13. It wasn't so much the weight of strike talk, and the fact that it was dividing our locker room, that sank us late in the game. It was Roy Green, again, and his prolific quarterback, Neil Lomax. They hooked up for two of those fourth-quarter touchdowns.

The next weekend we went to New York to play the defending Super Bowl champion Giants and somehow pulled out a 16–14 win. It was after that game that the call came to strike. So we packed our things at Valley Ranch and walked out the door for who knew how long.

This time, though, the union had decided to actually march against management, just like we'd seen steelworkers and autoworkers do. We got picket signs. We practiced some chants. We got a bullhorn or two.

We assembled outside Valley Ranch's main entrance on Cowboys Parkway and marched and chanted with our placards while television cameras rolled, newspaper photographers clicked away, and reporters took statements from us about what we were doing. It was local news and national news.

By then Ron and his family had moved to Cleveland, where he was trying his hand in the construction business, but he couldn't help but follow the strike, because it was national news, and Dallas was ground zero. He saw me mentioned in some news reports as leading the strike in Dallas and called me once with words of caution: that I shouldn't get branded as a rabble-rouser lest I wind up like him, summarily dismissed from the league.

At first the strike was like a big party. We were like the Grambling Marching Band, and I was the drum major. I'd never led a group before in my life, and there I was front and center. Almost everybody showed up, except those like Randy White and Don Smerek who had already expressed misgivings about a second strike.

As is typical with any protest, I guess, our band of merry protesters began to thin out as the days went by. The enthusiasm began to wane a little bit. After that first week, guys started going home. But I did my best to keep my troops' morale up.

Management was even more prepared for a strike this time. They had a strike fund, and we didn't. Management decided they weren't about to lose ticket sales weekend after weekend, so they used their strike fund to hire other guys at $1,000 per game to take our place on the field; they continued on with the season without us. It reminded me of a documentary I'd seen called *Harlan County U.S.A.,* about coal miners going on strike only to have management bring in other miners to take their place. That gambit hadn't worked for the mine owners in Harlan County, and our union was determined not to let it work in the NFL.

The NFL was a league of the very best football players in the world, and we didn't think football fans wanted anything less. But the owners' strategy to replace us with a bunch of guys who weren't good enough to play in the NFL was drawn up by one of the league's major innovators, Dallas's own Tex Schramm. Schramm had the Midas touch when it came to the NFL. Every idea he had come up with to make the NFL more successful had worked—merging with the old American Football League, creating the Cowboys cheerleaders in 1972, and having a league-controlled talent-scouting convention called the Combine.

I hated that Combine. The general managers and coaches got all the potential draft picks together and measured them and ran them and tested their strength in order to decide who would be picked where in the draft. With so many black players out there, it always reminded me of a modern-day slave auction. It was yet another reason I came to dislike management.

That was what we were up against. The owners opened their locker rooms—no, *our* locker rooms—to guys who couldn't carry our jockstraps. They gave them our equipment and uniforms and playbooks and prepared them to play our games in our stadiums across the country in just a couple of weeks.

The situation was especially dramatic for the Cowboys because we were America's Team and were presided over by the guy who came up with this whole replacement players' ploy. "Replacement players" was what the league called the guys they imported in our stead. We called them what they were called in that coal miners' movie: scabs.

In Washington, loyal fans and the real Redskins nicknamed the replacement Redskins the Redscabs. The Miami Dolphins became the Dol-Finks. The Los Angeles Rams were called the Shams. San Francisco was home to the Phony Niners. Most every team had a derisive, though comical, nickname like that, except the Cowboys. The replacement games weren't to be laughed at in the NFL town that invented them.

The league canceled the slate of games scheduled for week 3 and announced the resumption of the schedule in week 4. They were just going to pretend as if nothing had happened. Their show would go on, real players be damned. We kept marching.

Our quarterback, Danny White, was replaced by a guy named Kevin Sweeney, who played at Fresno State. Dorsett was replaced by a little guy named David Adams from Arizona. Our wide receiver Mike Renfro was replaced by a little guy, too, Cornell Burbage out of Kentucky. A guy from Indiana named Alex Green pretended to be me.

The replacement Cowboys' first game was October 4, back in New York against the Jets. They won 38–24, and Sweeney and crew became overnight celebrities in Dallas. That was the last thing we on the picket line had wanted to see.

The next game was scheduled in Dallas against Philadelphia. It was the home opener, because the week 3 home opener had been canceled.

We cracked.

One morning on the picket line leading up to that game, Randy White pulled up in his pickup truck with Don Smerek riding shotgun. We slowed our march, and Randy stopped his truck. He appeared to be waiting for an opening to drive through, and we didn't give him one. Then, just like a scene from that coal miners' movie, Dorsett and a couple of others marched to a stop in front of Randy's truck and blocked off the entrance.

Randy was nicknamed "Manster" for good reason. He wasn't the biggest guy, at six-four, 250 pounds, but he was the orneriest. He played at Maryland but was from Pittsburgh and carried that tough-guy steelworker attitude from the steel town. He topped it off in Dallas with a cowboy hat and was easily set on edge. Smerek, sitting next to him, was bigger, at six-seven, and at some point in his life had suffered a gunshot wound in the leg. He was nobody to mess with either.

But there they were, and Dorsett and some guys were standing in front of their running pickup truck with a guy called Manster at the wheel. Randy and Dorsett had already needed to be separated once over this strike, and now it looked like they needed to be separated again.

Randy started gunning his engine and popping the clutch, making the truck jump forward before rolling back. Then he stuck his head out the window. Some words were exchanged. Randy was one of the team captains, and guys started yelling, "Captain Scab! Captain Scab!" Dorsett and his posse joined in.

Finally, Dorsett and his crew moved aside, and Randy gunned his truck, tires screeching and smoke emanating, down the driveway toward the locker room entrance. I wiped a little sweat from my brow.

Randy and Smerek wouldn't be the only veterans to cross the picket line. The ironic thing was that before that week was out, Dorsett followed Randy. So did Danny White and Too Tall Jones and a few others.

The league had scared them by threatening to withhold something the union had won for the players a few years earlier: annuities. I had one. Doug Cosbie, our tight end, was the first player I knew to have one. The annuities were funded by the management, and payments were delayed, if all went well, until retirement. Owners were letting it be known that they were going to stop funding those annuities for players who refused to suit up. So Randy and Dorsett and some other guys got cold feet and busted the line. Some other stars around the league broke their team's picket lines, too.

It hurt to see Dorsett walk by me. He was one of my best friends on the team, and he was Ron's best friend, too. I was worried that if fans saw the stars cross over, they would turn against those of us who stayed outside.

It was frustrating, but I knew the Cowboys brass were cutthroat. I believed the union was right, and I wasn't about to give in. I couldn't give in. I never had before, and I wasn't about to now.

Some of the guys who didn't cross the picket line started going home instead. One morning there was a picture in one of the Dallas papers of me manning the picket line by myself. It wasn't the only morning I was alone. I had warned guys that what we were getting into was a long-haul struggle. There wasn't going to be a quick fix. But a lot of guys couldn't hang tough. They didn't have the fortitude or the cash. It became embarrassing for the union.

Dallas was never a union town anyway. Philadelphia was. It was invigorating to those of us still on the picket line to see the Eagles show up at Texas Stadium with a roster that didn't have a single NFLPA player on it. Meanwhile, Coach Landry trotted out several veterans, including Dorsett, who had a touchdown run in the third quarter of what was a 41–22 blowout win for the Cowboys.

Buddy Ryan was coaching the Eagles then, and he criticized Coach Landry for using veteran Pro Bowl players against his guys who just a couple of weeks earlier weren't even playing amateur football. He said he couldn't wait to get back at Landry in a few weeks in the rematch if the strike was over.

The next week, more stars and veterans crossed picket lines around the league. Almost one hundred went across by October 14. The inertia of players going back to work was too much for the union to bear, and it called off the strike the next day. We were to resume real games on October 25.

I was devastated. But I wasn't making the orders; I was carrying them out. This wasn't about me; it was about my brethren, even the ones who were too shortsighted to see what we needed to do.

There would be just one more scab game, but for the real Cowboys on the team, it became the most important game they'd played in years.

Our hated rivals from Washington came to town, and, like the Eagles, they didn't have any veteran players on their roster either. No Art Monk or Darrell Green or Dexter Manley. Washington coach Joe Gibbs had convinced his veterans not to cross the line. He believed so strongly in the idea of being a team that he successfully pleaded with his stars to keep the real squad together on strike. He didn't want any of the divisiveness he saw developing on teams like the Cowboys, where fights nearly broke out between guys wearing the same colors.

So Gibbs leaned on a quarterback named Ed Rubbert from Louisville and a little running back named Lionel Vital from Nichols State, which wasn't far from Grambling, in Louisiana.

Coach Landry couldn't have cared less about Buddy Ryan's criticism going into this game: He put his veteran stars on the field right away. When the starting lineups were announced, Danny White and Dorsett ran out, and the 60,000 people who turned out at Texas Stadium for the game booed them. They booed Danny because they had never really liked him. They booed Dorsett because of his previous holdout and his original stand with the strikers. It was the most unbelievable reception I had ever seen at Texas Stadium. The fans had turned on their own.

Then the truly unimaginable happened. Washington took control of the game to the delight of Cowboys fans, who started chanting "We want Sweeney," in reference to the starting replacement quarterback from a week earlier. They booed Dorsett again just about every time he was given the football.

Washington took a 3–0 early lead and then stymied the Cowboys the rest of the afternoon. Dorsett fumbled twice. Danny White was intercepted. That Vital guy scampered for 136 yards. And when Rubbert got knocked out of the game, a black quarterback named Tony Robinson, who was on a work release program from prison following a drug conviction, entered and lit up the Cowboys defense for 152 yards passing despite two interceptions. He engineered two scoring drives for ten points and led Washington to a 13–7 win and a dancing celebration near the blue star at midfield.

That game was the beginning of the end of the Cowboys regime—Tex Schramm, Gil Brandt, and Coach Landry—who were as much a part of the NFL as the red-white-and-blue logo shield. They had underestimated the importance of team when they gave Ron, the locker room leader, the boot. Now they had done it again, for the last time. Schramm & Co. never got the egg off their faces from that game.

It was hard for players who had broken the picket lines to look those of us who hadn't in the eye, and vice versa, after the strike ended. Relationships changed; friendships fractured. Guys who had been greatly respected lost that respect. Guys who lost a lot of money were angry with union leaders rather than with management. It wasn't a good formula for team chemistry unless what you were trying to make was something explosive. The teams that had to deal with the strike fallout for the rest of 1987 didn't fare well, and those who didn't did. The teams that had stuck together on the protest line played well together, like Washington, which went on to win the Super Bowl that season just as they had in the '82 strike year.

We learned that when Buddy Ryan's Eagles whipped us in Philadelphia 37–20, in the first post–replacement players' game, just as Ryan warned they would. A couple of weeks later, the lousy Lions beat us 27–17 in Detroit—a union town where the Lions remained loyal to the union. Danny White was picked off four times.

We lost four consecutive games down the stretch and finished 7 and 8, our second losing season in a row. Bum Bright, the owner, publicly questioned Coach Landry. Tex Schramm claimed to have reached the lowest point in his long career. Dorsett had his worst season ever. Danny White lost his job to Steve Pelluer.

The next season, we went 3 and 13, then 1 and 15 with a new owner from Arkansas, a hotshot oilman named Jerry Jones, whose first act with his new business was to dismiss the CEO, Coach Landry, and bring in his buddy, Jimmy Johnson.

It was a disastrous season personally for a lot of guys, me included. I lost at least $90,000 during that stretch. I was already entering the second half of my career, and now my combativeness with management had been spread throughout the locker room. It wasn't likely that I'd get another big contract, and I had to start thinking about life after football.

☆

Gene Upshaw and his legal team made a tactical gamble that paid off, not unlike the strategy Ron had come up with years earlier to get me a new deal. Upshaw had the union decertified—had it "retired"—in response to a court ruling on the union's antitrust lawsuit against the league that said the union's labor exemption protected employers from complaints. The union reorganized as a professional organization and filed for a second time its antitrust lawsuit, charging the league with unlawful restraint of trade by refusing free agency.

It took a few years, but we won that case, and the league was forced to sit down at the negotiating table and come up with a free agency plan. In exchange, we agreed to a salary cap.

It turned out to be a tremendous lesson about sacrifice for those of us who had stayed on the picket lines. I had realized that selfishness has its limitations. Selfishness does not make for great friendships and doesn't provide a foundation you can build on. It was a lesson I'd draw on when Ron was in need.

# 11

# Ron at the Reins

There are two entities who have plans for you: God and NFL general managers. I didn't know what God's plan was for me in 1990 heading into my tenth year in the league. I did, however, begin to learn then what general managers had in mind for me: take a hike.

First, the Cowboys refused in February 1990 to sign me to a new contract, and they cast me into the waters of unemployed free agents for the first time in my career. Two months later, I signed a contract with the New York Giants.

Then, early in the 1992 season, the Giants decided they had no more use for me, and they cut me, too. This time the Cleveland Browns picked me up, and I finished the season with them.

Cleveland was a bit of a reunion for me because its coach was Bill Belichick, who was three years into his first head coaching job after having been my defensive coordinator on Bill Parcells' Super Bowl–winning Giants staff. He was more than happy to have me, because I was a veteran who knew his system and thrived in it. I was content playing for someone who would welcome me aboard in the midst of a season that was already going surprisingly well.

The Browns were a .500 team when I got there, after six games of the '92 season. Due to injuries, however, they were going through quarterbacks—first Bernie Kosar, then Mike Tomczak, finally Todd Philcox—like bad draws on the blackjack table. But Belichick got better at his specialty, coaching defense, as the season petered out to a 7–9 finish. The last couple of games were something to build on in '93, and we did just that, getting off to a surprising 3–0 start, the club's best since 1979.

We beat San Francisco, which had been in the NFC title game the season before, on a Monday night. Then, in a game against the Raiders that seemed lost, Vinny Testaverde came in for Kosar and engineered a come-from-behind win.

After seven games, we were 5 and 2. We were in first place! I had been holding down the left corner spot, and we were playing well on defense.

Then I got a phone call from Belichick. He told me the team would be moving ahead without me. I was surprised. So was he, I think. It didn't make sense that Belichick would let go of a guy who was helping hold down the fort. There had to be something else going on, and there was. Belichick was taking orders from on high. It was his first job, and he couldn't go against the boss, Art Modell.

Modell, the owner, was losing money and looking to move the team. He had decided to shed salaries no matter what and was whipping his first-time head coach into line. So I was out. Then Kosar was cut loose. Modell knew exactly what he was doing; he skirted a union rule by making sure to boot us before the eighth game so that, in accordance with the collective-bargaining agreement, he wouldn't be liable for our salaries for the rest of the year.

Browns fans were up in arms. Their favorite team lost its next four games and wound up winning just two more the rest of the year.

I was ticked off. I knew I wasn't playing as well as I used to, but I also knew I was playing as well as anyone else in the defensive backfield. All of a sudden, I felt like I was being disrespected the way I had been coming out of high school and my "Negro League" college.

I went home to Dallas, and my agent started making calls around the league, looking for a defensive-back opening. He found one in San Francisco a few weeks before the playoffs were to commence, and the 49ers asked me to come out for a workout. I did. They decided they didn't want me. That was it.

Thirteen seasons. Fifty-seven interceptions. Two *Sports Illustrated* covers. One touchdown. One Super Bowl ring.

I was thirty-three, and I was finding out how Ron had felt when the Buccaneers didn't bring him back. And Ron had been just thirty then. He'd had more left in his body at that time than I probably had left in mine now.

It was hard letting go of the game. Football had saved me as a teenager. It got me to college. It put me under the wing of Coach Rob, the greatest football coach ever in my mind and a lot of other guys' minds. Football brought me a nice living with one of the most storied teams in the NFL, which just happened to be located within walking distance of the house I grew up in. It gave me some fame. It helped make me who I am.

I wasn't ready to stop playing football. Most players never are. I felt as good as ever. I wasn't suffering from any debilitating injuries. I'd only been hurt once in all my years playing this violent game, and it didn't linger long. When I was with the Giants, I caught a knee in my side from a bruising running back with the Eagles named James Joseph. His knee came up right in the kidney and spleen area like one of those body punches that put down fighters. It had put me right down on the ground. I just rolled over.

I came back in the game and got an interception, but after I got home that night, blood started running through my urine. I told the Giants trainer, Ronnie Barnes, and he ordered me to the hospital. The doctors found I was bleeding internally. My back hurt from the blood pooling in my torso. I didn't play the last two games of that season, and that gnawed at me. I detested not being able to play.

Quitting isn't part of a pro athlete's nature to begin with, and if it is, it's trained out of us. I remembered how Washington's quarterback Joe Theismann tried to get someone, anyone, to let him come back after he suffered a horrible broken leg on a sack by Lawrence Taylor, who had starred with Ron in high school back in Williamsburg, Virginia, before becoming a Hall of Fame linebacker with the Giants. Theismann's broken leg, once it healed, was shorter than his other leg, and he was still trying to convince people he could play.

I understood that now. For a pro athlete, your sport is all you've done for most of your life. People tell ex-athletes to get a life. Well, our sport *is* our life. Everything after that is an afterlife.

What was I supposed to do now? What could I find to be so passionate about that would fulfill me as much as my game?

For me, it was what I'd moved away from when I went to work in New York and Cleveland. It was family. It was friends. It was home.

I realized it when I looked at Charis and Cameron. She was nine, and he was five. They'd grown up so fast it seemed, probably because I hadn't seen them every day the way I did when I was playing for the Cowboys. Instead, I'd been gone about six months of the year for the past three years, living and playing football in New York and Cleveland while Shreill and the kids were in Dallas. It was long-distance fatherhood and quite a phone bill. I brought Shreill and the kids to New York at least once a month and for every holiday. They loved New York. I got them to visit me in Cleveland almost as frequently. I say almost because they weren't quite as fond of Cleveland. Had Ron and Adriane and their kids been in Cleveland when I got there, my family's visits to Cleveland would have been more frequent. But Ron and Adriane were in the nation's capital by then.

I could see Shreill and the kids were happy to have me home, Shreill especially, because she'd been a single mom with two kids for half a year each season I was with the Giants and Browns. We'd made that choice because we didn't want to uproot the kids from school, but the fact that the decision was a conscious one didn't make her situation any easier. I missed football, but now I realized how much I'd been missing the kids and Shreill before. In their arms was where I wanted to be more than anyplace else. Just being with my family after leaving football behind, and before doing whatever I would do next, was the best hiatus I ever took.

☆

I didn't do much of anything for quite a while. I watched football on television the rest of that season, but it was hard to stomach with the sting of being cut from the league still fresh. I drove the kids to and from school and to sports practices and games and whatever other extracurricular activities they had. I did the honey-dos that Shreill piled on me. And I worked out. Not because I anticipated one last shot at playing. I just had always valued exercise. There was no way I was going to be one of those guys who stopped playing and started piling on the pounds.

I hadn't talked to Ron in a while, but I knew what he was up to because Shreill and Adriane still spoke all the time. Ron, Adriane, Ayra, and Asley had tried living in Tampa when Ron landed there, but Adriane didn't enjoy it. Then they'd moved to the Cleveland area while Ron tried his hand in the construction business. But they had moved from Cleveland by the time I landed there.

Now they were in a suburb of Washington, D.C., where in 1991 Ron became an assistant to Steve Wilson, the defensive back we played with in Dallas who was now the head football coach at Howard University, Wilson's alma mater. The move allowed Ron to have his son, Shawn, who moved up from Williamsburg, Virginia, live with the rest of his family for a few years. In '93, Shawn graduated from Springbrook High School in Maryland and accepted a football scholarship to Ron's old school, Ohio State, where he became a freshman defensive back for Ron's Buckeyes.

Ron and Adriane and their girls, Shreill mentioned, were interested in moving back to Dallas. They were tired of the winters on the East Coast. And, though Shawn was there, they didn't want to move back to Ohio either, because it got even colder there than in Maryland.

They had always liked Dallas, though, and their best friends—Shreill and me and our kids—were together in Dallas again. Ron could plug back into the construction business, which was booming again after a bust in the late '80s. They liked the school system in Plano, the suburb north of Dallas where we lived. Dallas trumped everything else they were thinking about.

So I wasn't surprised one day when Ron called and said he wanted to visit for a few days to scout out the area. He visited, all right. He stayed with us for a month! I let him drive my Cowboys silver-and-blue Mercedes convertible, and he was gone so much in it, I started to think of it as his.

I was really happy to have Ron come down. All I had was time, and so did he. We hung out with each other like we did in the old days. We talked about the league and how it had screwed us in the end. We watched games on TV and told each other what we would do to some of the new players if we were on the field.

We also talked about what we could do together in business if Ron did move his family back to Dallas.

Ron found a house he thought Adriane and the girls would like about a mile and a half from where we lived, and after school let out in Maryland, they made the move back to Texas. It was like a big family reunion: Ayra and Charis, Ashley and Cameron, Adriane and Shreill, Ron and me. Same schools. Same neighborhood. Same friendships, renewed.

When school started up in Texas, the closeness that Ron and I had as Cowboys regenerated. Part of this was by necessity. We were in the same petri dish: the carpool.

After all those years of working as pro football players while the wives stayed at home rearing the kids, the roles were now reversed, at least temporarily. Shreill and Adriane both had taken jobs again. Ron and I didn't. We called ourselves "entrepreneurs," which was fine with the wives as long as we broke away from our "entrepreneuring" long enough to take the kids to school and pick them up.

Sometimes I dropped the kids off, and Ron picked them up, or vice versa. Then there were the days when Ron and I rode together and used the time to brainstorm business possibilities. Usually it was Ron's brain creating a storm of ideas that rained down on me. That was one thing about Ron. He always had a knack for seeing a business deal or making an existing one work better.

I first witnessed Ron's business acumen in the spring of 1984 when we were part of the Hoopsters, the off-season Cowboys basketball team created by another teammate with a great eye for business, Drew Pearson. I was not surprised many years after Drew retired to see him start a business bearing his name that manufactured licensed sports caps and became so successful that *Black Enterprise* magazine in 1994 named it Company of the Year. The Hoopsters was a brilliant concept.

Drew's idea was a creative way to cash in on our celebrity in Texas at a time when players' contracts weren't exorbitant enough to allow players to spend the off-season doing nothing but playing golf and hanging out in some resort like they do now. He'd dispatch the team to cities and towns all over the state, and we'd play games against college teams, top-notch recreation-league teams, or maybe the local volunteer fire department to raise money for a charity—say, for instance, the volunteer fire department. The Hoopsters would get a cut of the ticket sales, and the charity would keep the rest. We were America's Team, so it was almost always a win–win situation. The players made plenty, and the charities were always satisfied, too. It was an idea not unlike the national Hoop-It-Up three-on-three basketball tournament, which was also born in Dallas. Drew was ahead of his time.

Back then it was a lot more fun working for the Hoopsters than just working out or taking a summer job doing something else. It was right up my alley, basketball being my first love and my preferred summer workout anyway.

Ron liked to hoop it up, too. His game was as different from mine as our positions were in football. I liked to play around the perimeter and shoot jumpers, just as you might expect of a cornerback. Ron liked to play inside and impose his girth and strength on guys, just as you might expect of a fullback. He always said he was like famed NBA center Moses Malone, but I never wanted to give him that much credit because he'd actually start believing his own hype, which was hilarious.

Because we were just playing games around Texas, or sometimes in Oklahoma, where we were no less adored, if not worshipped, we usually traveled by chartered bus. It was easier and less expensive than going to the airport to catch a flight. It was also safer than having everyone drive themselves separately or carpool to wherever a game was scheduled. It was also a heck of a good time hanging out with all the guys and listening to everyone's newest tall tale.

A perfect example of how we often got around occurred in March of 1984. We were on a bus coming back from a Hoopsters game in Oklahoma. It was pretty late at night, later than it should have been, because the bus driver had gotten lost. Everybody was really tired. The games we played were usually pretty competitive, and we played a lot of them during the summer, as many as three events each week. But with all the travel, it seemed like we were playing every day. We played at least thirty off-season games in a single summer—that's more than a third of an NBA season or an entire college season. We were like that black baseball team in Richard Pryor's movie *The Bingo Long Traveling All-Stars & Motor Kings.* I remember specifically that Drew was really wiped out after this particular Oklahoma game. He was trying to stay awake by smoking a cigar, playing cards, and rapping to the guys. He hadn't even been drinking, and still he was struggling not to doze off.

We finally got back to the parking lot at the Cowboys training facility, and everybody kind of trundled down the stairs of the bus and onto the asphalt. We reminded each other to be back at the parking lot the next afternoon for our next game, at wherever that was—the location didn't seem very important at the moment. We just wanted to go home and get some sleep.

The next morning we heard that Drew hadn't made it home. He was at Presbyterian Hospital in Dallas awaiting surgery. His 1984 Dodge Daytona had slammed into the rear of a parked, steel-loaded tractor trailer on a Dallas freeway at 1:30 in the morning.

Worse, his brother, Carey Mark Pearson, was riding with him and hadn't survived the collision. We couldn't believe it.

Drew went into the operating room that afternoon, and it took doctors almost two and a half hours to close a softball-sized hole in his liver. Coach Landry flew in from Hawaii, where he was attending NFL meetings, to visit Drew.

"He fell asleep while he was taking his brother home from a basketball trip," Landry told a newspaper about his best receiver.

A police officer added that Drew's car was speeding and that the tractor trailer it struck had its flashers on.

Coach Landry told a newspaper that day that he and Drew had recently discussed Drew's retirement. Pearson was thirty-three then.

☆

The Hoopsters were shaken, and so was everybody else with the Cowboys and in and around Dallas. It wasn't something you ever envisioned happening to players. It was one thing to get hurt on the field—we were always prepared for that. But getting hurt off the field so severely wasn't something we thought about. It was as if we thought our supreme athleticism made us invincible. That sense of invincibility pervaded other aspects of our lives and our health, too: the way we drank and ate so much fried food and, for some in retirement from the game, stopped exercising and allowed the fat to pile on the body. Years later, looking at Ron, I remembered how shortsighted about life we were then.

The Hoopsters had to go on, though. We tried to approach it as if Drew had gone down in a football game during the season. This was just a time-out. We had to regroup and refocus. The only problem was we didn't have anyone who immediately wanted to step into Pearson's role as manager of the team.

Then Ron volunteered.

There were contracts in place, commitments to uphold, phone calls to make, travel to be arranged. Ron picked everything up and carried it through.

Four months later, just before training camp was to open, Pearson announced his retirement. He said the doctors told him he risked severe and possibly life-threatening injury if he attempted to play after the damage his liver had suffered. The Hoopsters were unofficially bequeathed to Ron that day, and Ron didn't allow a charity to miss a fund-raiser or the Hoopsters to miss a paycheck.

Now, shuttling our kids through the Dallas suburbs in the mid-'90s, Ron took inspiration from Drew's original vision for the Hoopsters as we kicked around business ideas. He took confidence from his ability to run the Hoopsters successfully. He figured we could replicate that model of raising funds for charity while making a living for ourselves.

The market for Cowboys was bigger in the mid-'90s than it ever had been. Jerry Jones's ownership and Jimmy Johnson's coaching had turned out to be a brilliant combination and had brought the Cowboys to a height they'd never even achieved in the '70s. Troy Aikman, Emmitt Smith, and Michael Irvin were the current stars every fan wanted a piece of. Ron and I were two old Cowboys stars for whom Ron figured there was either still a market, or one could be created.

We knew basketball games alone wouldn't sustain such an operation, so we considered golf tournaments, which were becoming all the rage with the business community. We also imagined incorporating autograph sessions and speaking engagements.

After a couple of months of incubating the possibilities in our two-man think tank, Ron and I launched a business called Players Ink II. It wasn't "Inc.," because the players' union had copyrighted "Players Inc." as its brand name to sell union paraphernalia, and we didn't want to get sued. We added the roman numerals to further distinguish us. But the crucial distinction between us and Players Inc. was that Ron and I were marketing the opportunity to rub shoulders with actual former NFL players, rather than caps or T-shirts or likenesses.

We started in towns in Texas, putting together our first deal in 1995. We moved into Oklahoma. Then we found ourselves in New Mexico, at a town I'd never heard of, called Gallup. We got as far as Ohio, where we did an event in Cincinnati.

It was going so well that we had a waiting list of former players who wanted to be involved, and they weren't just former Cowboys. We brought in a few guys Ron had played with in Tampa Bay—the tight end Jimmie Giles, the linebacker Hugh Green, and the running back James Wilder. Wilder had us put on an event in Sikeston, Missouri, his hometown.

Our events became so popular that one weekend we scheduled two in different cities, which meant Ron and I had to split up to cover our bases. I don't recall where Ron dispatched himself that weekend, but I ran our event in St. Louis, where we played a local high school all-star basketball team as part of a Seventh-day Adventist convention.

So many guys wanted to participate because Ron's formula was so great. We were raising money for all kinds of good causes—recreation centers, needy kids, and health care causes—and we were paying the guys who helped us out and doing well for ourselves, too. Guys liked to play golf anyway; now they got to play golf, help others out, and pick up a paycheck in the process. You couldn't beat it.

We didn't travel with more than ten guys. They'd get a few hundred dollars for each appearance from the charities, and the charities took the balance. When we were just starting out, we helped groups bring in maybe $10,000 or $12,000. After a couple of years our earning power per event had gone up to about $30,000. We were doing really well, and a big part of that was due to Ron's personality.

Ron is the ultimate people person. He can find a way to get along with just about anyone and takes it as a challenge when he encounters someone who doesn't immediately warm up to him. There is something innate in Ron, too, that makes him want to help people, just like he did with the kids in need of winter coats, and people could sense that.

Our business was a lot of work, or at least a lot of meetings and dinners and flying around. We didn't have an office or a secretary or a staff. We'd get up early and fly somewhere to meet someone interested in what we were doing. There were morning meetings and lunch dates and afternoon meetings and dinner dates. It seemed like we were away on meetings more than when we were playing. There were phone calls to make and schedules to arrange and plane tickets to buy and hotel rooms to secure.

We kept adding things to what we could do, creating a kind of à la carte menu. We started offering sponsors of charities the opportunity to have Dorsett or Too Tall Jones, or some other former Cowboys player of their choice, come to their place of business and give a motivational chat to their staff.

It was a lot of fun. It beat working nine to five in some staid office. It gave Ron a chance to do what he did best: work his magic with other people, especially strangers, the way he did when he walked into my dorm room—into my life—at training camp my rookie year.

After a couple of years, though, we got tired. It was just Ron and me every day, every waking moment, weekends included. We were coming back on a flight from Cincinnati in the summer of 1998 when Ron and I just looked at each other and decided to call it a wrap. We didn't want to make another phone call or take another trip. I think both of us had been waiting for the other guy to say the words, but each of us knew the decision would be met with absolutely no resistance.

We weren't just tired of traveling. It showed more on Ron than with me. He wasn't staying in the same athletic shape he had when he was playing football. He seemed to be tiring more easily than me and complaining of what seemed like small ailments. I didn't think much about his changing condition; I figured it was just all those football miles, getting tackled and smashing into big ol' linemen, catching up with him. I didn't think otherwise until later on when Shreill reminded me about a New Year's Eve party we all attended a few years before. I'll let her tell it here:

*It was New Year's Eve 1995, and Cubby and I joined Ron and Adriane at our friend Kim Catching's house to say good-bye to that year, which had been a really fun one. The year had been like old times, especially for me and Adriane. We were working and running the kids around whenever Ron and Cubby couldn't. We were talking on the phone till the wee hours of the morning and hanging out with the few old friends we'd come to trust, like Kim, whose home we were gathering at that evening to toast the beginning of 1996.*

*I've often thought about that night because it turned out to be so different from the other times when we'd gotten together. Ron was anything but the life of the party we'd all come to expect and love. Instead, he was sitting quietly at a kitchen table with his hands folded in front of him. He seemed to be resting on the table. His head was bent down as if he were about to nod off to sleep. His shoulders were hunched forward as if he were trying to stay warm.*

*Everyone kept asking Ron if he was feeling all right, and he kept repeating that he was fine. But we all could tell that something was wrong.*

*Cubby and I didn't stay too long after the ball dropped, and we were at home in bed sound asleep when the phone rang. It was going on three in the morning. It was Adriane.*

*Adriane said she had to go to the emergency room, because Ron had started convulsing when they got home. We got up, threw on some clothes, and took off to meet Adriane at the hospital. When we saw Ron, his face was broken out with little bumps that were oozing some sort of fluid. The doctor said it was toxin escaping Ron's body.*

*It was the first time we'd really witnessed Ron being sick, and it was disconcerting to say the least. Adriane was scared and frightened for her and Ron.*

*Ron remained in the hospital for several days. It was the beginning of what became a very painful trend that unfurled over his life and Adriane's for the years to come. For Ron, being in the hospital started becoming almost normal. In fact, ten years later, it began to be more unusual for him to spend an unbroken week at home.*

*We would eventually joke with Ron that he'd been in every hospital in Dallas. We were not exaggerating. That was how sick he became by the turn of the millennium, after he and Cubby stopped traveling with the fund-raising business they'd started.*

At the end of 1998, I had no idea I was witnessing in Ron a serious illness gaining ground on him. I just thought our business was slowing us down. But we were tired of being away from our families so much again, too. Family was always a thread that tied Ron and me together. When we shelved Players Ink II, Ron started a construction business with his son, Shawn—the Springs family could really work together. Ron called it FASON, which stood for father and son, and he decided to throw all his energy into construction again, this time with the bonus of ramping up his connection with Shawn, who was in his second season as a pro football player, starting at cornerback for the Seattle Seahawks.

But Ron and I didn't go our separate ways in our personal lives. It was just like when he moved his family back to Dallas after I was done playing. We had pretty clean slates again, and the wives hadn't stopped working. We returned to dropping off and picking up the kids whenever we could and talking to each other about what we each were going to do next.

I wasn't sure what to do. I started drawing on my annuity, since I was retired again. I listened to Ron talk about the construction business and wondered if I could do something in that industry. There were a number of former Cowboys in Dallas, particularly Roger Staubach, who had become very successful in the commercial real estate industry, developing properties all over the country and eventually the world. An idea started percolating in my head about building an entire community based on health and well-being, but I knew it would take a while to figure it out.

I thought for a short while about putting my degree in accounting to work. After my second season with the Giants, I started studying for the exam to become a stockbroker and got an internship with Dean Witter, but being stuck in an office for eight hours wasn't something I ever warmed up to. After that one summer in a corporate office, I never went back. All I knew was that I wanted to do something that brought me in contact with more people, different people, just like playing football and running around with Ron and Players Ink II had. And I wanted to do something that really helped others somehow.

I liked what we'd done with Players Ink II, and there were still people asking us to come to events. I couldn't do it all by myself and didn't want to, but I could provide a little something. If it was a business or group that wanted a guest speaker, I thought I could do that. I'd done it once before—by accident—and ended up enjoying it.

Way back at the end of my rookie season with the Cowboys, I got a call from the people who ran the Sheridan Broadcasting Network. Sheridan made radio programs for black radio stations. They also put together a top-twenty poll for black college football teams that everyone at black colleges followed. At the end of every college football season, Sheridan held a banquet, usually somewhere in the South near a black college, to celebrate black college football by naming a black college All-American team for the season. It honored me after my senior year, and after my rookie season I was asked back as a guest at its banquet.

I didn't think I was going to be able to make the banquet because it was scheduled around the third weekend in January when, if everything continued to go well, I was going to be practicing for my first Super Bowl. We were 12–4 division winners and favored by a lot of people to have tickets punched for Pontiac, Michigan, where the Super Bowl was being held January 24.

We crushed Tampa Bay 38–0 to start the playoffs the day after New Year's. Ron had a great day against the Buccaneers. He ran the football fifteen times for seventy yards and scored a touchdown. We knew we were on our way to the Super Bowl.

But the next weekend, The Catch happened in San Francisco, and all of a sudden my schedule was wide open. I accepted Sheridan's invitation to be a guest at its season-ending banquet.

I was a prize for a company like Sheridan then because I was the hottest thing to come out of black college football. I made the Pro Bowl as a rookie in the NFL, where I led it in interceptions. I was a big deal. A lot of people were calling for me, and a lot of people in the media were calling Coach Rob and asking him about me. Coach Rob fibbed the whole time, too, telling them he knew from the first time he saw me that I was going to do great things.

So I packed for a flight from Dallas to Jackson, where I'd played when Grambling met Mississippi's black college teams, like Alcorn State, Jackson State, and Mississippi Valley State. People were headed to Jackson for the banquet from all over the country. Some I learned were coming from Washington, D.C.

There was a plane crash that week in Washington. A flight headed for Florida took off in a bit of a snowstorm and fell into the Potomac River. I remember seeing it on television. People jumped into icy water to try to save others. It was scary. Seventy-eight people were killed, and just six people survived after getting rescued from the water.

I learned once I got to Jackson that some of the guests from Washington were stranded at the airport because of the accident. One of them was scheduled to be a speaker at the banquet. So someone with Sheridan asked me to pitch in at the last minute.

I agreed even though I'd never done anything like that before. I didn't have a clue what to say or how to say it. That was when I met a talkative guy at the hotel before the banquet from South Carolina State who had graduated just a year before I had. He said his name was Armstrong Williams. Boy, could he talk. His mouth ran just like Ron's, and he asked a lot of questions. He wanted to know all about my time at Grambling and what my life was like now that I was a star in the NFL.

I asked him why he was at the banquet, and he told me he'd won public speaking contests. I told him what I had volunteered to do, and he said not to worry, he'd write something out for me, and he did just that, right on the spot during the cocktail hour that preceded the dinner.

When my time came, I approached the dais, introduced myself to the audience, and proceeded to read what Armstrong had written for me. I don't remember what it was. I just remember I got through it, and the crowd applauded.

Then Armstrong got up and made a speech to all these black people about how he was a Republican and his father was a Republican and how black people needed to remember that it was the party of Lincoln who freed the slaves. The crowd groaned, and I was stunned—I was a Democrat like most black people were—but the political differences between Armstrong and me didn't matter much after what he'd done for me. We'd seen each other from time to time over the years. He invited me to some dinners when I was on the East Coast. Once,

I remember, Armstrong introduced me to a friend of his he said was going to become famous one day: Clarence Thomas.

Now, in the mid-'90s, when people called asking about Players Ink II, I told them we were no longer in business, but that I was available if they wanted a speaker. Some did, and I started speaking at awards banquets, most of which were tied to charities, and at business meetings. I wasn't confined in an office. I was meeting different people. I was writing things to say about my experience playing for Coach Rob and the Cowboys and winning a Super Bowl.

But really, I was killing time trying to figure out what I was going to do next, what I was going to do with the rest of my life. I had no idea that sharing my experience in life, especially Ron's friendship, with the rest of the world would be such a big part of it.

# 12

# My Father's Hand

I've believed in God for as long as I can remember. I believe in him now more than ever, if that's possible. I pray every night and give thanks every morning. I keep His book within easy access, on the top of a dresser in Shreill's and my bedroom. I believe in God because He has proved to me that He exists and believes in me, too. I've felt His presence in my life at different points when things seemed, against all odds, to turn out for the best. I also believe because I've heard God speak through powerful voices—people who, no matter what their faith, were able to serve as representatives of God's love in the world.

First Baptist Church of Hamilton Park in Dallas was born with the neighborhood in the early 1950s. It was the brainchild of a minister named Jesse Lee Foster and his wife, Annie Pearl Foster. It started in a living room and shortly afterward moved to a condemned auditorium that the Reverend Foster convinced the Richardson School District to donate to Hamilton Park.

On my fifth birthday, December 28, 1964, First Baptist broke ground to build its own sanctuary. The lot it would be constructed on was just a stone's throw from the house I was growing up in. Our family had been members of the church since it was in that old school auditorium, and the church's new building was a cause for celebration.

You could say that I grew up at First Baptist as much as I did in my own home. I can't recall a Sunday when I wasn't sitting in a pew with Mom, Eartha, Gigi, and Dad, listening to the Reverend Foster extol the virtues of the good book.

Reverend Foster was a classic black Baptist preacher. He would start a sermon calmly with a little story from the Bible and build to a crescendo with a booming voice and all sorts of histrionics, arms flailing and feet kicking. He was the kind of preacher who, when he finished his sermon, left you with chills running up and down your spine.

Just before my NFL career ended, Reverend Foster was honored by the legendary Dallas theologian W. A. Criswell, who once headed the Southern Baptist Convention. Criswell gave Reverend Foster an honorary doctorate from Criswell College. It was the first time Criswell, who was white, had ever conferred such a degree on a black preacher. "J. Lee Foster," Criswell said of the man who had mesmerized me from his pulpit every Sunday, "is a perfect example of a biblical vine dresser in the modern world. He plants the seed with the word of God, he waters the seed with the Holy Spirit, and he cares for the increase."

With Reverend Foster's nurturing, this particular young sprout grew to be someone who liked going to church. I learned to respect the discipline of regular worship, and now that I'm back in Texas I still go to First Baptist just about every Sunday.

Because Shreill is Catholic, with her Louisiana roots, she and I sought out a Catholic church to attend at Grambling. It wasn't hard to choose because there was only one—St. Benedict.

The St. Benedict we knew was the creation of the Reverend James Lyke, a black priest who came there in the mid-'60s. The building that housed St. Benedict was erected long before Father Lyke assumed it, but he made St. Benedict's Church something wholly different from just another Catholic church.

The word was that Father Lyke was very active in the civil rights movement in Louisiana. He'd been thrown out of restaurants that had refused to serve black patrons, chased by the Ku Klux Klan, and been the target of bomb threats in other Louisiana towns he lived and worked in.

About the time I arrived at Grambling, Father Lyke was returning to campus from a period of ministering in Memphis. He was an instigator of the black Catholic movement that infused the traditions of Protestant African-American worship into Catholic services. He added something else, too, to St. Benedict—he added the words *the Black* to its name. We learned that the historical St. Benedict was born the son of African slaves in Sicily in the 1500s and was adopted by Franciscan friars, for whom he became a beloved cook and spiritual leader.

Father Lyke himself was, not surprisingly, a Franciscan brother. I never got to know him well—he left after my sophomore year. But I did get to know his assistant, the Reverend Edward Branch, the younger black man who took over St. Benedict the Black.

Father Branch conducted Sunday services according to the vision of Father Lyke, and it was less like any Catholic church I'd ever been to and more like what I was accustomed to at First Baptist. It was energetic and lively. The songs weren't solemn; they were upbeat, funky almost. The congregation was just about all black; I'd never seen so many black Catholics, and neither had Shreill, whose home church back in Dallas was mostly white.

The only person at Grambling who was more influential to me than Coach Rob was Father Branch. He wasn't an imposing figure like Coach Rob. He was a little guy. But his messages resonated with me as much as a lot of the things Coach Rob told me.

Father Branch's St. Benedict the Black became a refuge for me. When I was stung my freshman year by being left off the traveling squad when the Tigers went to Tokyo, I went to Father Branch's church and heard him preach about the need to stay positive, which was something he himself did at all times. After that, a visit to Father Branch became a routine for me anytime I felt disappointed on the football field or in the classroom. He had a way of lifting my spirits and just about anybody else's, too. He restored my faith in myself anytime it wavered. I visit him whenever I'm in Atlanta, where he now ministers to the Catholic Center for the black colleges—Spelman, Morehouse, and Clark—that make up the Atlanta University Center. The Catholic Center is named Lyke House after Father Lyke, who died in 1992.

Father Branch is one of many people who've helped me on my path. It's always seemed that someone else was there for me—someone who saved me unexpectedly, or gave me an unforeseen opportunity, or answered my prayers.

When I went to juvenile jail, I thought I was going to be there all by myself with a bunch of thugs. I was pretending to be tougher than I was, to ward off potential attackers. But I hadn't been locked up for too long before I saw a familiar face. It was Gayle Warren, a deacon from First Baptist. I hadn't known that he happened to be one of the supervisors at the jail. I couldn't have been happier to see someone behind those walls who I knew and, more importantly, who would look out for me. I felt embarrassed that Deacon Warren saw me there, but I didn't feel alone.

Before I got my scholarship to Grambling, the recruiting season was already over, and the signing dates for new college athletes had passed. Mom couldn't afford to send me to college. But somehow, some way, Coach Rob had one more scholarship left, and he decided, with great persuading from my mother to give it to me. It didn't hurt that I was the boyfriend of the niece of one of his assistant coaches, but the odds against his still having a spot left so late in the game were pretty great.

The only odds that may have been greater were those I beat by making it into the NFL as a free agent—and winning a starting job on top of that—with one of the most renowned teams in the league, which just happened to be in my hometown. And when Jimmy Johnson dumped me from the Cowboys after we finished with a league-worst 1–15 record in 1989 in his first season as an NFL head coach, I was taken in by Bill Parcells's Giants, who went on the next season to win the Super Bowl that landed me on that *Sports Illustrated* cover.

☆

Sometimes people talk about a script that no writer could create. My life's script tells such a fortunate story that no mere mortal could have written it. There just have been too many times in my life when a potential disaster was turned into a windfall for me to think it has all unfolded by chance. I don't take what has happened to me for granted. Something else has had a hand in guiding my life, and I believe that hand is God's:

> My sheep hear My voice, and I know them, and they follow Me. And I give them eternal life, and they shall never perish; neither shall anyone snatch them out of My hand. My Father, who has given them to Me, is greater than all; and no one is able to snatch them out of My Father's hand. I and My Father are one.
>
> John 10:27–30

I believe I've been touched by miracles. I think Charis, Shreill's and my firstborn child, was a miracle. Today she's a beautiful twenty-four-year-old after having been born two and a half months premature.

I think my mother is still with us today through a miracle, because in 1996, when she was just sixty-three, I thought I was about to lose her. It was the Wednesday before Super Bowl XXX in Tempe, Arizona, where the Cowboys were meeting the Pittsburgh Steelers. It was late afternoon, and I was home getting my things together to fly to Arizona the next morning to watch the game and make several paid appearances. My phone rang. It was Eartha.

She and Mom had been chitchatting over at Mom's house when Mom's words slowly started turning into gibberish. Then Mom passed out, falling to the floor, Eartha said.

An ambulance was taking Mom to the hospital, and Eartha was getting ready to follow it; she wanted me to tell everyone else to meet there. The first person I called was Dad. In fact, he was the only person I called, because I couldn't even finish telling him what Eartha said before I lost my composure.

Luckily, Shreill was home. She saw me sobbing into the phone and helped me pull my mama's-boy self together and get down to Presbyterian Hospital, the same hospital where Charis was born, as fast as we could.

Mom was still unconscious, and the doctors had her hooked up to all sorts of bags and machines. They said she had suffered a brain aneurysm and needed surgery as soon as possible, which would be later that night. They said they were worried about permanent paralysis or worse, assuming she pulled through the surgery.

They described to us what they would have to do. It included opening Mom's skull. I'd never been so scared in my life.

One of Dad's cousins from East Texas was a minister, T. C. Walls. He came up and gathered the family and friends for prayer. Shreill's parents were there. I recalled the prayer that Coach Landry had said for Charis when she was born. I remembered how fervently Pastor Foster had once talked about keeping faith in the face of doubt.

I prayed harder and longer than I ever had. I pleaded for whatever help Mom needed. I recited the words of prayer Dad's cousin offered for Mom and for our family.

We stayed at the hospital most of the night and went home for just a few hours after Mom was taken into surgery. When we returned early the next morning, the doctors told us the procedure had gone well. They had even better news for us: They didn't believe Mom had suffered any paralysis, and they were pretty certain she was going to make a full recovery. They expressed surprise at their work and Mom's resilience. It was such a turn of good fortune that I can only ascribe it to divine intervention—to the prayer we offered and the response it got.

I was scheduled to leave that day, Thursday, for Arizona, but I kept pushing back my flights because I didn't want to leave Mom's side. Shreill was there, along with my sisters and their kids, and they all kept assuring me that Mom would be fine under their watchful and caring eyes.

Then Ron showed up. Shreill had called Adriane, and Adriane had relayed what was happening to Ron. He walked in as loud as always and put me and everyone else at ease. He started entertaining the entire wing and had people who didn't even know him, especially the nurses, laughing along with him.

Ron told me that he'd take over the vigil while I went to Arizona and that I didn't have to worry. I took him up on his offer, although once I got to Arizona, I was calling back to the hospital constantly.

Ron was true to his word. He hung in there like a rock for my family and friends until Mom woke up and started regaining awareness.

That my mom eventually left that hospital and is here with me today without much of a trace of what happened that week is, I think, a miracle. My mom survived that aneurysm. A few years later my father suffered a heart attack that he survived. The Wallses are a fortunate family. Even my grandparents lived long lives. My life doesn't have to be this blessed. Things could've turned out a lot worse.

I see that only now that I've stepped away from the selfishness that possessed me for so long as an athlete. With the wider view of life I have now, I can look beyond the resentment I used to harbor over any disrespect I suffered during my career. I used to think of my circumstances in a negative light: that I'd had to grovel for a scholarship; that I didn't get drafted; that I had to march for commensurate pay. Now I can reframe those experiences in terms of what was lucky and God-given about them. I still get mad sometimes that I haven't come close to getting elected to the Pro Football Hall of Fame, despite being tied with Mel Blount for tenth on the all-time interceptions list. Blount, who starred for the Steelers Steel Curtain defense in the '70s, is in the Hall. I have one more pick than Lem Barney, Willie Brown, and one of my contemporaries, Darrell Green, and all three of them are enshrined in the Hall. Why not me? Who doesn't like me? That disappointment shouldn't consume me as much as all the blessings God has provided for me. It is something I struggle with mightily.

I've never been evangelical about my beliefs or proselytized to others. I've always kept my religion to myself. I think faith is personal, and everyone should handle it in a manner that is comfortable for them. I respect others for what they believe and how they choose to pray, or whether they believe at all and don't pray. My relationship with God is special to me, and I think everyone else should be allowed to have their relationship be special, too. I've never invited others to join my way of worshipping, even though I enjoy it and am so inspired by it.

Ron is just the same. Growing up in a religious home back in Williamsburg, Virginia—a Protestant home—it was just as unusual for him not to be in church on Sunday as it was for me. His sisters sang in the choir. Ron just preferred a different type of church than I did.

He came to like big churches with pastors he considered to have some fame. He joined me on Sunday once or twice in Hamilton Park but liked to tease me about how small my church was and that its flock all came from the neighborhood. He liked to have the same level of bravado about his religion as he had toward the rest of his life.

Ron also teased me about my minister, Gregg Foster, after he met him, and I told him that Gregg and I had actually grown up together. Even though one of Ron's brothers grew up to be a minister, Ron thought it odd that I allowed us all to be preached to by a peer—a homeboy, of all people. I think Ron had trouble respecting Gregg as a minister partly because we were all about the same age. Little did Ron know, but Pastor Gregg was going to play a key role in helping me help him.

I didn't take offense at Ron's joshing about my church and pastor. Ron liked to have a little fun with every situation. He didn't see any sacred cows.

In a way, I could understand his uneasiness about my being ministered to by Pastor Gregg. Pastor Gregg and I don't have a normal pastor–parishioner relationship. We can't, no matter how hard we try. We went to elementary school together. We ran around Hamilton Park together chasing girls and playing sports. His younger brother, Anthony, was right there with us, and today he is Gregg's associate pastor. If you'd told us all then that they'd grow up to take over their father's ministry at First Baptist, we'd have said you were an order of french fries short of a Happy Meal.

But Pastor Gregg studied his father's craft and his devotion. He attended and graduated from Criswell College, which had awarded his father that honorary doctorate. Then he went to Tyndale Seminary in Fort Worth and Landmark Baptist Seminary there, too. He has enough college degrees to make up a new chapter in the Bible, and his preaching is more an expression of that learnedness, unlike the ferocity of his father's. Pastor Anthony has the gift of whoop, as they say of that style of black preaching. Pastor Gregg got his dad's looks, and Pastor Anthony got his dad's fire. A few days before I went under the knife myself for the very first time in my life, it was Pastor Gregg who I called for counsel.

# 13

# God's Body

Pastor Gregg was already well aware of what was about to happen between Ron and me, but not because I sought his counsel early on. He found out just like everyone else—through the media. Ron's son, Shawn, told a *Washington Post* writer one day that his father was planning to receive a kidney from me. The story rushed through the Internet and was picked up by broadcast outlets in Dallas, and the chatter started.

The first Sunday after the news broke, I was in church, and Pastor Gregg pulled me aside in the vestibule. He told me how proud he was of me—as part of his flock and as a friend. I heard a lot of that sentiment that day. It all buoyed my belief that I was doing the right thing.

I didn't just thank my friend-grown-up-to-be-my-pastor for his kind words. I asked Pastor Gregg if he would sit with me and Shreill, the kids and Mom, and Eartha and Gigi in prayer before I underwent the surgery. Of course he would, he said. He then invited me to bring the family to the church on the eve of my hospitalization.

There was no way I was going to lay my life down for Ron and his family without going before the Lord first. I had to hold His hand in order to maintain my courage, and I wanted my family to hold on with me. The magnitude of what I was about to do was sinking in fast. I knew we needed the extra strength that only God can provide.

It was the first time in my life I'd ever called on a spiritual leader to pray for me. I didn't even do it when Charis was fighting to get out of that hospital and home to us as a preemie. I should have found the time for that between football practice in the morning and afternoon and spending evenings and nights at the hospital at Charis's side. This go-round I decided that I was going to make the time to gather my family in prayer. I wasn't scared, but I needed the extra girding that only prayer could give me. It's called faith.

I had learned in church that you have to possess hope before you can apply faith. I felt as if I had more than just hope that Ron would get better if he received a kidney from me, since I was not only a match but in outstanding health. After all the medical testing and counseling from doctors and therapists, I felt prepared to enter the operating room with an assurance that Ron would get better if everything went according to plan.

That isn't to say that going through the process of becoming a living donor isn't unnerving. It can be after you undergo the battery of physical and psychological tests and you learn all the ins and outs of the donation process. My doctors were not shy about telling me the risks of bleeding and infection that can result from donation and, in extremely rare instances, even death. But they also reminded me that those were risks anyone undergoing surgery faced.

They told me in detail how the day of surgery would unfold from the moment one of the staff started an intravenous line in me for the sedation medicine to the second I awakened upward of five hours later. They told me that once I was asleep, a breathing tube, connected to a machine, would be inserted in my mouth and throat, because under general anesthesia, I would need help to breathe. They explained that a catheter would be inserted into my bladder so that I could undergo a specific type of donation surgery called laparoscopy.

They said a few small incisions would be made in my abdomen, and a laparoscope containing a miniature camera to help guide the surgeon would be inserted into the incisions. Other small laparoscopic tools, they said, would be inserted in the incisions to sever the kidney, and an incision of no more than four inches would be made for the removal of my kidney. Then they would stitch me up, roll me to the recovery room, and allow me to regain consciousness.

I knew I was in good medical hands. I just didn't want to forget to ask God for His hands, because with His hands I knew everything would be all right. That's having faith.

And faith gives you courage. Faith gives you that strength to do what is before you because you believe—no, you know—that God is watching, and He rewards your belief in Him with eternal light.

Ron reached out for God's hands, too. He and Adriane had their pastor, Gordon Banks, from Covenant Church in Carrollton, Texas, come by the hospital the morning of the transplant. Covenant is one of those very large churches that Ron likes. But the Reverend Banks was one of Ron's peers and friends, just like my pastor. Banks was a former teammate of ours with the Cowboys, a wide receiver who traded his football uniform for the cloth.

I needed as much of that as I could get going into a surgery during which I would have one of the organs God gave me, an organ that had helped me become a fine enough physical specimen to make a nice livelihood by slamming my body into others, removed and given to someone else.

I was never afraid of my decision to donate a kidney to Ron or afraid that it wouldn't work; I was worried about what would happen if we didn't take the chance that it could fail. I remember hearing a preacher say once that sometimes God's will just comes over you, and you are helpless. When I think about it, that is what happened to me with Ron. I couldn't help but react as I did when he told me yet another potential donor had fallen through. I was overtaken with a frustration and anger that, I believe, was God's way of working through me to help Ron and his family.

I think Pastor Gregg anticipated that I would request a special prayer session, because he didn't have any meeting or travel on his schedule that would conflict with this last-minute counseling. That, too, was probably the work of the Lord.

Shreill and I and the kids drove down from Plano to First Baptist. Eartha and Gigi with their kids picked up Mom at the house and drove her to the church. First Baptist hadn't been a couple of blocks from Mom's house for twenty years. It had outgrown the red-brick sanctuary the flock built in 1964 and moved to a new facility in downtown

Richardson in 1986, becoming the first black church in that suburb. We didn't dress up for this occasion in our Sunday best. It was a weekday, and Pastor Gregg wasn't dressed up either when he greeted us at his office. Everyone looked very relaxed, which was exactly the way I wanted them to be.

Pastor Gregg led us into the sanctuary. I don't think I'd ever been there when it was so empty and quiet and serene. I heard everyone's footsteps as we walked in and took our seats in the first row or two, and Pastor Gregg stood before us.

"Cubby," Pastor Gregg said, sounding more like the kid I grew up with than the minister he had become, "I am honored for you to be led by the spirit."

I nodded and said, "Thanks, Gregg." Mom wiped away a tear.

Pastor Gregg then asked us to bow our heads in prayer. And for the next ten minutes or so, the only words we heard were his.

I don't remember exactly what Pastor Gregg said except that he emphasized what I wanted everyone to hear, especially Mom, who was still struggling with the idea that I was actually going to give part of myself to a teammate. Pastor Gregg said that what I was doing was an example of what God said we should all do for our neighbor. He said that giving of oneself voluntarily for the well-being of another is a Christian duty. He talked about how there is a mandate from the Lord, that is motivated by compassion, to aid those who are in need of healing. He talked about the nobility of putting the needs of another before your own.

I had never thought until that moment about what I was doing in quite those terms. To me, the organ donation procedure seemed to be part and parcel of my faith, an ultimate expression of loving thy neighbor, and I hadn't really needed to articulate the reasons for myself. But the way the gift of this procedure could be part of a Christian life needed to be spelled out, because there were those among us—in our neighborhoods, in our workplace, in the pew next to us—who believed that organ donation was more the mutilation of a body God had created than the saving of a life he granted.

> Do you not know that your body is a temple of the Holy Spirit, who is in you, whom you have received from God? You are not your own; you were bought at a price. Therefore, honor God with your body.
>
> 1 Corinthians 6:19–20

I can't argue with the Bible. I can only continue to read it and listen to what is read from it. I believe that I am not my own, as Corinthians says, and to me that means I am here to be shared with those who need me in life and in death. I think I can honor God that way. I don't think a greater act of compassion exists than the donation of an organ to another.

Pastor Gregg's message underscored to me the importance of the movement for organ donation that Ron and I had joined. We hadn't sought it. Few people who join it do. It found us, and we just happened not to turn away.

We were unique because of our relationship and unusual because of our race. Black folks need organ donations more than any other group, and they find fewer among them who are willing to volunteer. Ron and I wanted to show our people that we can lift each other up in this way.

Nothing about this impending transplant struck me as more poignant than what Pastor Gregg did in those few minutes that afternoon. It affirmed in front of everyone else who is close to me how strong my belief was in what I was doing. It confirmed it to me, too. He washed from me any lingering second thoughts I might have had remotely tucked away.

I felt then that I had done everything I possibly could do to prepare to be an organ donor. I felt I'd done everything I could for everyone else, too. I also realized I was doing something for people beyond Ron and our two families.

As a result, the next day, February 28, 2007, was a calm one for all of us, including Mom and Adriane and the Springs kids, as Ron and I were anesthetized for what turned out to be a five-hour surgical procedure. When the surgical team finally broke their huddle over us and walked out of the operating room and into the waiting room where our families were congregated, one of the doctors, Ronald Aronoff, announced that everything had gone smoothly and that my kidney was perfect.

"Praise God," Shreill said softly.

"Amen," Adriane responded.

It took me about two weeks of recovery after the surgery before I could return to Pastor Gregg's church, my church. It was for a Sunday service, and my abdomen was still quite sore. Pastor Gregg spotted me, of course. He announced my presence from his pulpit and said a few words about what I'd done.

From somewhere among the pews came another "Amen."

# 14

# Somebody's Got to Do It

When I was in my early teens, I spent a lot of time in Garland, a Dallas suburb just east of Hamilton Park. My dad lived there for a while after he and Mom separated, and I lived there with Dad for part of one school year.

I never liked Garland as much as Hamilton Park while I was growing up. Compared to Hamilton Park, it seemed like the country, and I didn't like the country. I got enough of that when we took weekend trips to East Texas, where my parents' family roots are and where we stayed with relatives who had outhouses for bathrooms. I was too much of a city boy for that.

Garland wasn't *that* backward. At least everyone had indoor plumbing. And we had a lot of family in Garland, a bunch of cousins my age, that made visiting there, even living there a short while, a little more tolerable. One Garland family we were related to was the Armstrongs. My mother was an Armstrong, one of seven brothers and sisters. Several relocated from East Texas to Garland, so there were several sets of Armstrong households, including one where my cousin Dennis lived.

Dennis and I were about the same age. We hung out with other kids in Garland and played some pick-up sports against them. But Dennis wasn't nearly as good at sports as I was, and he had a knack for getting other guys mad at him and winding up in fights he couldn't win and didn't. It seemed to happen with regularity, and I got tired of standing up for him. I got so tired of having to come to Dennis's defense that I complained to my mother about him once.

Mom listened to me rant, and then, I'll never forget, she said, "Dennis is family. Don't give up on him. You take care of family."

There has never been anything more important to my mom than family, which is a good thing, since we have so much of it. There are me and my sisters and my two cousins at Uncle Robert's house, where Dad stayed for a while. Uncle Robert is one of my Mom's brothers. There are my cousins in Garland, like Kato Armstrong, who played basketball at SMU in Dallas, and Herkie Walls, who played wide receiver at Texas before being drafted into the NFL and playing three seasons with Houston and a fourth in Tampa Bay in 1987, a year after Ron left the Buccaneers. Then there are Herkie's brothers, Phillip and Tyrone.

Out in East Texas, where Mom and Dad grew up, I have even more family in cities like Longview and towns like Elysian Fields. There are so many people in our family that sometimes I bump into someone I don't know, and after we start talking, we find out we share a relative.

Shreill is the same way. She has four siblings. Whereas I'm the youngest of my parents' kids, she's the oldest. Shreill's family is just as big as mine, but they hail from Louisiana, in the Baton Rouge area, just a little farther east of my family's homestead in East Texas.

Her family is Creole, descendants of French colonists and Africans. Shreill said her great-aunt and grandmother would always sit at the kitchen table and gossip about people in French.

Shreill's grandmother taught at Southern University Lab, a college-prep high school tied to Southern University. She lived a block away from the university. Shreill's mom went to Southern, which is part of the reason our daughter wound up going to Southern. It makes for an awful lot of fun trash-talking during the Bayou Classic, the Grambling versus Southern football game every Thanksgiving weekend.

☆

I had to remind my mother of the importance of family after I made up my mind to try to save Ron's life by giving him one of my kidneys. I knew she was going to be the one person to question the wisdom of my decision, and I'd sworn ever since my juvenile jail stay that I'd never disappoint my mom again.

I didn't think Mom would object to the idea of my donating a kidney. I thought she would object to the idea of my donating a kidney to someone outside of our family.

Mom clutched family so closely to her heart that she all but adopted my dad's son Greg, from dad's marriage to Annette, whom he married after Mom. She accepted Greg as her own and led me to accept him as my brother. Mom always said that he was innocent, that he had nothing to do with Dad's leaving us and had done nothing to deserve being shunned.

Mom has a big heart. I remember when I started getting interested in girls, and I didn't have Dad to turn to every day because he had moved on. I was living the life of a single mom's kid. I only had Mom to talk to about the opposite sex. One day I asked her what to do if a girl liked me who I didn't think looked very good.

"You can always find something good about a person," Mom told me. That always resonated with me.

Mom taught me and Eartha and Gigi to respect other people and do the best we could not only for ourselves but for others, too. Mom was always helping other people and looking out for others' well-being.

I decided to do that for Ron: look out for his and his family's well-being. Adriane doesn't like to hear me say it, but what I decided to do for Ron was as much about her and the kids as it was about Ron. It was really for Ron's family that I decided to do what I did.

Ron rarely, if ever, talked about how he was feeling as his body deteriorated and surgeons chopped away at it. I didn't want him to talk about it either. It would have just been depressing. I felt that the best thing I could do for Ron then as a friend was give him something else to think about, so I avoided talking about his condition, just like he did.

Ron knew, however, that I understood how tough a time he was having because he was right there in his house listening to his wife talk to my wife about everything, and I was in my house hearing the same conversation. I couldn't ignore the conversations I overheard Shreill have with Adriane on the phone, and if I tried, Shreill would fill me in anyway. I learned about dialysis and what Ron was going through at a dialysis center in Dallas from Shreill:

*Ron's illness wasn't just bringing him down. It was pulling Adriane under like a whirlpool in the ocean. I could see it in her face, which became drawn and broke into a smile less and less. I could hear it in her voice, which was growing wearier. I could see it in her eyes, which every now and then looked overcome by the emotion of watching the man she'd come to love, the father of her children, struggle with the onslaught of diabetes.*

*Diabetes wasn't just beating Ron down physically, it was hurting Adriane, too. Slowly but surely, it was turning her into a caretaker for her husband. She was already a forty-something mom with two girls going through those all-important teenage years, years that would have been exhausting for her in the best of circumstances.*

*I could see that Adriane was weary from the emergency visits to the hospital that were cropping up more and more, not to mention the weekly visits to the doctor's office—sometimes the same doctor and other times a new one. One doctor would refer him to another doctor, or specialist, for some new problem that had appeared. That new doctor might send Ron to yet another specialist.*

*Diabetes just causes so many problems. The kind of diabetes Ron had, type 2, meant that his body wasn't processing carbohydrates properly, because of a lack of insulin. This meant that there was a lot of extra sugar in his blood, and it was literally eating away at his other organs. The kidneys are hit first, because they work to clean the blood, producing urine. The kidneys start working overtime trying to deal with all the bad blood coursing through them. But they can't handle the job, and they start to fail. Then the bad blood gets out into the rest of your system. Ron had to have his heart checked because diabetes increased the risk of heart disease. His nerves were in danger of damage. His eyes had to be checked because diabetes could cause blindness. He was at greater risk of having a stroke. So he needed an army of doctors to keep an eye on him.*

*Adriane was tired of watching Ron get stuck with needles to have his blood drawn and get tethered to tubes and cords to yet another bank of medical machinery to test something else in his body. She was tired of sometimes having to handle this hardware herself. Adriane was just "sick and tired of being sick and tired," like the civil rights leader Fannie Lou Hamer has written on her tombstone.*

*Once, I remember, Ron was being treated with antibiotics from an intravenous bag that his doctors allowed to be administered at home. They didn't dispatch a nurse. Adriane did it instead. I watched her change the bag and attach the tube. She looked so expert doing it that I told her she should have gone to medical school. But that wasn't what Adriane wanted to be doing then; it was what she had to do.*

*Adriane kept track of all of Ron's medications. Sometimes, Ron would suffer diarrhea from the drugs he was taking, and Adriane would have to clean him up. After one emergency hospital visit in 2004, when Ron's kidneys shut down for the first time, Ron was ordered to start dialysis, and that became a new duty for Adriane. She had to get him to the dialysis center three times a week and pick him up.*

*As diabetes continued to ravage Ron's body, surgeons had to amputate first his toes and then his foot, and the disease also slowly gnarled Ron's hands into virtually unrecognizable fists from poor circulation and nerve damage. I would look at Ron's balled up hands sometimes and imagine that it was anger welling up inside of him, trying to fight the disease that was ruining his life and that of the woman he loved.*

*It is never easy to feel what someone else is going through unless you're going through it, too. I never felt the totality of Adriane's burden until the one time I picked up Ron from dialysis because Adriane had something else she really had to do. She was trying to keep her job in downtown Dallas and take care of her daughters and keep house and care for Ron. She was like Superwoman, but even she needed to ask for an extra hand every now and then, and I was only too happy to help.*

*I drove over to the dialysis center to pick up Ron, who now was all but wheelchair-bound. Some assistants at the center helped me put Ron in his wheelchair and roll him out the door. Then it was on me.*

*I had to help Ron get out of the wheelchair and shove his body into the car. Then I had to fold up the wheelchair and stuff it in the truck. Once we got to his house, I had to do the reverse. I unfolded the wheelchair, rolled it around to the passenger door, and steadied Ron as he got out of the car so that he could plop down into the wheelchair. Then I rolled him to the front door and inside the house.*

*That was the only thing I had to do that day, and it absolutely wore me out. But here Adriane was doing that at least three times a week—dropping Ron off in the morning and picking him up in the afternoon. Other days, she might have to go through the same routine several times, if Ron had other medical appointments or tests. That meant Adriane would have to drive from her downtown Dallas office back home, take Ron to and from where he had to go, and drive back to her downtown office to finish her work.*

*Adriane's normal workweek day began with her rising at 4:30 in the morning to get herself ready for work and get Ron ready for whatever he had to have done that day. She had to prepare his breakfast for him and sometimes feed him first because his diabetes was making his hands more and more useless. On the mornings when she had to get him to dialysis, he had to be at the center by 6:00, which meant he and Adriane had to leave the house by about 5:30.*

*Adriane had to make sure Ron always had a snack or lunch with him to keep his blood sugar regulated. She had to make sure, on those increasingly rare days when he didn't have to leave the house, that he had his cell phone nearby in case he needed something, even if it was just to talk, to break the monotony of fighting and praying to stay alive.*

*Adriane would get home around 6:00 and make some dinner for Ron, bathe him, make sure he took his medication, and prepare to start the process all over again at 4:30 the next morning.*

The more I learned from Shreill and, later, my own research about the complicated, terrible turn Ron's and Adriane's lives had taken, the more amazed I was.

Dialysis is an extremely invasive procedure. In Ron's case, it was more like a slow death. The process includes having all of your blood extracted from your body, filtered, and then inserted back into your body. It's not only invasive, but it's time consuming as well. Each session lasts four to five hours a day, and Ron endured that three times a week, for three and a half years.

I knew things weren't getting any better for Ron. I knew how it was all weighing on Adriane. Eventually she had to take a leave of absence from her job as a civil rights investigator for the federal government to care for her husband. Adriane and Ron are a lot alike. They share the gift of gab. Both are very strong in the headwind of a challenge. Shreill would turn to me after talking to Adriane on the phone and just shake her head in amazement. She couldn't imagine how Adriane remained so stoic in the face of what was happening with Ron.

We could count on one hand the number of times Adriane appeared to let the emotion she must have had bubbling inside her spill over.

It was no different for Ron's and Adriane's oldest daughter, Ayra. She was away at Ohio State and worried every minute about her dad and what her mom had to do to care for him. She had that awful feeling of wanting to help and being unable to because she was so far away.

We never saw Shawn much because after seven years playing football in Seattle for the Seahawks he was living in Washington playing football for the Redskins, having relocated there for the 2004 season. But we knew how concerned he was about his dad when he volunteered to donate his kidney, only to have his father reject the idea. Ron told Ayra and Ashley, his younger daughter, not to dare think about giving him their kidneys either. Ron had decided he'd rather die than have his life extended with a transplant from one of his kids.

All the strain may have been the reason Ron began to show his religiosity a little more as time went by. He started attending Covenant Church in the north Dallas suburb of Carrollton more and more, where our former teammate, Gordon Banks, was a minister. Ron never said so to me, but he may have been thinking of the end as things seemed to get more dire. He had stopped drinking just before he underwent his first amputation. He started playing gospel music all the time and reading the Bible more and more. I remember Shreill and I stopped by to visit him one Friday as we headed to get some happy hour margaritas, and he scolded us. He started attending Bible class at a friend's house and humming hymns sitting in his wheelchair watching TV. Ron was having a life-changing moment, and he wasn't going to go through it without being close to the Lord.

Ron was getting scared, but he wasn't going to admit it. He didn't want to admit it because doing so would go against being the big, tough football player he'd always been. He also couldn't admit it because he thought that would show a lack of faith.

Ron wasn't an old man, after all. At the time he became wheelchair-bound, in November 2006, he was just hitting his fiftieth birthday, just three years older than me. He was a former fullback in the NFL who wasn't suffering from any debilitating injuries to his neck or back or knees from all that hitting and being hit. If it weren't for this damned diabetes wreaking havoc on his body, Ron would have been looking forward to a long, normal life just like the rest of us.

That was one thing Ron pointed out from time to time to me as a way of saying he didn't want me to feel sorry for him. He would say he lived a blessed a life even though his hands were slowly gnarling into knots, his arms were atrophying, and his toes, feet, and legs were starting to disappear. Ron would say what a great wife he had in Adriane. He would point out that all his kids made him proud—a rich, football-playing son, a daughter graduating from his alma mater, and another daughter excelling in high school. He would talk about the life that he and I had lived as professional football players, which had provided us with incomes, taken us places, and introduced us to people whom others idolized.

The odd thing was that Ron's testimonial about his blessings had the opposite effect on me from what he intended. It made me more and more determined to do something for Ron and his family. I started to see more than just my friend Ron wasting away. I was seeing an entire family erode, a family that was also an extension of mine. It was a dire situation, but a situation for which I had been prepared for my entire life to tackle.

This is what happens when you are reared by someone like my mom, who sees an importance in lending a helping hand to those who need it and deserve it. This is what happens when you realize how many times in your life others have done something, big or small, for you. This is what happens when you realize you are being overcome by that instinct of human nature—to help.

God puts you on earth for a purpose, and you exercise that purpose. I was beginning to think that maybe Ron was my purpose in life, that maybe this was our fate.

We were brought together by football for just a few years. Our wives grew to be best friends and created and maintained a bond between our families. Ron and Adriane liked my hometown of Dallas so much that they decided to move back and live within a mile of our house. Ron got deathly ill, and of all the few people who could save him, I was one who was right at his side. I couldn't let such a fateful opportunity pass.

I wasn't a blood relative. Ron and I were the best of friends, but I wasn't Ron's *best* friend, and he wasn't mine either, at least not in the beginning of our relationship. Ron's best friend was the man he bunked with and blocked for on the Cowboys: Tony Dorsett. My best friends were the guys I bunked with during my rookie season, Angelo King and Michael Downs, and T. from Stultz Road.

But Ron and I had grown close enough to be godparents to each other's kids. Ron and I went into business together. It was Ron who had taken me under his wing so many times when I needed guidance. Now he needed something that I could deliver.

So when he told me on that fateful day at the gym in October 2006 that his latest potential donor, his nephew Chris, wouldn't be able to bail him out, I said, "What would I have to do, man, to go through with this?"

"You gotta go through a lot of stuff," he said. "I'll tell you what. You really wanna know? I'll give you a number. You call them, and they'll tell you all about it. They're gonna give you a written test . . . they're going to give you a bunch of medical tests . . . they're gonna ask you if you're crazy . . ."

Ron didn't express any elation. He'd been down this road too many times, when someone had promised him a kidney, and it wound up being a road to disappointment. He didn't even follow up with me in the days after my impromptu decision, probably because he was afraid I would say I'd changed my mind.

I didn't go about exploring my possible kidney donation to Ron with any excitement either, for much the same reason. I knew that anything could happen to disqualify me. I knew I had a mother to convince that this was the right thing to do.

When I got home that day, Shreill was in the kitchen. She'd just made some dinner and was standing near the kitchen island. I kissed her hello, perhaps put some of her cooking on a plate, and walked over to the couch in front of the big TV and plopped down.

"Hey, I decided I'm gonna go ahead and help Ron out," I said as I prepared to take a bite. "I think I'm gonna donate my kidney to him."

All I could hear for several seconds was whatever was playing on TV. Finally, Shreill responded.

"Really?" she said softly.

"Yeah, somebody's got to do it," I said, pointing out that Chris's donation had fallen through. "I think Ron's out of options."

That was the extent of our conversation, or my announcement, as it was. I didn't tell anyone else immediately what I was contemplating.

Shreill didn't question me, and I would've been shocked if she had, because I knew that anything I could do for her best friend, Adriane, Shreill was going to appreciate:

*I think the downward pressure on the family sank them to their lowest point after Ron was forced to have the lower part of his right leg amputated. It was the first time it appeared that Ron could no longer deal with what was happening to him. He had lost hope and resigned himself to death, maybe even hoped for it.*

*Ron wouldn't acknowledge visitors to his room after that amputation. He refused even to open his eyes. He went on his own little hunger strike, pushing away his hospital meals.*

*It made me so mad. I was mad because I knew what his struggles were doing to Adriane and what his newly adopted defiance was doing to every-*

*one, not to mention to his own health. So I paid a visit to Ron one day when I knew Adriane and the girls wouldn't be there.*

*I walked in and closed the door to Ron's room behind me and drew shut the curtain to the hallway window. I walked over to Ron without pity and with purpose. He looked worse than I could remember. His hair wasn't combed. He wasn't clean shaven. He hadn't allowed the nurse to brush his teeth.*

*"You know what?" I told Ron in the stern voice I had only ever used toward my kids when they didn't act like Cubby and I expected. "You need to straighten up."*

*He opened his eyes and blinked. He was startled.*

*I told him how the way he was acting was affecting his family and everyone else. I told him he was being selfish and that everyone who was helping him deserved better from him.*

*I grabbed his toothbrush and brushed his teeth. I got a towel and washed his face.*

*I told him, "Would you rather be with a leg and looking cute in your coffin, or without a leg and sitting up straight? C'mon now."*

*He muttered something, but he knew what I was getting at. Ron loved Adriane and his kids, and he knew they'd rather have him around to care for than not to have him around at all. That was why Adriane was doing everything that she was doing. That's why loved ones anywhere do the same thing. That's what my mother did for my father when he first got ill with diabetes and was forced to go to dialysis. That was what I knew I'd do for Cubby if, God forbid, he ever went through something like what Ron was going through.*

*Cubby heard Adriane's pain seep through my voice whenever I talked about all that she was doing, bearing that cross that had descended on her shoulders. I talked about it all the time, because it was the theme of most of my conversations with Adriane. The days of talking about shopping and what the kids were up to and the latest gossip surrounding some ex-Cowboy's wife we knew were long gone. What more was there to talk about than the situation her husband was in?*

*That's the thing about a disease like diabetes. It consumes everything around it. Ron's illness consumed Adriane. It consumed his kids. It consumed my friendship with Adriane, which was closer then than any I'd had with anyone. Sometimes Adriane and I would be chatting on the phone, and I'd hear Ron scream in the background, "Adriane, Adriane! I gotta go to the bathroom." And she'd tell me, "Why didn't he tell me that before I got on the phone? Let me call you back."*

*The sicker Ron got, the more Adriane and I talked, and the more Cubby realized what she and Ron were going through. If it wasn't for the closeness of Adriane and me, Cubby really wouldn't have known how bad things had become because he and Ron didn't talk nearly as often, and when they did, it was generally about any topic other than the dread hanging over Ron.*

*Cubby only witnessed what was happening the few times he ferried Ron to and from dialysis, or just spent time with Ron at Ron's house or at the gym once Ron had summoned enough spirit to strengthen his body for that life-saving transplant.*

*Adriane was doing what she had to do, and wanted to do, because she loved Ron, and Ron loved her. It was proof of what I always said: You never know what you can do until you have to do it. What Adriane had to do was keep her husband alive. Cubby watched Adriane's purpose in life become that. He realized at some point there was something he could do and that he would have to do it.*

*Cubby decided to see if he could donate his kidney to Ron. He wanted to save their family. He wanted to relieve Adriane of her enormous burden. And he wanted to help Ron return to being the husband and father and friend he'd always been.*

I made my first inquiry about organ donation the day after I made Ron my offer at the gym. A few days later, I was at a transplant center taking a test to determine if I was of sound mind to be a donor. There must have been five hundred questions to answer. I'd never seen anything like it. It was an attempt to determine if I was, among other things, suicidal. I didn't understand how someone hoping to save another person's life could desire to end his own.

I was then asked to attend a class on organ donation at the center. There were about fifteen other people in the class. What stood out most for me about the class wasn't the step-by-step explanation about the surgery but the warning that some donors suffer emotionally from not feeling appreciated enough for making their sacrifice. It was called a "hero syndrome." A hero was the last thing I wanted to be seen as.

Finally, I had to undergo a physical test of my kidneys to make sure they were both healthy enough—one healthy enough to be donated, the other healthy enough to do twice its normal workload when the other was gone. I had to drink eight cups of water, then drink some iodine. The iodine was mixed into a soft drink, but it still tasted so bad it had me on the edge of heaving. That was followed by another round of water shots, at least another eight, maybe as many as ten. After a few minutes, I was dispatched to the bathroom to provide a urine sample. Then I had to repeat the process a couple more times, all the while fighting the urge to throw up and trying hard to keep from peeing on myself for the requisite time period. I hadn't been so uncomfortable since that hit to the spleen I took in a game that had me pissing blood. This particular kidney test made me think for the first time that Ron better appreciate what I was doing.

When I was done with all the testing, I told my father about my decision. It surprised him, but he didn't say what I knew my mother would say as soon as I mustered the strength to inform her: He didn't say don't. But Dad and I had never had the type of relationship Mom and I do. Mothers and sons get along a lot differently than fathers and sons. I am still a mama's boy after all these years.

I kept Shreill informed during every step of the pretransplant trials. It was all so foreign to me that I wanted Shreill's input to make sure I was asking the right questions about what I was being asked to do and how the surgery was going to be done. One of the things I love about my wife is that she always has great suggestions.

Shreill suggested I call a couple of people we knew who had gone through the same thing. One was Lisa Allen, the girl we grew up with who donated a kidney to her sister Gwen when I was at Grambling. The other person was the wife of the comedian George Lopez. Ann

Lopez and Shreill had met during a charitable program she and Ann were involved in some years ago through Southern Methodist University in the tony Dallas enclave of Highland Park. Ann gave George a kidney in 2005, after his kidneys started deteriorating due to a genetic condition, rather than from diabetes.

I'd lost track of Lisa, but I knew my best friend growing up, Mike Terrell, who was Lisa's boyfriend back in the day, would know where to find her. He did. I told T. why I wanted to talk to Lisa. He was the only person other than Shreill and Dad who I'd told at that point.

Lisa was surprised to hear from me after all those years and happy to learn what I was planning to do. I filled her in on what I'd been through to that point, and she assured me that it was all ordinary.

Then I called Ann Lopez, and she affirmed everything Lisa said. My peace of mind returned.

It took me about four weeks to go through the testing that was required of a potential organ donor. Ron's insurance paid for it all and would pay for the surgery, too. Shortly afterward, I got a call from Ron's doctor, Dick Dickerman. He asked me to meet him at his office in South Oak Cliff.

He greeted me when I got there, and before he closed the door to his office, he asked one of his nurses to step in with us. She did and walked over to a corner behind a chair, where I took a seat. A rush of worry came over me. I began to think that the news Dr. Dickerman was about to deliver to me wasn't that I failed the test to be a donor, but that the test had found something wrong with me.

"Everson," Dr. Dickerman said, "I know you're committed to doing this, and I know how forceful Ron can be, because he really wants this to happen. Now that we know you're compatible, I want you to know that it's not too late to pull out. I'm giving you an opportunity right now to make a final decision."

It was as if I were being questioned on the football field all over again. I know Dr. Dickerman didn't mean it that way, but that was the way his questioning struck me. I didn't realize this final chance to back out was standard procedure in the transplant business. I just heard it as an expression of disbelief that I could be as good as I appeared, that I could be ready to do something that had actually never been done before in history: give an organ to someone who was related to me only through a few years of playing a professional sport together.

"I can still make you look like a hero," he said. "I won't let anyone know that you decided not to do it at the last minute. I can tell them that you weren't compatible—the test results are confidential."

I exhaled. Then I laughed.

"Doc, c'mon, man," I said sinking back into the chair with relief. "I'm not going to change my mind now. When can we do this?"

A smile sprang up across Dr. Dickerman's face.

I was relieved because that was the moment when I realized I really didn't have any second thoughts about what I was planning to do. I knew that what I was doing was right. I knew what I was doing was safe. I knew that I was in good hands, God's included. All I had to do next was get my affairs in order, which included making sure my own insurance was sufficient for my recovery, as well as letting the rest of my family in on my secret and telling Ron I had passed.

But things quickly got out of hand. Before I caught up with Ron, he caught up with me.

"Walls," I heard Ron shouting through my phone, "you compatible!"

Ron was at the transplant center several times each week for therapy, and a nurse there had given him the heads up.

Ron was showing his eagerness now, because he knew I wasn't the type to break my word. He wanted to set a date and wanted it set for as soon as possible. I understood, but I'd also been advised during the transplant class not to allow pressure to dictate the donation, and I had some work to do, most lucratively at the Super Bowl on the first Sunday in February 2007. I told Ron the transplant had to wait until after then. I couldn't jeopardize a paid appearance because my finances at the time weren't as healthy as my kidneys. I hadn't been doing anything regularly since Ron and I had shut down Players Ink II in 1998. I'd been pursuing a real estate dream, but it was still just that, a dream. Ron understood.

Then before I could break the news to my kids and my sisters, Shawn Springs told a couple of reporters at the *Washington Post* that his father's old teammate, me, was going to give his dad what hopefully would be a lifesaving kidney transplant.

It was mid-December, and Charis happened to be home from college when a local television reporter, Jeff Crilly, knocked at our door and asked if I was home. I wasn't. The reporter then asked Charis what she thought of what I was about to do, and Charis had no idea what the guy was talking about. He then showed her the story he was writing on his laptop.

Charis called me. I was mad. I called Ron to tell him his son had broken the news. Ron was mad. We were trying to keep this as far off the radar screen as possible. After all, publicity wasn't the reason I'd decided to donate my kidney to Ron.

I didn't realize at the time that what we were doing wasn't just admirable, it was newsworthy. Organ donation is something everyone should be aware of, because so many need it, and it's not that hard to make it work once a donor is found. Yet it's not something you hear about very often. Many people are capable of being organ donors, but they've never thought about it before. Those people just need a nudge in the right direction. That was the case with me.

With Shawn having unveiled my plans unexpectedly, my first priority was to get over to my mother's house before the media did and before she heard about Ron and me on the radio or on TV.

It was early in the afternoon, and Mom's house was quiet when I walked in. She was babysitting some young kids, and they were napping, so Mom, fortunately for me, didn't have the TV on.

She was sitting at the kitchen table, and I took a seat across from her and told her that I was going to donate a kidney to Ron. She sucked in her breath, shook her head, and groaned like a pain had just shot through her.

"Cubby, why would you do that?" Mom said. "What if I need a kidney?"

I just laughed. That wasn't something I'd considered.

"Mom, you're seventy-two," I said. "And you don't have any kidney problems. What are you talking about? If you need a kidney, you can get it from one of your grandchildren."

"But why? Why are you doing this?" Mom asked.

"Mom, you're the one who always talked to me about caring for your fellow man," I said. "You're the one who told me to be conscientious. I can't turn my back on Ron," I told her. "You want me to live with him dying when I could do something about it? I can't do that."

Mom was quiet. She understood. She wasn't happy about it, though.

I knew what troubled Mom deep down inside. It was that I had such a charmed life and that she was so much a part of that charm—from getting me out of juvenile jail to getting me a college scholarship that led me to a nice living as a pro football player. She didn't want me to risk that life no matter how many assurances we got from the doctors that everything would go without a hitch. She didn't want me, her baby, to get used.

I thought in the weeks that passed over the holidays and into the New Year that Mom had gotten over her resistance to the idea. Ron and I held a press conference. Local and national reporters picked up our story and told it as the remarkable fruition of a friendship. They talked to Ron and me and Adriane and Shawn and some of the old Cowboys and the doctors and champions of organ donation. They talked to just about everyone—except Mom.

Mom is not an envious person. She is a proud person, though, and almost on the eve of the transplant I learned that she was stung by being overlooked in the story about Ron and me.

It was two days before the transplant, and I'd just had my last presurgery checkup. Everything was great. I was there at the same time as Ron, and he was yelling from his room into mine, "Don't change your mind now!" Everyone in the doctor's office was laughing. My spirits were high. I decided to stop by Mom's house to see how she was holding up.

I opened the door, announced my presence, and walked over to where Mom was, but she didn't turn around and acknowledge me. I felt my breathing stop. I knew something was wrong.

"I don't appreciate everyone calling the Springs family and calling you and thanking you," Mom said. "No one has called me."

Then she turned around and looked at me.

"You are *my* son," Mom said very pointedly. "You are *my* son who is going to be on that operating table. I'm not happy that no one is considering my feelings. No one has said, 'Thanks for raising a great son who is going to be doing this.'

"Why is no one coming to me?" she continued. "You are my *only* son."

I was deflated. Mom's displeasure was a punch in my gut.

I stayed for only a few minutes. I couldn't take her being upset. I thought we'd cleared that hurdle, and all that was left was the surgery.

I hopped in my car and pulled out of Hamilton Park onto Central Expressway to drive home. On the way I called Adriane and related my mom's feelings.

Adriane immediately called my mom and warmly expressed her family's gratitude. Two days later, the most heartening thing happened, although I wasn't there to witness it.

I'd already been rolled down the hall to the operating room and told Mom, Shreill, the kids, Adriane, and Ron that I'd see them in a few hours. Ron was still in his room. He wasn't scheduled to join me until I was prepped and ready to go.

So our families moved over to Ron's room to send him off after doing the same for me. As is his nature, Ron upstaged the send-off.

Just as they were rolling him out, Ron called out to my mom.

"Miz Walls, Miz Walls," Ron hollered, to get her attention as well as everyone else's. "I want to thank you for having that son. If it wasn't for you having Cubby, I'd be in trouble right now."

Those who heard Ron's heartfelt expression said it gave them goose bumps and that Mom smiled, ever so slightly.

# 15

# It's about the Others

When we were done putting in a Sunday afternoon or Monday night's worth of work at Texas Stadium during my Cowboys days, we'd strip our gear and tape, get treatment if we required it, shower, dress, answer questions from reporters, and, finally, head out of the sanctuary that was our locker room onto a long ramp leading up from the field and eventually out of the stadium. The ramp was always teeming with people.

There would be members of the media, stadium workers, and Cowboys employees moving equipment from the field to storage and shuttling bodies back and forth to the interview room. There would be people I'd never seen before and people I recalled seeing before who were related to some of my teammates.

And somewhere among them all, I would find my family, too, or they would find me. Shreill would be there. Charis would be there toddling along. Cameron wasn't born until my last season with the Cowboys, but sometimes my mom would be there to congratulate me for playing well, for making an interception if I'd done that.

During the seasons when Ron and I played together, Adriane and Shawn would be there. Ron and Adriane's daughters weren't yet born.

Win or lose, it was always a joyous moment. I was always happy to see my family, and they were always happy to see that I'd survived another knock-down, drag-out scrap with some other toughs from another NFL team.

Fourteen years into retirement, I'd forgotten all about that feeling until the middle of the last afternoon of February 2007, when I slowly awakened in a fog. Everything around me seemed to be swirling by or dancing about, slowly coming into focus. I was on my back, and the first thing I saw was the ceiling passing above me, illuminated by white fluorescent lighting. Then I glanced to my side and saw the walls going by. It took a moment before I realized I was being rolled down a hospital hallway, from where and to where I wasn't quite sure yet.

I was dazed, not unlike I'd felt after a good collision on the football field. I was woozy. It took me a few seconds more to remember why I was there. My memory started coming back as I heard some voices that sounded familiar.

"Cubby," I heard someone say. I focused my eyes. It was Shreill.

Other faces I recognized started to appear in a growing gaggle of doctors and nurses and orderlies I didn't immediately recognize, just like it used to be outside the Cowboys locker room at Texas Stadium after a home game. I was picking out my family one by one, or they were picking me out.

Charis was there. My mom was there, too. This time they were happy to see I had survived my first hospital stay, my first surgery, and my first organ donation. I was happy, too.

I was wheeled into my private hospital room from the recovery room where I was parked immediately after the surgery. I was still drifting in and out of sleep. At some point I opened my eyes, and from a small gathering in the room Ron's son, Shawn, came to my side. He was very happy to see me. The whole hospital was very happy. It was a celebratory atmosphere, a party, just like the locker room always was after a big win. And this was a big win.

I don't think I showed my elation in those early moments after the surgery. I was just too groggy. It was going on four o'clock in the afternoon. I was coming to after being under anesthesia for the first time in my forty-seven years of life. I'd been in surgery with Ron for five hours and in the hospital since the night before. I was only 150 grams lighter. That's how much a kidney weighs. But I felt like I was missing a lot more than that.

I felt drained. I was tired. I hadn't felt so drained since shoving that blocking sled at Grambling for one hundred yards in that unforgiving Louisiana sun. I hadn't felt as tired since those days as a kid playing basketball at Hamilton Park into the wee hours of a summer's morning when I was left gasping for air, bent over, hands on knees or gripping the hem in my shorts.

I was in pain, too. It was the worst pain I'd felt since that time I got kneed in my side with the Giants in 1991. During the preliminary testing for the donation, the doctors had said they noticed one kidney suffered bruising at some point. I suspected it was from James Joseph's knee.

The doctors that time hadn't kept me in the hospital. But here at Medical City Dallas Hospital after giving one of my kidneys to Ron, I was required to do a sleepover. When I was playing, I always wondered what it would be like to have to undergo surgery and stay in the hospital. Now I was finally learning. It was not fun.

The Medical City doctors wouldn't let me do anything Wednesday night after the surgery. They wouldn't let me get up. They wouldn't let me eat what I liked to eat. Instead, they were feeding me soft foods like oatmeal. They let me have something to drink that was so bland I don't recall it. And it seemed like every time a nurse came by it was only to stick me with another needle. I wanted to go home.

It wasn't until the next morning that I was allowed to get up and start walking around. The doctors actually suggested it then. That brightened my mood a little.

But it wasn't just the pedestrian exercise of walking around that lifted me. It was what I discovered as I poked my head outside my little room and walked down the hallway toward what sounded like a party going on in another room not too many doors away. Turned out, it was Ron's room. I hadn't seen him since before we were rolled into surgery.

Ron was awake, that's for sure. He was dining on salmon, and his room, despite our being boarded in the intensive care unit, was packed with people. It reminded me of that ramp outside the Cowboys locker room at Texas Stadium after Ron and I were done with a game.

The most amazing thing was that it wasn't just Ron's family and friends stuffed into his little room. It was most of my friends and some of my family, too. They were in his room because I hadn't been much company until then, I was sleeping so much.

My best friend growing up T., Mike Terrell, was in Ron's room. Tony Hill was in Ron's room. Angelo King was in there with his wife. Robert Newhouse, who we'd played with, was in there. There were eight, ten, a dozen people in there. I didn't even think Ron could see me walk into his room for all the other people, but I was wrong.

"Boy, what you doin' walkin' around?" Ron said in his typical boisterous style in between bites of salmon. And vegetables. And wild rice.

What could I say? I just laughed and shook my head in disbelief at the scene.

My stomach was on empty and growling. Ron was gorging himself. I'd forgotten what the doctors told me the immediate recovery would be like. They had said that Ron's healing process would be faster than mine because he was getting something good added to his body rather than having something taken away—the new kidney just kicked right in, and he could eat heavy foods the next day, whereas I had just lost a kidney, along with a lot of blood, and my system was trying to adjust.

My body was depleted and needed time to heal. I had to introduce more substantial foods gradually. I remember when they finally moved me up to grits after a day. Grits! Ron may have been on filet mignon by then.

It all kind of reminded me of that Robin Harris joke about somebody stealing your car and getting out of jail before you get a new one. You're at the bus stop, and the thief is driving by. Ron hadn't stolen anything from me—I had given him my kidney. And now he was eating everything in sight and laughing, and I was eating oatmeal and grits and had a pain in my gut. I couldn't help but chuckle, no matter how much it hurt to do so less than twenty-four hours after having my kidney cut out of my side.

The discomfort I felt physically was no match, however, for the warm feeling I was experiencing spiritually and emotionally.

This was the moment when I realized what organ donation was all about. This was when I understood what organ donation can do.

It isn't about saving a life or extending it. Clinically speaking, it is, I guess. But it's about much, much more.

Organ donation is about saving families. It is about bringing happiness and comfort to so many more people than just the recipient. I saw it, so I know. Everybody around me and Ron saw it, so they know. The impact of organ donation is palpable; it reached out and touched me.

Ron was happy. Adriane was happy. Their kids were happy. Their extended family was happy. The doctors and nurses and everyone in the hospital who was aware of what was going on were happy. The city of Dallas was happy. The transplant organizations in Texas were happy that another success story in organ donation had blossomed, a story that captured a lot more attention than most transplants. Even the people in the media who wrote about it or reported on it for newspaper and television and radio news reports were happy. This was what they call a feel-good story. Good news, for a change. It felt great.

My family was happy, even though it wasn't my life that was being given that second lease. Shreill was happy that the husband of her best friend was saved and that their family was kept intact. Charis and Cameron were happy that the father of their best friends growing up, Ayra and Ashley, were relieved. They were happy that their godfather, who had shuttled them to and from school and practices and made them laugh so hard, would still be there for them.

My mom was happy. I don't think she had been so happy since the day Coach Rob told her that he was giving me his last scholarship and that I was guaranteed that college education my mother just wasn't going to be able to afford, happier than that day when I walked out of juvenile detention after two weeks with my record as clean as before I was wrongfully charged with robbery.

Actually, I don't think that there was anyone in that hospital whose glee about how everything had turned out was more evident than my mom's, and this after I'd been so reluctant—scared, to tell the truth—to let her know what it was I was planning to do. I had been right that she would be upset. But I also knew that in the end she would understand why I decided to do what I did. I was right again.

My most vivid memory from when I was waking up from the anesthesia was my mom's face coming into focus as I glanced around. Her eyes were glazed with tears. She was at my side, and she was absolutely beaming. That pretty smile of hers was spread across her face.

After she had resigned herself to the process, which she knew she couldn't stop, Mom had been there with me every step of the way, from the moment I was rolled out of my room toward the operating room to that moment when I came to.

"Oh, Cubby," I think I heard her say.

I'd heard those words from her before. It was a sign that she was more than just happy. It was a sign that her happiness was steeped in relief.

We all were relieved. But Mom had harbored the darkest nightmares about what could happen. What mom wouldn't? What dad wouldn't? My dad had never expressed any reservations, though. He was a football player like me and Ron. He was too tough, at least on the outside.

Mom is strong, too, but she also is sensitive when it comes to her children and all the children in our family. So she was more relieved than anyone else that her biggest fears hadn't come true and that her baby boy was, as I told her I would be, just fine. She felt better knowing that all the hard work she put into rearing me, making sure I got a college education and made the most of what talents I had been given, had not been lost.

After it all sank in, what Mom became, more than anything else, was prouder than ever. Isn't that the feeling most parents want from their kids? I know my heart fills with pride when my kids do something well that makes them stand out, like when Cameron brought home an award from school and when Charis tried out for *American Idol* and did well. I know my heart breaks when they do something I'm not proud of, like when I broke my mom's heart by disobeying her and getting into trouble as a teenager.

Like most parents, Mom wanted Eartha, Gigi, and me to be special. Like most parents, she wanted to take pride in her children with the knowledge that she was the influence in our lives that made the difference. For all that she did for us, she was a difference. What I did for Ron and his family was proof.

I know that's what she felt as she stood in that hospital room looking and listening as all these other people praised the Lord for what happened, before turning around and thanking me for being the one who actually carried out the Lord's work. That was pretty good company I was in, especially in the eyes of the woman who made sure I was in First Baptist Church of Hamilton Park every Sunday growing up.

Mom at that moment could see what my intentions were all along. She could finally relate to my desire to save not just Ron, but a family, a family that extended beyond Ron's own and even enveloped my own, my mom's own. That wasn't something Mom could see when I made her the last person close to me to know I was about to become a living organ donor. All she could see then was danger.

It was understandable, of course. "How dangerous is donating a kidney?" "Weren't you afraid?" "What if something had gone wrong?" I heard the same questions from a lot of people trying to understand how I came to be a living organ donor. From my mom I heard all those questions with emotion sometimes bathed in tears.

I asked those questions, too, but from another perspective. I wondered how dangerous it would be for me *not* to donate to Ron, if I could. I wondered how frightening the outcome would be for his family if I came up short like others had. I worried about what would happen if Ron's body rejected my organ.

The real danger wasn't to me, I tried to tell Mom. The most frightening possibility was his family being without him. The biggest thing that could go wrong was with Ron.

The reason it was all worth it, I figured, was that we would witness a scene like the one that developed in Ron's hospital room after the surgery, with him sitting up eating salmon and running his mouth at everyone just like the best of times.

Mom just soaked it all in, just like she had when Hamilton Park was buzzing about Coach Landry awarding me—her college graduate son living with her in the room he grew up in—a starting job as a rookie. She was bursting with pride just like she was when I was named to my first Pro Bowl and when I finally won that Super Bowl ring.

This was a different kind of elation. This time she was soaking in the accolades from people talking about what a wonderfully selfless thing it was for her son to donate a kidney. She was being showered with compliments about her son, who was so compassionate that he would give up an organ to someone he wasn't even related to by blood—at least not before that last day of February 2007.

☆

Attention and adulation certainly weren't among Ron's or my intentions when I reared up off that gymnasium floor and, in a moment of anger at Ron's physical predicament, made my first promise to him that I would try to help. We only talked about what we were doing between ourselves and among our family and closest friends. We never called a newspaper reporter or a radio sports talk show to announce my decision. The only person in the media we'd let on to about what we were considering was a Dallas television reporter, Nita Wiggins. She'd covered Ron's failing health first and followed up several times, so Ron and I told Nita that we'd talk to her and her only when everything was done.

I didn't know about Shawn's leak until I was walking through Dallas–Fort Worth International Airport the day the story appeared for a flight to New York to do Stephen A. Smith's ESPN television show. I noticed that a lot more people than usual were looking at me. I often got recognized in Dallas, but it had been a while since I had attracted this many glances. Then my phone started ringing with inquiries from reporters wanting to know if it was true that I was going to become a kidney donor to Ron. It wasn't until later that I realized the people looking at me at the airport must have seen the story on their computers or heard it on the radio.

That was when I called Ron and told him our secret was no more. We didn't even have a date yet for the surgery.

That was also when Ron and I began to realize that what was about to take place between us was greater than us. It was greater than what either of us had gone through, Ron's years of pain and misery and my brief period of physical and psychological tests.

It was at that moment that we knew we would be linked forever by more than just the blood we would share with the new kidney in Ron's abdomen. We knew there would be another bond beyond even our families and the long friendship we had that began when we had played together for four seasons long ago.

The media onslaught was similar to the way the doors would open to the Cowboys locker room and let in the flood of reporters who wanted to know how we'd won or lost. All of a sudden, everyone was interested in this new game. Stephen A. Smith asked me to talk about the breaking news on his show, and I did. It was the first time I had spoken in public about organ donation.

Ron and I couldn't hide anymore and, looking back on it all, we shouldn't have.

Within a day or two of Shawn's spilling the family beans in the national press, Ron and I got together and laid out a strategy just like we had all those years working together with charities. We decided we would hold a press conference. We hired a public relations consultant.

Then we made the second biggest decision in our joined lives: We figured it was time to start a foundation to, as we wrote in our mission statement, educate people about ways to prevent chronic kidney disease and to dispel any myths about the living donor process. We wanted to save as many lives as possible with the ultimate remedy, if necessary: kidney donation.

It all made perfect sense. It was the type of thing that was a natural extension of what Ron had been about so much of his life, from the time he took over the Cowboys' charitable basketball team when Drew Pearson got hurt to the past several years, in which he'd been involved with a diabetes charity in Dallas. Ron has always wanted to help someone else, including that cocky rookie cornerback from the

Negro League whom he embraced in the summer of 1981 with the Cowboys—me.

Ron had already been on television with Shawn championing the need for awareness of diabetes and suggesting how to keep the disease at bay. What he decided to do now was add organ donation to the cause that adopted him and enlist me as part of the campaign.

I wasn't sure I was being called to dedicate myself to this new cause, beyond the act of donation. It wasn't until we got closer to surgery and more people found out and reacted with so much amazement and gratitude that I realized the rest of my life was taking almost as much of a turn as Ron's was.

It was ironic: What I had come to be known for in my career was taking things from others—passes intended for someone else. Fifty-seven times I'd snatched a football out of the air as an NFL cornerback. Only nine other men in the history of the league had intercepted more. Eleven times during my senior season at Grambling I picked off passes by opposing quarterbacks. No one in college football that year grabbed more. Even as a senior in high school, the only year in high school I played football, I led our district in interceptions.

What I had done as a professional made me an all-star. What I had done in college made me an All-American. What I had done in high school had caught the attention of a few college recruiters.

Now what I was about to do attracted the interest of everyone. I was being recognized for giving to another person rather than taking something away. It seemed to dwarf the recognition I had received as a football player.

I remember shortly after I got home from the hospital, Shreill and I went for a walk around the neighborhood. I joked with her that this was the only time she had ever been in better shape than I was. I was itching to get outside, and the doctors said it would be fine for me to walk around.

We tried to stay off the beaten path, but a few people spied us. A Suburban slowed down, and the guy who was driving stuck his head out the window. "Hey, Everson!" he shouted, and gave me a thumbs up sign. It wasn't the first time a stranger had stopped me on the street. It happened from time to time during and after my playing days. There was nothing like being a member of the Cowboys in Dallas or elsewhere. To be one of the celebrities on America's Team was always special. Playing for the Super Bowl-winning Giants a few years before I retired never compared to sporting the silver and blue.

But the recognition from helping Ron was altogether different. I ceased being a football player in most people's eyes. Now they looked at me as a humanitarian. I was accustomed to people stopping me to talk about who inspired me to play sports, the famous coaches I played for, playing in the Super Bowl, and, of course, The Catch. Now they wanted to know who influenced me to make this decision with Ron and what it was like to prepare for it. I was getting more attention than I did when I was playing football, and it was for something that hadn't even happened yet.

Everything was so accelerated that Ron and I never even took time alone to talk about what we were about to undergo. Instead, we were doing interviews and attending to our separate medical appointments and being with our families.

Every reporter asked us what it was like when we were alone after I was given the go-ahead to donate to Ron. They wanted to know if Ron embraced me and I embraced him and had that heartfelt discussion that the closest of friends might have around a moment like this. They wanted to know if some tears had been shed, if that emotional thank-you everyone can envision had been given.

But Ron and I never had those moments, because we literally never had the time.

And if you want to know the truth, Ron's not that kind of person, and neither am I. I teased him about that, too, even though I knew I didn't want to be seen boo-hooing over what we were doing. I was a football player. He was a football player. We were just meeting a challenge, we told ourselves, which is what football players do.

We knew by then that we were doing more than simply coming up with a game plan for one day. But it didn't feel necessary to talk about that at the time. We were looking at the board, at the X's and O's and arrows, figuring our strategy, getting ready to be as tough as we knew we needed to be. But months later, when Ron and I looked around Ron's hospital room that first day when we saw each other after surgery, we couldn't ignore the magnitude of what we had engaged in. It was all right before us. We were fielding questions from media everywhere and receiving well wishes from people we didn't even know.

That was when Ron and I began to understand that we'd really done the right thing. We weren't thinking just about what I'd been fortunate enough to do for him and his family. We were also thinking about what we'd done for others. We were now joined forever in a cause.

It hadn't been our idea. After all, Ron never planned on getting diabetes and losing body parts, and I had never envisioned giving up one of mine while I was still alive. It just happened, like a great block at the line of scrimmage that opens a hole to the goal line or a quick break on a deep pass that results in an interception. It all just kind of happened.

My giving a kidney to Ron wasn't just about Ron and me. It was about all those afflicted with diabetes or some other crippling kidney malfunction. It was about all those people we saw in the dialysis center with their bodies being chipped away by amputations. It was about all those people we saw there with their lives ticking away with every spin of the wheel in those machines that whirred on, sending their blood through a rinse cycle. It was about all those people in the dialysis center who we'd see regularly and, all of a sudden, not see again.

What Ron and I did was about the families and loved ones and friends and coworkers of those in need of the gift for a continued and better life.

So Ron and I looked at each other in his hospital room with some amazement. It was not unlike the time years earlier when we saw that reporter talk to the kid without a coat to stay warm on a cold Fort Worth street corner. We knew we had to do something, to do something more. So we did.

We had already decided to entertain media inquiries that were pouring in, and we did. We had already decided to publicize what we'd done, and we were. We had already decided to let others in Ron's situation and mine know that they could pursue the solution we had, and we were using our hospital beds as bully pulpits to do just that.

We decided to call what we were doing the Ron Springs and Everson Walls Gift for Life Foundation.

# 16

# Ron Lives

On March 2, 2007, Ron and I sat down at a long table at Medical City Dallas Hospital before a thicket of television cameras, a hedge of photographers and reporters, and a forest of friends and well-wishers, to tell them how we'd come to be where we were, recovering from a transplant of my kidney into Ron's abdomen. Our families were at our side, including my mom.

Our plan was to talk about how we stood for what being teammates was all about and how we were blazing a trail as athletes for others to follow as organ donors. But that plan melted away.

Ron was rocking back in his chair, sticking out his barrel of a chest like he always did. I was leaning a little forward, about to say a few words. Except for the amputations, of course, Ron looked better than he had in years. His complexion wasn't as dark. His eyes were bright. "Before Ron went in," I told the crowd about the day we were rolled into the operating room, "something very powerful happened. He made a statement to my mother about how he wanted to thank her . . . "

Suddenly, I had to swallow. My eyes welled up. Tears began flowing down my face.

" . . . for having me," I struggled to say, under the current of emotion that enveloped me. "'Cause her having me saved him. And she deserves that thanks."

From that moment, Ron and I weren't just hard football players anymore. We had graduated to something else, and no one that day was looking at us as football players, anyway. They hadn't gathered to see us as old number 20 and number 24 telling stories about Coach Landry and Danny White and Too Tall Jones. They'd come to see us as the best friends two people could be. They'd come to see us as an inspiration for life itself. Now they wanted to know who influenced me in life.

Ron's life and mine were headed in a direction we never conceptualized and one that's irreversible. It was as if we'd been transformed, or spirited away to another place.

Our relationship even shifted a little, because now it was I who had done something for Ron for which he would be forever grateful. Nothing was the same for us anymore except our close friendship.

☆

It was quite a whirlwind Ron and I went on after Ron was finally released from the hospital following the transplant. We obliged countless requests from radio and television stations for interviews.

ESPN came out to do a story on us. HBO came out to do a story. The NFL Network came out. Reporters from all over the country called, and some paid visits. The Cowboys set aside part of their home opener against the Giants on September 9, 2007, to honor us at Texas Stadium. Someone from Oprah Winfrey's show contacted us about coming to Chicago to tape a program with her.

No one wanted to talk to us about playing professional football. They all wanted to talk about our friendship, Ron being brought back from death's door, and my decision to donate my kidney.

Invitations came in from all sorts of organizations that wanted to honor our friendship and cite me for becoming a donor. A congressman from Missouri, William Lacy Clay, even told me he planned to introduce a bill called the Everson Walls and Ron Springs Gift for Life Act of 2007, H.R. 3635, to start a national organ tissue donor registry. He then invited me to come to Capitol Hill and testify to the House Committee on Oversight and Government Reform about what I'd done and why others should consider being organ donors.

So I traveled to Washington, D.C., early on the afternoon of September 25, 2007, and sat down at a table in a conference room in the famous Rayburn Building, just like I'd seen really important people do before, and testified. Here is some of what I said:

*Congressman Clay and ranking member [Michael] Turner,*

*I want to thank you for giving me the opportunity to testify before your committee. I am humbled and honored to present Ron Springs's and my story to you. Ron is unable to attend this hearing in person because he is still going through rehabilitation, but he is doing well and is on the road to recovery. I am here representing both of us and our newly formed foundation—the Ron Springs and Everson Walls Gift for Life Foundation.*

*Winston Churchill once stated, " To every man there comes a time when he is figuratively tapped on the shoulder and offered a chance to do a great and mighty thing, unique to him and fitted to his talents; what a tragedy if that moment finds him unprepared or unqualified for the moment that could be his finest hour."*

*I am not a hero, nor have I sought the spotlight since my retirement from the NFL in 1993. But I received my tap on the shoulder in 1981 when I met Ron Springs. We were on opposite sides of the ball—me on defense as a cornerback and he on offense as a running back with the Dallas Cowboys.*

*Ron was a very unique athlete. He had size, speed, and the intelligence it took to become a leader on and off the field for the Dallas Cowboys. I was able to relate to Ron not just on the field, but off the field as well. Our friendship was strengthened by our family's bonding with each other.*

*After Ron and I both retired from the NFL, the relationship between our families became stronger. I realized how important teamwork was as a player, and I have always tried to transfer that from on the field to off the field. I learned those lessons from playing for great coaches such as the great Eddie Robinson from Grambling State University, Tom Landry of the Dallas Cowboys, and Bill Parcells of the New York Giants. But I also learned much more from my fellow soldiers that fought in the trenches with me. Ron Springs was one of those fellow soldiers.*

*Ron had been diagnosed with diabetes years ago, but the disease became more acute with time. He had been placed on a national transplant waiting list in 2004. His health was challenged by chronic kidney disease. There was failing eyesight, lack of circulation to his limbs, and ultimately kidney failure. One of the strongest athletes I have ever known began to show weaknesses that could not be imagined a few years earlier.*

*I, like most people, was very naive about the symptoms of chronic kidney disease. I was fortunate that diabetes did not run in my family. Because of the many afflictions affecting my friend, I began to take a crash course on the subject of chronic kidney disease. I was very surprised at what I found out.*

*There are millions of Americans that are afflicted with chronic kidney disease, but minorities are affected disproportionately.*

*You have limited choices when you are afflicted with chronic kidney disease. One option is to start taking insulin; another option is to take dialysis. There is another option that is only for the fortunate, and that is to undergo a kidney transplant procedure. There are two types of kidney transplants. One is to receive the organ from a cadaver, the other, and more favorable procedure, is to receive the organ from a living donor.*

*Fortunately for Ron Springs, I volunteered to be his favorable option. On February 28, Ron and I underwent a successful living organ donor transplant procedure. Because of this, Ron has no more dialysis treatments and has a chance at a better quality of life. Although he has a long way to go, as far as rehabilitation is concerned, our lives and our families' lives are much richer because of my decision to lay down my life for my fellow human being.*

*There is a lot of misinformation surrounding organ donation that needs to be dealt with. Minorities, especially Blacks and Latinos, are extremely hesitant to register for organ donation. Some of it stems from religious reasons and others from some of the terrible things our government has done in the past, such as the Tuskegee experiments [during which African-American men were used as guinea pigs to study the ravages of syphilis].*

*N.F.L. Commissioner Roger Goodell and Dallas Cowboys owner Jerry Jones have pledged their support to us and our foundation to take our message across the country. They both have submitted letters of support to you for inclusion in the official record of this hearing.*

*We want to work closely with the Department of Health and Human Services, as well as the pharmaceutical industry, to take our campaign nationally. Any help you can provide in meeting with these organizations would be greatly appreciated.*

*When I received this tap on the shoulder, what a tragedy it would have been if I was unqualified or unprepared for the moment that could be my finest hour. I thank God that I was able to give and extend the life of my dear friend, Ron Springs. Of all the success I have obtained both on and off the field, being used as a vessel of God is by far my finest hour.*

I dabbed a little sweat from my forehead after I finished my testimony. I didn't think I'd be nervous about what I agreed to do, but I'd never spoken to so many strangers about something so personal.

☆

Ron and I stopped working out at the gym together because Ron was going through extensive physical therapy. We were both also occupied by all the requests to appear here or talk there.

It wasn't until a couple of weeks after I got home from Washington that Ron and I finally sat down with each other and chitchatted pretty much alone like in the old days.

It was a Thursday evening, October 11, 2007, and Ron came by the house. Adriane dropped him off while she was running some errands, and Ron walked into the house—by himself. The wheelchair was gone. He was getting stronger.

His walk wasn't steady, and it wasn't fluid. It was sort of a stumble, and as happy as I was to see him maneuvering on his own, I was frightened he was going to topple over. So I hurried to his side.

With a little help from me to steady him, Ron sat down on the sofa off to the side of the big TV screen in the family room. I sat where I always do, on the other couch facing that TV.

In fact, we weren't totally alone: Shreill and Charis were there. But that was family. It was like old times. Ron was running his mouth like he always did. You could hear his rejuvenation as much as you could see it. He was teasing Charis. Charis was talking about some hip-hop celebrity gossip that she was writing about on a blog that she had started. Ron was all ears and told Charis he was going to sign up for her blog so he could follow the latest gossip that we all knew he wasn't interested in.

We were all laughing. We didn't have a care in the world anymore. Our biggest fears had evaporated. I'd even forgotten Ron was headed for another surgery the next morning until he mentioned it before leaving. He gave me a football to sign for a charity, and then, with some help from me again, he stood up from the sofa and walked out the front door. Adriane helped him back in the car, and they drove off.

Shreill had mentioned to me at some point that Ron was going in for another procedure, but I hadn't really made a mental note of it because it wasn't anything serious. He had a cyst on one elbow that was preventing him from exercising one of his arms in rehab. His arms had atrophied a little; otherwise, he could have been driving himself around already. He would be able to resume physical therapy and get his arms straightened out after the doctors removed the cyst. Pretty simple, it seemed, especially after all that Ron had been through.

The only concern was that Ron was still diabetic, and the doctors said that made him more susceptible to infection. So they had to be extra careful. That was it.

We'd already been through this once before. Ron was suffering from a sports hernia after the transplant and needed an operation to repair it. He went in and came out without a complication. This would just be another tune-up to help him get back in shape.

The next afternoon, Friday, Shreill asked me to pick her up from the women's clothing store she's worked at for years at North Park Shopping Mall, just a few exits down from the exit I take off Central Expressway to go to my mom's house in Hamilton Park. I was hanging out that day with Charis, so the two of us went to pick up Shreill.

It was a little before five o'clock and no more than a few minutes after Shreill got into our car, when her cell phone rang. It was Adriane. She was calling from the hospital where Ron had gone for the extra bit of surgery. Shreill spoke to Adriane much more briefly than she usually does, said "OK," and hung up. Shreill turned to me and said Adriane wanted us to come by the hospital.

It was a beautiful room-temperature day in Dallas. If there was a cloud in the blue sky, I don't remember it. The day had us in a mood to go somewhere, maybe an outdoor cafe, where we could enjoy the day a little longer. The last place I wanted to be was in a hospital. I'd had my fill. I never liked hospitals anyway.

We were actually headed in the opposite direction from the hospital when Adriane called Shreill again. Shreill said I would have to turn around.

"What?" I said to Shreill. "C'mon. Can't we go later?"

Shreill insisted with a serious tone, and I reversed our course.

I started joking with Shreill: "This fool better not need any more blood from me. I've given him all I'm giving!"

Charis chuckled. I noticed that Shreill didn't.

The rest of that drive to the hospital, which wasn't that long, seemed like forever, and we remained unusually quiet until I finally asked Shreill what was wrong. Shreill just shot back, very seriously, "I don't know."

Everyone went quiet again. I was trying to figure what Adriane could possibly need us for. We were still on a high from the transplant that was done just six months earlier. Everything was going so well. The foundation was up and running. Ron had been over at the house only the night before, walking on his own. I hadn't experienced any discomfort from the donation except for the pain of healing, and that was soothed by the overwhelming joy of seeing Ron still with us and the happiness on Adriane's face and his kids'.

But here we were exiting Central Expressway and winding around a road toward the parking lot of the hospital wing where Ron had gone to get his elbow fixed, and a sense of uncertainty was hovering over us. We walked through some glass doors, through the lobby, and to a bank of elevators for a ride up to Ron's floor. The elevator doors opened, and I stepped out first. I stuck out my chest and threw back my head, and I saw Adriane a little way down the hall. Her back was turned.

"What the heck's going on in here?" I blurted out, fully expecting Adriane to respond by telling me to be quiet because I was in a hospital.

Adriane turned. I stared. She said nothing. As I got closer, I could see that her eyes were red and the skin around them puffy. She'd been crying.

Before I could say, "What's wrong?" Adriane said, "Here they come."

I looked down the hallway over Adriane's shoulder and saw three doctors walking our way. All I could hear at that moment was the clicking of their shoes on the floor. The closer they got, the more I felt limp, as if the air was leaving my body and blood was draining from my limbs. The hallway seemed to be closing in, and all I could see were these three figures getting closer and closer until they paused in front of me, and I just stared waiting for someone to say something.

They looked at me for a moment, and I looked at them. One introduced himself as a cardiologist. Another introduced himself as a plastic surgeon. The third said she was the anesthesiologist.

I'd all but forgotten Adriane was standing there with Shreill and Charis. It was as if I were in a trance.

One of the doctors said something about how Ron had been stabilized. Someone, maybe the same doctor, said something about Ron having flat-lined. Another voice said something about having brought Ron back.

I heard my mind whirring like the machines in that dialysis center. I felt dizzied by all that was being said, as if I'd just had a head-on collision on the football field. I tried desperately to grasp the words and their meaning.

"Stabilized from what?" I said. "Brought back? Is he awake?" I asked, hoping that I could go see him.

They started talking more. One doctor said Ron wasn't awake. One doctor said they had minimized the amount of time Ron's brain was without oxygen.

I took a step back, seeking extra space that would give me the air I needed to breathe that was suddenly in short supply. My nerves sent me into a brief quiver. I tried to gather myself. I struggled to listen to every sentence, every word, that the doctors uttered in hushed, measured tones. As I pieced each bit of information together, I felt a part of me collapse inside.

"When can we see him?" I asked.

They said we'd have to wait. So we did.

I don't know what it feels like to be shot and have to drag your body, your wounded limbs, out of harm's way. But it can't be much different from how I felt as I took one difficult step after another down that cold hospital hallway toward a lounge with the weight of all the horror, all the fear, all the uncertainty, that had just been dumped on my back.

I collapsed into a chair. Shreill and Charis and Adriane dumped their bodies onto the couches and chairs, too. And we waited. For exactly what, we weren't sure. Not much was said.

The hour that passed before a nurse retrieved us seemed like an entire day. We dragged ourselves back down the same hallway to a hospital room, where we were led in. In the bed under white sheets lay Ron.

He was asleep, they told us, but his eyes kept opening up, blinking quickly. He looked as if he were having a seizure.

A doctor standing at Ron's side assured us that his fluttering eyelids were a good sign, an indication that oxygen was getting to his brain. I just stared. His eyes blinked open and closed, open and closed, open and closed, over and over and over again. I couldn't watch anymore. I turned and walked out of the room.

Just as I did, another doctor walked down the hallway in a great hurry toward Ron's room. I recognized him as Ron's regular doctor and asked him what he knew about what had happened. He was angry. He said what he saw in Ron was not good. His assessment left me, left all of us, frightened like we hadn't been before. Three months later, Adriane held a press conference with Shawn at her side to announce the family was suing for malpractice two of the doctors involved in Ron's arm surgery.

Ron has been the same every day since he went into the hospital for that arm surgery, upwards of two years as I write these words. I haven't changed from the day I decided to give him my kidney.

☆

Two months before Ron's arm surgery, Ron and I were interviewed by Frank Deford on Bryant Gumbel's *Real Sports* program on HBO. The segment was scheduled to be aired on October 23. It was supposed to be the ultimate feel-good story about what we were—two guys who worked together and became the best of friends and then shared our lives in order to save one of us. It was supposed to be about hope and selflessness. It was supposed to be about refusing to be sad and sorry. It was supposed to be uplifting.

I was determined our story still would be an inspiration, because it was.

HBO called after the news broke about Ron's setback and asked if I wanted to sit down with Deford again to update the story, or if I just wanted to drop it. I said I wanted to update it, and did.

It was the most important thing—*the most important thing*—I could do now for Ron, because I knew what some people out there were thinking. It was only human nature. They were wondering if all I'd done had been worth it.

They were wondering if, with Ron fallen into a coma from which it sounded as if he wouldn't return, what I'd done was wasted, whether I'd squandered my kidney for a man who now had no use for it, if I'd unnecessarily endangered my life and sacrificed my good fortune for nothing.

Those thoughts were born out by some others in the media who had sought out Ron and me before but never called back. We were no longer a feel-good story. We were a sad story.

Even Bryant Gumbel expressed the futility of it all after Deford finished his piece, wondering if there was nothing to do but let Ron die peacefully. A friend of mine, Raynard Jackson, was so upset that he wrote Gumbel to complain. Gumbel responded November 1, 2007, in an e-mail Raynard shared with me:

> *Mr. Jackson—*
>
> *I'm sorry if you took offense or found the question callous and/or insensitive. If you know me as you say you do, you must know that was clearly not my intent. I have the utmost respect for Mr. Springs and would never choose to dishonor him or his family in any way. Nor would I ever presume to tell anyone how they should or shouldn't deal with issues of life and death. My question to Frank Deford was prompted by the limited information we had, information which led me to believe that Ron was being kept alive artificially and that his death was imminent. Please forgive me.*
>
> *Peace . . . BG*

Gumbel was not alone in his initial thoughts, which couldn't have been further from the truth. There was nothing Ron and I had done that was for naught.

It may seem counterintuitive, but in the aftermath of Ron's last surgery, in all the uncertainty and tragedy it is wrapped in, I feel more convinced of the value of what we did than ever before. I feel fully vindicated in the face of any doubters.

If Ron could talk right now, he would say the same, and probably add several observations of his own.

After all, Ron is still here. He is still breathing. His eyes still open and close. He coughs and twists and turns. He needs a haircut and a shave and a trim of his mustache. He needs beads of sweat on his brow wiped away from time to time. He still looks like he will wake up at any moment, which is at once as encouraging as it is frustrating.

My kidney is still working inside Ron to help keep him alive. Adriane, Ayra, Ashley, and Shawn are still able to see their old man and care for him. There isn't a day that goes by when Adriane or Ashley or Ayra doesn't spend time with Ron and tend to his needs. They are able to talk to him when he opens his eyes and looks their way. They are able to maintain hope for his recovery no matter how difficult it may be for them to see him in his state of hibernation.

Ron lives on.

But Ron lives on not just in his bright, airy room on the fourth floor of Medical City Dallas Hospital for his family and friends. He lives on far beyond Dallas and Texas. He lives on all over the country. He lives on all over the world.

He lives on for countless others who only know of him through the foundation in his name and the encouragement we've given others to do what we've done. He lives on for the people who've come up to me and embraced me in tears to tell me what our story has meant for someone close to them, who is still with them thanks to the selflessness of a living donor.

Organ donation and transplantation itself are not miracles. That is one message Ron and I want to convey. A miracle is something out of a mere mortal's reach. Donating an organ is something almost any healthy person can do.

That's why all this was worth it from the beginning and will be worth it forevermore. This is a mission now, a mission for life. Ron and I found that second stage in life, or it found us, that we were looking for while carpooling the kids around Dallas after our football careers ended.

Ron always said, and he was so right, that what we'd done was about all of us, neighbors, families, and strangers. It was about Gwen and Lisa. It was about Shreill's grandmother. It became about all those suffering with diabetes and all those families who were grieving watching their loved ones wither away before their eyes.

If we'd just stopped because Ron wound up in a coma, we'd be doing Ron, and all those who've come to believe in us, to count on us, a major disservice.

I don't believe that just because Ron is in a coma he doesn't know what's going on. I believe that he thinks we've already spent too much time fretting over him and not enough on spreading the good word of our foundation.

What Ron and I went through the past few years made me think about something Coach Rob always asked of the newcomers to his Grambling football team. He'd gather the team around before the first practice of summer and ask a simple question:

"When you go through life," Coach Rob asked, "will you leave a footprint in the sands of time?"

We'd all sort of stare at Coach Rob wondering what the heck he was talking about. Now I know. Coach Rob wanted our time on earth to leave an impression for all who come after us to follow.

Ron and I have left our footprint in the Creator's sand.

# Index

# About the Foundation

On September 9, 2007, seven months after Ron Springs received a kidney transplant from Everson Walls, Ron and Everson announced the creation of the Ron Springs and Everson Walls Gift for Life Foundation. Their goal is to educate the public about early detection and prevention of chronic kidney disease and build awareness about the organ donation process, particularly in communities of color, where diabetes affects people at a higher rate than the general population and is compounded because there are fewer donors. The Gift for Life Foundation is based in Frisco, Texas, and can be contacted through its Web site at www.GiftforLifeFoundation.org.

> *Everson's selfless act of donating his kidney to Ron was life-changing for Ron, everyone in our entire family, and those who are close to us. Every day that goes by I ask God to richly bless Everson and use him as an inspiration for others to muster the courage, strength, and love to give a gift for life.*

—Adriane Springs,
wife of Ron Springs and
co-incorporator of the Ron Springs and
Everson Walls Gift for Life Foundation

# About the Authors

**Everson Walls** is a four-time All-Pro NFL cornerback who played thirteen seasons and recorded fifty-seven interceptions, the tenth most in NFL history. He played his first nine seasons with the Dallas Cowboys before joining the New York Giants in 1990 and starring on its Super Bowl winning team. He retired in 1993 with the Cleveland Browns and returned to his hometown of Dallas, Texas, where he lives in the suburb of Plano with his wife Shreill. They have two children, Charis and Cameron. Everson has been inducted into the Southwestern Athletic Conference Hall of Fame, the Grambling State University Athletic Hall of Fame, the Louisiana Sports Hall of Fame, and the Texas Black Sports Hall of Fame. He is co-founder of The Ron Springs and Everson Walls Gift for Life Foundation that educates the public on the dangers of kidney disease and the need for organ donation.

☆

**Kevin B. Blackistone** is a national columnist for AOL Sports' *FanHouse*, a regular panelist on ESPN's Around the Horn, and the Shirley Povich Chair in Sports Journalism at the University of Maryland. He is a former award-winning sports columnist for *The Dallas Morning News* who has covered sports across the United States and around the world. He was born in Washington, D.C., reared in Hyattsville, Maryland, and graduated from Northwestern University and Boston University. He resides in Silver Spring, Maryland.